Shattered Illusions

D0770527

SECURITY AND PROFESSIONAL INTELLIGENCE EDUCATION SERIES (SPIES)

SERIES EDITOR: JAN GOLDMAN

In this post–September 11, 2001, era, there has been rapid growth in the number of professional intelligence training and educational programs across the United States and abroad. Colleges and universities, as well as high schools, are developing programs and courses in homeland security, intelligence analysis, and law enforcement, in support of national security.

The Security and Professional Intelligence Education Series (SPIES) was first designed for individuals studying for careers in intelligence and to help improve the skills of those already in the profession. However, it was also developed to educate the public in how intelligence work is conducted and should be conducted in this important and vital profession.

For a complete list of titles in the series, please visit https://rowman.com/Action/SERIES/RL/SPIES or scan the QR code below.

Shattered Illusions

KGB Cold War
Espionage in Canada

Donald G. Mahar

Foreword by Ward Elcock

ROWMAN & LITTLEFIELD
Lanham • Boulder • New York • London

Published by Rowman & Littlefield
A wholly owned subsidary of The Rowman & Littlefield Publishing Group, Inc.
4501 Forbes Boulevard, Suite 200, Lanham, Maryland 20706
www.rowman.com

Unit A, Whitacre Mews, 26-34 Stannary Street, London SE11 4AB

British Library Cataloguing in Publication Information Available

Library of Congress Cataloging-in-Publication Data Available

Names: Mahar, Donald G., 1947- author.
Title: Shattered illusions : KGB Cold War espionage in Canada / Donald G.
   Mahar.
Description: Lanham : Rowman & Littlefield, [2017] | Series: Security and
   professional intelligence education series (SPIES) | Includes
   bibliographical references and index.
Identifiers: LCCN 2016041392 (print) | LCCN 2016042969 (ebook) | ISBN
   9781442269132 (cloth) | ISBN 9781442269149 (paperback) | ISBN
   9781442269156 (electronic)
Subjects: LCSH: Espionage, Soviet—Canada—History. | Canada—Foreign
   relations—Soviet Union. | Soviet Union—Foreign relations—Canada. |
   Brik, Yevgeni Vladimirovich. | Spies—Canada—Biography. | Spies—Soviet
   Union—Biography. | Soviet Union. Komitet gosudarstvenno?i
   bezopasnosti—History. | Cold War. | Mahar, Donald G., 1947- |
   Intelligence officers—Canada—Biography.
Classification: LCC F1029.5.S65 M35 2017 (print) | LCC F1029.5.S65 (ebook) |
   DDC 327.71047—dc23
LC record available at https://lccn.loc.gov/2016041392

Printed in the United States of America

My inspiration emerges from
the imagination and love that springs
forth from my wonderful grandchildren,
Gibson and Autumn.
This book is dedicated to you.
Carol Anne, Scott, and Marta,
you are the loves of my life.

From Stettin in the Baltic,
To Trieste in the Adriatic,
An iron curtain has descended
across the continent.

Winston Churchill
March 5, 1946

Contents

List of Illustrations

Yevgeni Brik at his Portraits by Soboloff studio in Verdun, Quebec, 1953.

Brik's Birth Certificate. He was born in Novorossiysk, USSR, November 25, 1921.

Nikolai Alekseyevich Korznikov, KGB First Chief Directorate, Directorate S, Illegals Department.

Leonid Dmitrievich Abramov was Brik's initial KGB trainer and first Illegal Support Officer in Ottawa.

Brik's home and photo studio at 5381 Bannantyne Avenue, Verdun, Quebec.

KGB officer Vladimir Pavlovich Bourdine, Canadian Prime Minister Louis St. Laurent and Soviet Military attaché P. Komin at Soviet embassy reception.

One of Brik's agents provided classified reports on the CF-105 Avro Arrow.

KGB officer Nikolai Pavlovich Ostrovskiy was Brik's third Illegal Support Officer. He also ran RCMP Corporal James Douglas Finley Morrison.

James Morrison was a member of #1 Canadian Provost Corps (RCMP) for which he served with distinction during WWII.

James Morrison and his son at RCMP Detachment, Moosomin, Saskatchewan.

Gwynneth Morrison (nee Vidian-Jones) met Morrison in the UK at her parent's home during World War II.

James Morrison approached KGB officer Ostrovskiy at the Grand Hotel, Ottawa.

Foreword

Given the immediacy and violence of the threats posed by various terrorist organizations over the last two or three decades, it is perhaps not a surprise that the threats posed by various Soviet Bloc intelligence services during the Cold War have receded into memory. While the writers of spy novels, and indeed most intelligence services, are focused largely on the activities of various terrorist organizations, the reality is that there are a number of intelligence services around the world, some with their roots in the Cold War, that are a threat to Canada and Canadian interests. Today those threats spring more often from cyberattacks on various government or private institutions, but sometimes events remind us that traditional foreign espionage is still a threat. One has only to recall the conviction of naval officer Jeffrey Delisle in Canada for espionage, the arrest of eleven Russian Illegals in the United States in June 2010, or the arrest of two Russian Illegals in Toronto in 1996 living under the identities of two deceased Canadian children.

Mr. Mahar's book tells the story of one Canadian counterintelligence operation, code-named KEYSTONE, dating from the Cold War. It is a story that Mr. Mahar, first as an officer in the Security Service of the Royal Canadian Mounted Police and then as an intelligence officer in the Canadian Security Intelligence Service (CSIS) working against Soviet Bloc intelligence agencies, such as the First Chief Directorate of the Komitet Gosudarstvennoi Bezopastnosti (KGB) or its successor the Sluzhba Vneshney Razvedki (SVR), knew well. While the story, or rather a part of it, has been told before in John Sawatsky's book *For Services Rendered: Leslie James Bennett and the RCMP Security Service*, Mr. Mahar's book tells, for the first time, the story of that operation from start to finish.

It is the story of GIDEON, a Soviet Illegal placed in Canada by the KGB and then recruited by the Security Service. LONG KNIFE, a Security Service officer in need of money, then betrayed his recruitment to the KGB. GIDEON, who had already been recalled to Moscow for other reasons, returned home, unsuspectingly to be arrested. Given the unforgiving reputation of the KGB, it is perhaps not a surprise that when GIDEON disappeared from view everyone believed that he had been executed. Many who were thought to have betrayed the KGB were executed, often brutally. However, the story did not end quite as one might have expected. It is the rest of the story that Mr. Mahar, as a participant, wanted to tell.

More broadly, there is an image of the intelligence world that it is about "lying and stealing," as one international news magazine recently described it. In other words, it is a somewhat less than honorable profession. Unfortunately that view is sometimes reinforced by the reality that news stories about the intelligence world are rarely about successes and often about real or often perceived failures. I know that there are good stories about both counterterrorism and counterespionage successes, most of which will never be told. Mr. Mahar's book is an example of one story that can now be told and offers a more realistic view of the profession.

It is also a story about one of the most often questioned aspects of intelligence work: the reliance of intelligence agencies on human sources. While the questioning is perhaps understandable given the often disreputable reputation that is ascribed to sources, as one of my colleagues once said to me in the context of concerns about an alleged source whose identity had been revealed in media reports: "If we want a better class of sources, we need a better class of targets." Whatever their reputation, sources are an essential part of intelligence work. Their motives are as varied as the levels of risk that they may be exposed to, but their contribution is often crucial to success. Intelligence agencies therefore make every effort to protect and support their sources. While the Security Service was unable to protect GIDEON from betrayal by one of its own, this is the story about the efforts that the Security Service and CSIS made to protect and assist a key counterintelligence source.

In sum, Mr. Mahar has written the story of a major Canadian Cold War counterintelligence operation that is about the people involved but also about the intelligence world. As an intelligence professional himself, not an observer, he both knew the people and understood how the world they inhabited worked, and he tells the story well.

He also tells it honestly, describing both successes and failures along the way, which is the reality of all intelligence operations. Rarely do they go as planned. Ultimately, however, Mr. Mahar's book is one of those rarities of the intelligence world, a good story that can be told that helps us to better understand the intelligence world and reminds us that while intelligence agencies are properly focused on terrorism as the priority, there are other threats of which we need to be aware and be prepared to address.

Ward Elcock
Director of CSIS (1994–2004)

Preface

Yevgeni Vladimirovich Brik was a Soviet Illegal who was dispatched to Canada with instructions to establish himself in the Montreal area as a Canadian watch repairman. His KGB codename was HART. Royal Canadian Mounted Police (RCMP) corporal James Douglas Finley Morrison, a man who distinguished himself in Europe during World War II, had a brief but significant encounter with Brik. The consequences of that fateful meeting and the subsequent actions taken by Morrison changed the course of espionage and counterintelligence in Canada for many years. In 1953 when the RCMP Security Service learned of the existence of Brik, Inspector Terrance (Terry) Guernsey, the officer in charge of counterintelligence, took control of the developing case and named it Operation KEYSTONE. Concurrently, he assigned the codename GIDEON to Brik. Two years later, he assigned the codename LONG KNIFE to RCMP corporal Morrison. Those names remained classified top secret and were protected by the RCMP Security Service and the government of Canada for decades.

There has never been a comprehensive account written about this historic Soviet KGB Cold War espionage operation in Canada nor the RCMP Security Service counterintelligence operation to combat it. This book changes that landscape. Over the years, various authors in the West and in Russia have dedicated individual chapters or passages in their respective books in an attempt to expose this extraordinary case. Journalists have dedicated columns in the print media but only managed, for the most part, to engage in circular reporting. Much of what has been written thus far is seriously flawed. The recorded history in the public domain is largely incorrect and leaves a false impression for those who seek the truth. These inaccuracies are regrettable but understandable when one recognizes that the various writers are outsiders to the intelligence world. They have never had direct access to Operation

KEYSTONE classified intelligence files, nor had they ever been exposed to GIDEON, the Soviet spy who is the primary antagonist in this story.

Respected British author and historian Christopher Andrew, working with the late KGB/SVR archivist and defector Vasili Mitrokhin, produced the most accurate, albeit brief account of this story in their book *The Mitrokhin Archive: The KGB in Europe and the West.*

As a senior intelligence officer of the Canadian Security Intelligence Service (CSIS), I was an insider working at the heart of the Counter Intelligence (CI) branch. The director general of CI at that point, Mr. Geoffrey O'Brian, assigned this operation to me in 1992 when it literally rose like a Phoenix from the ashes. Of course, with responsibility for the case came the privilege of access to the original Operation KEYSTONE classified documentation. Ironically, it was the second time that I had been exposed to this historic case.

I was posted to RCMP Security Service at headquarters, Ottawa, in August 1976, having just spent seven years as an RCMP officer in the Province of Saskatchewan. Shortly after my arrival, the late RCMP inspector Bill Walker gave me dozens of historic operational case files to read, ranging from the late 1940s to what was then present day. One of the cases he gave me was Operation KEYSTONE. I devoured it page after page. Little did anyone know at the time, especially myself, that knowledge of GIDEON, LONG KNIFE, and this case would become so very important sixteen years later. That knowledge was critical for the operation we ran throughout 1992. I knew this troubled man personally for the ensuing nineteen years.

It is instructive to know that between my arrival in the Security Service in 1976 and the time Operation KEYSTONE erupted for the second time in 1992, the government of Canada disbanded the Security Service and established CSIS on July 16, 1984.

The Russian Intelligence Service has long held an iron grip and a stern countenance over the people of the nation. Prior to the Russian Revolution, Tsarist Russia came under the watchful eye and excesses of the Okhrana. It was created in 1880 as the Tsarist Intelligence and Security Service. The Okhrana served as a secret police force for the Russian Empire. It was a feared agency within the Ministry of Internal Affairs (MVD). Following the revolution in 1917, Lenin dissolved the Okhrana and arrested, incarcerated, and executed many of its officers and agents.

In its place, the new Soviet Socialist Republic established the All-Russian Extraordinary Commission for Combating Counter-Revolution and Sabotage (CHEKA) in December 1917. Since then the Russian Intelligence Service has reinvented itself numerous times. It evolved over the next thirty-seven years, taking on new names and bureaucracies. It had been variously known during those tumultuous years by Soviet acronyms such as the OGPU, NKVD, NKGB, and several other iterations. In March 1954 the Komitet Gosudarstvennoi Bezopastnosti (KGB, Committee for State Security) was created. Its primary functions included, but were not limited to, the collection of Foreign Intelligence (First Chief Directorate) and, secondly, Internal Security (Second Chief Directorate). With the collapse of communism in December 1991, the organizational structure and name changed once again when the KGB was disbanded. In its place two new intelligence organizations were born. From what had been the former KGB's First Chief Directorate came the Sluzhba Vneshney Razvedki (SVR), the Foreign Intelligence Service of the Russian Federation. Its headquarters, secluded by woods, is located in the Yasenevo District of Moscow.

On April 12, 1995, the Federal'naya Sluzhba Bezopasnosti Rossiyskoy Federatsii (FSB), with its headquarters at Lubyanka Square, Moscow, was established as the Federal Security Service of the Russian Federation.

For the sake of simplicity, I have chosen to refer to the Russian Intelligence Service throughout this narrative as the more widely known and understood KGB.

In a similar vein, the RCMP created a security and intelligence component within the force shortly after the end of World War II. It was established following the September 5, 1945, defection to Canada of Soviet intelligence officer and cypher clerk Igor Gouzenko from the Soviet Embassy in Ottawa. Gouzenko, a member of Soviet Military Intelligence (Glavnoye Razvedyvatelnoye Upravleniye or GRU), documented widespread Soviet GRU espionage in Canada and other Western countries. At the time of his defection, he removed 109 classified GRU documents from the safe inside the Soviet Embassy that identified GRU agents and operations.

Gouzenko further informed the Canadian government that the KGB had also established an espionage presence in Canada but that he did not possess intimate knowledge of their networks. In the wake of these revelations, the RCMP recognized that they needed to develop an enhanced security and intelligence capability to investigate, identify, monitor, and interdict these KGB and GRU clandestine agent networks.

Throughout various times in its history, the RCMP named its security and intelligence organization the Special Branch, Security and Intelligence Branch, Security and Intelligence Directorate, and the Security Service. Similar to the Soviet KGB model, I will use the generic term, the Security Service, throughout the story to lessen confusion for the reader.

The process of identifying classified government information and having it declassified for release and publication is a journey filled with angst over a highway infused with disappointment, potholes, and obstructions. For over two years I sought previously classified Canadian documentation by petitioning federal government departments and agencies by using Canadian Access to Information and Privacy Act (ATIP) legislation. The CSIS, the RCMP, and Foreign Affairs and International Trade Canada all contributed, to the extent the law would allow, to the body of knowledge with respect to this story. I am grateful for their assistance but, like any historical researcher, I yearned for more. I also traveled extensively across Canada interviewing people, while at the same time searching archives and libraries for hidden treasure. Open source information of all types and categories is invaluable and often leads to the discovery of material that one would have thought was contained only in classified records or would have been protected by privacy legislation. I also profited from a trip to Moscow where I was able to visit and photograph various KGB sites and museums as well as other locations of interest to this story.

One of my objectives in writing this story is to correct the plethora of inaccuracies that are prevalent in the literature today about this historic case. It was considered by those in the West who had knowledge of it to be one of the most important Canadian counterintelligence operations and penetrations of the KGB during the early period of the Cold War. It is an important piece of Canadian history about the early beginnings of the Cold War that has been buried in the archives. It was a historically important espionage operation for the Soviets as they systematically planted well-trained deep-cover Illegals throughout the West to support the intelligence requirements of the Kremlin.

One would be mistaken in thinking that Operation KEYSTONE is a relic of the past, a phenomenon of the KGB and the Cold War. Dispatching deep-cover Illegals to the West, and elsewhere, has continued under the current-day SVR. Recent Canadian cases that received broad media reporting include the 1996 arrests of Yelena Olshevskaya and Dmitriy Olshevsky in a CSIS operation dubbed STANLEY CUP. Using identity theft, the SVR assigned them the names of two Canadian infants who had died at birth. The Russian couple entered Canada individually and were later married as Ian and Laurie Lambert. There was also the 2006 PAUL WILLIAM HAMPEL SVR Illegals operation in Montreal. He was arrested in November 2006 at Montreal's Pierre Elliott Trudeau Airport as he was trying to leave Canada. The arrests in June 2010 in the United States of eleven SVR Illegals further illustrates the Russian Federation's continued adherence to using deep-cover spies to steal military, economic, high-tech, and political secrets from the West. This case, which featured the glamorous Anna Chapman, shocked America. It had a distinctive Canadian connection. Four of the eleven Illegals were posing as Canadians and were in possession of Canadian passports.

The KGB was under the illusion that GIDEON was their faithful, deep-cover Illegal agent operating clandestinely in Canada. The RCMP was under the illusion that LONG KNIFE was a dedicated patriot and undercover operative working against the KGB. Both organizations and their respective governments were about to discover that their trust and faith had been unwarranted. Their illusions were about to be shattered.

Acknowledgments

The research and writing of this book has been a journey of four years in the making. The task was a little daunting considering that almost all of the principals have been deceased for many years. And of course, a great deal of the information remained classified and rested in the vaults of the CSIS and within the classified holdings of our national Library and Archives Canada.

Anyone who has ever attempted a project of this nature knows that it takes the combined efforts of a multitude of people. This is not a work that has been written in isolation. I am deeply indebted to the many men and women of CSIS, from the senior executive to the operational and administrative officers, with whom I have discussed various aspects of this story. They gave of their time graciously. I say with the deepest of regret that, because of the nature of their duties, these fine Canadians must remain anonymous. I would like to thank a number of current CSIS employees for their continued friendship and interest in this book project. I am in their debt.

I am deeply grateful and honored to have former CSIS director Ward Elcock as the author of the foreword for this book. When asked if he would consider such an undertaking, he accepted immediately. Prime Minister Jean Chrétien appointed Director Elcock as the fourth director of the Service in 1994. He served in this capacity for ten years before being reassigned by government. He has a bachelor of arts degree in political science from Carleton University in Ottawa and an LLB from Osgoode Hall Law School in Toronto. I stand shoulder to shoulder with former Service colleagues who share great respect and admiration for him. He has always been a keen professional and fine gentleman.

I am grateful also for the very professional advice, encouragement, and assistance that I consistently received from Rowman & Littlefield's senior acquisition editor, Marie-Claire Antoine. She patiently handled my queries with aplomb and was always available when I called. I would also like to

thank Rowman & Littlefield's Monica Savaglia, Mary Malley, and Elaine
McGarraugh for steering my manuscript through production.

I am blessed to have three extraordinary brothers, professionals all, who
provided me with love, support, and encouragement. They listened to my
ideas, offered sage advice, and were always there for me when I needed
them. Bob (Cataula, Georgia), Dave (London, Ontario), and Ralph (Ottawa,
Ontario), I am deeply proud of the three of you. As I grow older, I recognize
how precious time is and how much the three of you mean to me. I know
Bob and Dave will agree that I need to express a very special thank you to
brother Ralph. He has been a pillar to me throughout this project. It is difficult to believe that I could have finished the book without his able assistance.
Ralph has devoted countless hours toward this undertaking. He is responsible
for tracking down the ownership and copyright of most of the photographs
that appear in this book. Additionally, he acquired the licenses needed that
allowed me to use these photographs. It was no small feat. A retired career
officer of CSIS and a former Royal Canadian Mounted Police (RCMP) officer, I benefited greatly from Ralph's deep knowledge and timely advice with
respect to all things Soviet. If that isn't enough, it was Ralph who steered this
technology-illiterate retiree through the intricacies of social media platforms
and other forms of book promotion. Thank you so much, Ralph.

I am deeply privileged to have received strong support from so many
others who are silently a part of the fabric of this book. I respect and ac-
knowledge your wish to remain anonymous. Soviet defectors, former Soviet
immigrants, intelligence professionals, and others have provided advice,
anecdotes, translation, and a meal or two while talking about this story. You
have my deep gratitude.

And a special thanks to the following individuals, listed in random order,
who met with me in communities across Canada and the United States during the research phase of this book. I thank you for your time and candor:
the late Ryan Vidion-Jones of White Rock, British Columbia, brother of the
late Gwynneth Morrison; Robert and Elizabeth Knuckle of Dundas, Ontario;
Allan MacDougall, Halifax, Nova Scotia; Sonja Matthys, Ottawa, Ontario;
Tanja Zivanovic, Ottawa, Ontario, who provided translation advice; Ann
Mahar, Cataula, Georgia; Joby Warrick, double Pulitzer Prize–winning
author and journalist with the *Washington Post*; Anthony (Tony) and Jonna
Mendez, Virginia; John Cummings, Ottawa, Ontario; Dan McNamara and
Laura Pizzale, lawyers, London, Ontario; Robert and Mary Ellen Gordon,
Orleans, Ontario; Tom Maybee and his wife, RCMP Deputy Commissioner
(Rtd.) Barbara George of Trinity, Newfoundland; FBI Supervisory Special
Agent (Rtd.) John W. Whiteside III, Pennsylvania; Deborah Theede, New
Brunswick; Michael and Suzanne Donnelly, Ottawa, Ontario; David and

Rochelle Greenberg, Ottawa, Ontario; Bruce McDonald, Ottawa, Ontario; Benjamin Dunn, archives analyst at RCMP Historical Branch; Alan Jones, Ottawa, Ontario; James and Dorothy Bruce, Etobicoke, Ontario; Sandy Mc-Callum, Petrolia, Ontario; Mike McAllister, Scarborough, Ontario; Geoffrey O'Brian, Ottawa, Ontario; Robbie McLeod, Campleton, New Brunswick; Gordon Gramlick, Pokono, Alberta; and Ambassador Gaetan Lavértu, Ottawa, Ontario. And a special expression of gratitude to the infamous retired Canadian and American intelligence professionals who I gather with annually for our spring summit at Finger Lakes, New York: Jim Ohlson, Bob Hallman, Joe Dickey, Phil Pounds, Tom Reilly, Bob Barrass, Dan Cameron, John Summers, and Peter Godin. May our bond of brotherhood and camaraderie forever endure!

A special thanks also to lifelong friends Ron and Sue Fenney, London, Ontario; Ken and Connie Fenney, Port Credit, Ontario; and Richard and Laima Cowburn, Burlington, Ontario. Your encouragement and friendship mean the world to me.

But it is to my family that I owe the most heartfelt thanks of all. I know I won the lottery the day I married Carol Anne Westran in 1971. She has been at my side for over forty-seven years, in Canada and abroad. Nobody has given me more love, support, or encouragement than she has. As with everything she does in her life, she encouraged me to finish what I started, to get out across Canada to conduct the interviews I needed to do, to get the photographs that would complement the story, and to spend the time at the computer to complete the manuscript. She played an active role prior to the exfiltration operation and assisted Yevgeni Brik to become familiar with life in Ottawa when he arrived back in Canada. For all that you have done, I thank you from the bottom of my heart.

To Scott, Marta, Gibson, and Autumn Mahar, you provide meaning and substance to our lives. We are so immensely proud of you all. You make our days happier, our weekends more fun, and family dinners a wonderful circus. Gibson and Autumn are the loves of our life and are a reflection of the love they get from their parents. Ewa and José Garcia y Artega and Agnes Westran, you enrich our lives and make family gatherings both fun and special. And Gary and Eleanor Morgan, your friendship is intertwined with our heart and soul. You are family to us in every respect. And we are the richer for it. Thank you so much for your editing help, for listening countless times about this story, and for always being there. A very large part of you is in this book.

I have strived to get the details of this historic Canadian story accurate. If I have failed, then the blame is entirely mine. All errors and omissions are mine and only mine.

Chapter One

Flight to Rio

Yevgeni Vladimirovich Brik locked his single-bedroom ground-floor apartment at 5381 Bannantyne Avenue in Verdun, Quebec. He knew he would not be returning to his home for at least a couple of months. If things went badly, perhaps not at all. The three-floor red brick building contained nine apartments and was located at the busy intersection of Bannantyne and Argyle in this blue-collar working-class municipality adjacent to Montreal. Construction workers, restaurant help, and delivery truck drivers were making their way to work this humid and sticky morning of August 3, 1955. Brik's apartment doubled as his residence and his fledgling photography business, Portraits by Soboloff. Luggage in hand, he walked to the sidewalk and entered the waiting taxi, which sat idling outside his door. It was just after 5:00 a.m. The Trans World Airlines flight he would be taking to Rio de Janeiro via Caracas, Venezuela, was fueled and ready and would depart in ninety minutes. He had plenty of time to get to the airport.

Brik, three months short of his thirty-third birthday, checked his suit pocket for his Canadian passport as the taxi pulled away from the curb. The photograph staring back was his likeness, but the name identified Brik as being Joseph Bugyi. The real Joseph Bugyi had been a Canadian of Hungarian extraction who had been born November 30, 1895, at Farmos, Pest, Hungary. Prior to returning to Eastern Europe to live permanently, he had been a resident of the small farming community of Rockfort, Saskatchewan, in the eastern part of the province north of Yorkton. He had been a permanent resident of Canada since 1923. He returned to his roots because of the economic hardship of the time.

The passport that Brik was carrying skillfully concealed any trace that the date of birth had been altered or that Bugyi's photograph had been substituted. It was one of many false identifications that Brik would be associated

1

with over the years. A few weeks previously the Joseph Bugyi passport had been discreetly passed to him by a man he did not know during a hasty, prearranged meeting in Ottawa, Ontario. That meeting was organized by Nikolai Ostrovskiy of the Soviet Embassy in Ottawa. Ostrovskiy, who did not attend that meeting, held the diplomatic position of First Secretary at the Soviet Embassy. In reality he was a clandestine intelligence officer of the Komitet Gosudarstvennoi Bezopastnosti (KGB), who had been dispatched to Canada by KGB HQ in Moscow commonly known as The Centre. He was formally attached to the KGB's First Chief Directorate (Foreign Intelligence) where he functioned as a Line N officer responsible for the intelligence operations of Soviet Illegals. Previous to his Ottawa posting, Ostrovskiy had been assigned to the KGB's Department V, which was responsible for the planning of sabotage missions and assassinations.

Brik, whose KGB codename was HART, had not spoken to the intermediary. The stranger who delivered the false passport was a member of the Communist Party of Canada and an established KGB agent of sixteen years.

Yevgeni Brik was headed to Dorval Airport on the outskirts of Verdun. The airport initially opened September 1, 1941, and quickly became internationally recognized as the primary staging base for Britain's Royal Air Force Ferry Command. Over ten thousand aircraft constructed in Canada and the United States had been delivered to the United Kingdom from Dorval Airport during World War II. It transitioned to a civilian airport at the end of the war in 1945. Yevgeni emerged from the cab and walked into what was then Canada's largest airport.

A diminutive man with a shock of brown wavy hair, Brik boarded the Trans World Airlines Super Constellation with its distinctive triple tail design and curved fuselage and was soon flying high above the United States en route to Caracas. The long hours on the "Connie" provided Brik with time to reflect on the unexpected events of the past few months. He knew his recall to Moscow for additional intelligence training and to reunite with his wife and parents was standard operational procedures. This had been explained during his initial training in Moscow years earlier. In the latest communication from Moscow, Brik was further advised that he should expect to return to Canada six to eight weeks later. Brik had securely locked his apartment and photographic studio, leaving everything intact. However, the surprising KGB assignment to go to Rio while en route to the Soviet Union was completely unexpected. No such contingency had been discussed prior to his dispatch to Canada in late 1951. The assignment itself was intriguing.

Yevgeni Brik was mildly surprised with the 80 degree Fahrenheit temperature and heavy humidity when he disembarked from the aircraft at Aeropuerto Internacional de Maiquetia Simon Bolivar. The airport, simply called Maiquetia by locals, was constructed in 1945 on the outskirts of Caracas. Brik had just flown 2,450 miles south of Dorval, which was almost the halfway point to his destination. He assumed it would be much hotter here. Caracas was merely a refueling stop. Those passengers who were continuing to Rio were able to go into the terminal for a change of scenery and to get a little exercise. Brik had never previously been to South America and was fascinated by the activity and crowds he encountered. Within the hour, the "Connie" raced back down the runway, lifted and banked southeast as it began its 2,800-mile journey to Rio. Brik focused on the details of the operation that Moscow had sent prior to his departure. He was skeptical, somewhat apprehensive, but a little excited at the same time. He was anxious to experience this exotic Brazilian city on the ocean. After learning that Moscow wanted him to travel to Rio, he began reading about the Latin music, the exciting women, and the laissez-faire attitude that prevailed in the city.

Darkness had fallen by the time the TWA Super Constellation began its descent to Galeao International Airport. The lights of the city sparkled like a billion shiny jewels.

Brik gathered his luggage, proceeded without difficulty through Brazilian Immigration and Custom's controls, and stepped out into the chaos of the arrivals terminal. The reception area was an assault on his senses. The sights, sounds, and smells of the terminal and the people in it were unlike anything he had ever experienced. There seemed to be no order; pandemonium ruled. Brik managed to push back at unwanted stewards who were grabbing at his luggage and spurned offers from unofficial taxi drivers inside the terminal to take him where he wanted to go. Outside the terminal he found what appeared to be an official, government-licensed taxi and jumped in.

Brik was very happy to discover that the taxi driver spoke very good English. He asked to be taken to an inexpensive hotel in the center of the city where it would be easy for him to get around. The drive to the city center was just as chaotic as the airport terminal. Within forty-five minutes Brik registered at the São Francisco Hotel as Joseph Bugyi using his false Canadian passport as identification. Although exhausted from the long day of travel, Brik showered and went out to explore the unfamiliar, exciting neighborhood and get something to eat. The brightly lit city electrified him and stimulated his senses. He visited several bars and happily discovered that they hosted many attractive women who were neither shy nor unfriendly. The music, cigarette smoke, and liquor embraced the crowds as they partied throughout the night. The bars, clubs, and beer halls remained open almost to daylight. Brik was only too happy to oblige them all and stayed until the lights were turned off.

The combination of a long travel day, time difference, a late night at the clubs, too much alcohol, and too many cigarettes caused Brik to sleep longer than he wanted or planned. It was early afternoon on August 4, and he had important preparations to arrange. Moscow had sent instructions for him to meet quietly with another KGB Illegal at a designated rendezvous site on August 7. Brik's first objective was to establish precisely where that meeting place was in relation to his hotel. Second, he needed to spend time in the rendezvous area familiarizing himself with the surroundings. Of particular importance, Brik wanted to conduct discreet surveillance in the rendezvous area to determine if Brazilian intelligence was in the shadows waiting for the two Soviet Illegals to walk into a trap. Brik had never met this agent. All he had been told was this new agent's codename was HECTOR and he was currently working on another intelligence assignment. Brik was also told that HECTOR would be relocating to Canada sometime in the future and would assist him in his espionage activities. Brik received instructions to go to the railing on Beiramar Praemona opposite Riobranko Street and to be there at 5:00 p.m. He was to carry a small parcel under his left arm with a green ribbon tied around it. He was also told to carry a local newspaper. Brik was provided with a backup plan that provided an alternative time and date to meet with HECTOR if he failed to show up at the first scheduled rendezvous. This too was standard operating procedure. Finally, Brik was told not to be alarmed if neither meeting materialized. HECTOR was very busy in another important theater of operations. If he was unable to meet Brik at either rendezvous, Moscow would send Brik back to Canada by way of Rio de Janeiro in several weeks' time, at which point they would ensure HECTOR's attendance. The backup plan gave Brik a sense of confidence that the KGB's intentions of having him return to Canada to continue his activities following home leave were intact.

Finding the rendezvous site in Rio proved less problematic than Brik had originally thought. Riobranko Street was one of the main and busiest streets. Without exerting a lot of effort, he found the railing on Beiramar Praemona and walked the area to get a sense of the buildings, alleyways, and side streets. He looked for and found a quiet place where he could sit and discreetly observe people in the immediate area in the hope of ascertaining whether there was danger lurking in hidden places. Having satisfied himself that the rendezvous site was easy to locate, Brik wandered off. He planned to return over the next few days, at different times, to confirm that the area was not under surveillance.

During the evening of August 4, and the following two days, Brik's capacity to function as a human being was greatly challenged. He attacked the bars with a vengeance and nearly drank himself comatose. He happily paid for the company of various willing ladies and otherwise spent money at an alarming rate. Brik was having the time of his life in a city and country far removed from Moscow or Montreal. It was particularly pleasing to him because he didn't know a single soul in all of Brazil.

Reality returned on the morning of August 7. Brik pulled himself together, showered, and dressed in fresh, clean clothes. In anticipation of his expected meeting later in the afternoon, he found an inexpensive restaurant and devoured a hearty meal. In spite of his earlier commitment to operational security, he never did return to the rendezvous site after his initial visit to observe if the area was under surveillance. He would make up for that failing by going to the site earlier this afternoon.

As he did three days previously, Brik walked the area to once again acquaint himself with his surroundings. He established a quick escape route in case local authorities initiated a trap. Satisfied that all was under control, he found a quiet place to sit, wait, and observe. The late afternoon shadows signaled it was time. Sensing no danger, Brik walked over to the designated railing a couple of minutes prior to 5:00 p.m. and began reading the newspaper he was carrying. The small parcel tied with green ribbon was tucked under his left arm. His anxiety level was heightened, but he felt in control. The hour hand passed the appointed time and kept sliding as the minutes rolled by. It was a pleasant afternoon with a clear sky and virtually no clouds or wind. Brik looked at his watch and saw that it was 5:45 p.m. He resisted the urge to pack up his newspaper and walk away. He knew it was the correct operational thing to do. He recognized he shouldn't remain in the target area too long. Nevertheless, he did. When 6:00 p.m. arrived Brik folded the newspaper and walked away from the rendezvous site. He privately wondered whether HECTOR encountered some unspecified problem. Had he been injured in a serious car accident? Perhaps Brazilian Intelligence or the local police arrested him, or worse, shot and killed him? Brik knew that the KGB in Moscow told him there was a possibility that HECTOR may not show up. In spite of that Brik felt uncomfortable. He wanted to get as far away from there as quickly as possible.

Early the following morning, in accordance with his backup plan, Brik returned to the rendezvous site by the railing on Beiramar Praemona. However, as was the case the day before, HECTOR failed to appear. Brik wasted no time. He quickly returned to the São Francisco Hotel and, without Moscow's knowledge, wrote and posted a short, cryptic note to a certain dentist in Ottawa. He neither knew nor met the dentist. Minutes later he placed his suitcase into a taxi, departed for Galeao International Airport, and boarded an Air France flight for Paris. He did not know that his arrival in Rio and his five days of partying had been under close KGB surveillance the entire time.

Chapter Two

The City of Light

Yevgeni landed in Paris in the early morning of August 9, 1955. Rather than exhausting him, the long flight from Rio had reinvigorated him as he thought about the city and its fabled nightlife. He was still in possession of the false Joseph Bugyi Canadian passport that had served him well in Brazil. The documents were of such high caliber that he gained entry into France without difficulty.

Brik jumped into the nearest taxi and asked the driver to take him to a small and inexpensive hotel in the center of Paris. Sizing up his passenger, the taxi driver suggested a discreet, out-of-the-way hotel that also served as a brothel. Yevgeni agreed and was happy with the choice. After all, he was spending KGB funds.

In his hotel room, Yevgeni wrote a short, cryptic note to a Parisian woman whom he knew by the KGB codename MARA. The attractive young woman, a French fashion designer, was serving as a "live letter box" for the Paris KGB Residency in the Soviet Embassy. Yevgeni's note to her confirmed his presence in Paris. However, it was one piece of intelligence he didn't need to provide. As had been the case in Rio, the KGB was already aware that he had arrived in the City of Light. Yevgeni's correspondence to her further stipulated the precise date and time when he would go to the identified Paris rendezvous site to quickly exchange travel documents with yet another unknown KGB intermediary.

In the meantime, Brik had other requirements to take care of. He needed a Finnish visa for the final leg of his journey back to Russia. But the Finnish Embassy was closed for a three-day weekend. Three additional days in Paris suited Brik's sense of fun.

Early Saturday morning, Brik left his hotel and headed for the rendezvous site. It was the proposed meeting date he had identified in his note to MARA, two days earlier. Brik walked slowly along the Avenue des Champs-Élysées en route to Place du Carrousel next to the Musée du Louvre where, according to plan, someone would approach him at 11:30 a.m. As stipulated by Moscow, Brik wore a sports jacket that had a European edition of the *New York Times* in his right-hand pocket with the paper's banner visible. It was a glorious summer morning, and Parisians and tourists alike were out enjoying the splendor of the city. The KGB operative would ask if he was staying at the Hotel Bristol. Brik was to respond by saying, "No, at the Hotel Milan." The contact would then offer greetings from Tony. In the meeting instructions he had received prior to departing Canada, Brik was admonished not to remain at the rendezvous site for more than ten minutes. If the contact did not appear, Brik was to repeat the exercise two hours later at 1:30 p.m. and to continue following this pattern for the next two days if necessary. If, at that point, the intermediary had still not shown up, Brik was to write another brief note to MARA and furnish another meeting date. As things evolved, the elaborate backup plan was unnecessary.

The brief contact between Brik and the unknown intermediary occurred precisely on time, at 11:30 a.m. In a discreet but quick movement Brik was handed new identity documents. He in turn relinquished the Joseph Bugyi passport that had served him well on his travels from Canada to Brazil and France. The intermediary disappeared into the crowd as quickly as he had appeared. And at that moment, Yevgeni Brik became John Hladysh for the second time in his life.

When the Finnish Embassy opened again after the long weekend, Brik showed up at the Consular Section early. Once inside the embassy he completed the official visa request form and paid the necessary fee. The middle-aged consular clerk on duty was a locally engaged French national. She reviewed the form for completeness, handed him a receipt for his passport and visa-processing fee, and instructed him to wait. He walked back out into the Paris sunshine a short while later with his passport and Finnish visa in hand.

Brik wrote two personal postcards to people he didn't know and posted them to addresses in London, England. The cards advised the respective recipients that he expected to arrive in Moscow within days.

Paris was drenched in sunshine the following morning when Brik boarded the Aero Finnair flight that would take him to Helsinki by way of a brief one-hour stopover in Brussels. The flight to Helsinki Airport, situated near Seutula, was pleasant and seemed to take no time at all. The new airport, completed in time to welcome the thousands who had arrived for the 1952 Helsinki Olympic Games, was the pride of the city.

After depositing his suitcase in a hotel, Brik went directly to the Helsinki meeting site that had been identified to him before he departed from Canada. He was greeted by a short but spry Russian-speaking man who had been assigned to assist Brik with his onward travel. The little Russian was actually smaller than Brik himself. The two finalized arrangements for Brik to get back into the Soviet Union using the John Hladysh documentation. Brik was questioned on how he would prefer to enter the Soviet Union. Did he wish to enter the country by using the "green path," a KGB euphemism for crossing the border illegally? Brik knew that choosing this method would mean that he would be smuggled into the country inside a concealed compartment in a specially modified truck or car. It would be designed in such a fashion that authorities could search the trunk of the vehicle and not see the secret compartment. Brik was not enthused with this idea. The alternative would be for him to fly from Helsinki to Leningrad and from there to Moscow. The disadvantage with this method was that the John Hladysh passport would have a USSR entry stamp in it. In spite of this Brik chose this alternative. He was advised that tickets would be provided to him the following day.

Fatigued from his travels and the frequent time changes, and suffering from the accumulated effects of his extracurricular nighttime activities, Brik cleared Finnish Immigration and boarded a Russian Tupolev, which landed a short time later at Shosseynaya Airport in Leningrad. Unbeknownst to him, Moscow had sent one of its burly officers from the notorious Second Chief Directorate (Domestic Operations) who would, if necessary, overpower and force Brik onto the aircraft. This tactic would only be used if Brik had a change of heart in the final moments and decided not to return to Moscow. However, this extreme measure proved to be unnecessary. An hour and a half later the aircraft began its final approach at Sheremetyevo Airport in Moscow. During those ninety minutes Brik was consumed with thoughts of his wife and parents. As the plane landed, he felt a wave of emotion and savored the prospect of seeing them after having been in Canada the past four years. It was August 19, 1955, and he was finally back home.

As the aircraft rolled to a stop on the tarmac, Brik caught a glimpse of a black ZIS Model 110 limousine with window curtains as it pulled up and stopped next to the front of the plane. Like all other Soviet citizens, Brik understood that the limousine was reserved for senior government officials. As he descended the steps leading from the aircraft he was astonished to see Nikolai Alekseyevich Korznikov step from the car. Korznikov, a senior KGB officer in Directorate S within the First Chief Directorate (Foreign Intelligence), was responsible for KGB Illegals' operations worldwide. Korznikov greeted him politely and motioned for him to enter the vehicle. Brik, with his brain racing and struggling to maintain his composure, knew instinctively that this was not a courtesy being extended to him. He had no idea why Korznikov was at the airport to pick him up. But he knew it wasn't a good thing. Yevgeni Brik's life was about to change forever, if not be cut short altogether.

Chapter Three

From the Baltic to the
Land of Liberty

Yevgeni Vladimirovich Brik was born November 25, 1921, at his parents'
home at 65 Vorontsovskaya Street in the Black Sea port city of Novorossiysk in Krasnodar Krai. His birth certificate, #N601/211, was registered on
December 2, 1921, by the Communist Party Executive Committee of Novorossiysk District.[1]

He entered this world barely three years after the Russian Revolution and
the Bolshevik murders of Czar Nicholas II and several members of the Ro-
manov family. Their hidden, mutilated bodies would not be discovered in a
mine shaft in the Yekaterinburg area of the Urals for more than fifty years.
Soviet Russia had emerged from World War I only to become embroiled in a
horrific civil war followed by years of appalling famine.

Yevgeni Brik was an only child. His father, Voldemar Ioganovich Brik,
was thirty-one years old and considered to be a quiet, studious man. He
was born in Libawa, Lithuania, in 1890 and was currently employed as an
accountant in a tobacco organization in Novorossiysk. Yevgeni's mother,
Nataliya Stepanovna Brik (nee: Lazareva), was twenty-four years of age.
She was young, slightly extroverted, and a very popular schoolteacher in the
community.

In 1921, Voldemar Brik received an appointment to the Soviet Ministry of
Foreign Trade. An opportunity of this nature would never have materialized
had he not been a trusted cadre of the Communist Party of the Soviet Union
(CPSU). Leaving his young family in Novorossiysk, Voldemar moved to
Moscow and obtained housing at Pervie Ostrovskie Pereulok, House No. 6,
Apartment No. 3. His wife and young Yevgeni joined him there a year later.
They were both exhilarated but a little frightened to embark on their new
adventure to join Voldemar in Moscow.[2]

Life changed dramatically for the Brik family in Moscow. Young Yevgeni no longer saw the deep-water port with its many ships from around the world or the high, round hills where his mother would take him on short hikes. The entire port with its busy ship traffic would be laid out below them when they reached the top of the hills. Family, friends, and other acquaintances labored at the port where grain and other commodities were received or shipped to other countries. Others worked in the nearby cement factory. It was the only life the Brik family knew.

Moscow was a massive, sprawling city with grand, high buildings and more transportation and people than Nataliya or Yevgeni had ever seen or imagined. If the change was overwhelming to Voldemar Ioganovich, he never showed or expressed it. The bustling Novorossiysk sea port and nearby hills were replaced by magnificent buildings such as St. Basil's Cathedral commissioned by Ivan the Terrible and the Kremlin, the former Citadel of the tsars that had been a symbol of Russian power for centuries.

In 1926, five years after commencing work with the Soviet Ministry of Foreign Trade in Moscow, Voldemar Brik was posted to New York City. He was assigned as a senior accountant at AMTORG Trading Corporation (Amerikanskii Torgovlaia). The Soviet company was established to consolidate the numerous USSR organizations engaged in trade between it and the United States. It opened in early May 1924 at 136 Liberty Street and quickly became a concern of the Federal Bureau of Investigation (FBI), the US Department of Justice, and the Office of the Attorney General of the United States. AMTORG offices were also situated at 261 Fifth Avenue and 165 Broadway in Manhattan. The company employed several hundred Soviets and was heavily populated with clandestine Soviet intelligence personnel. Trade between the Soviet Union and the United States began to rise dramatically. With increased trade came the need for additional resources. Voldemar Brik arrived in New York alone. His family remained in Moscow while he established himself in Brooklyn. He and a large number of accountants and administrators worked out of the AMTORG offices located at 165 Broadway.

Twelve months after her husband arrived in New York City, Nataliya and Yevgeni sailed past the Statue of Liberty, disembarked, and were processed at Ellis Island. Never in their lives had they imagined ever leaving Novorossiysk and moving to Moscow. A year after that move they were staring at the skyline of Manhattan. It was more than they ever could have dreamed of. They joined Voldemar in Brooklyn's blue-collar area of Flatbush at 1119 Foster Avenue.[3]

During the ensuing several years, Yevgeni attended American schools in Brooklyn, played ball on neighborhood streets, and grew older in the very same fashion as other children in Brooklyn. He learned English by simply speaking and making mistakes. As his English skills improved and he gained more confidence, it soon became difficult to distinguish him from American kids with Brooklyn accents. He learned English from everyone he came in contact with. He soon was helping his mother with the daily shopping trips in the community to get groceries and to do other chores. While at home the family spoke Russian, but once outside Yevgeni reverted to Brooklyn slang. He loved the language and was a very good student. To his parents' amazement, Yevgeni spoke Russian without any accent and spoke fluent English without any trace of Russian. Every day he became more and more like a normal American kid.

The Brik family returned to Moscow in 1932, and Voldemar Ioganovich resumed work at the Soviet Ministry of Foreign Trade. Yevgeni had thrived at school in Brooklyn. The move back to Russia was very difficult for him. He missed his American friends, teachers, and neighbors. He had no friends in Moscow, and he knew that any Russian kids he might meet would not be able to comprehend or relate to his stories of travel to America and the experiences that came with living in Brooklyn.

His parents recognized the advantages of continuing his education in the American school system. They subsequently enrolled him in the Anglo-American School in Moscow where he remained until 1936. As was the case while living in Brooklyn, Yevgeni's education during these years was in English. The situation changed at the beginning of the school year in 1936 when he enrolled back into a Russian school program where he remained for the next two years. Following in his father's footsteps, Yevgeni voluntarily joined the KOMSOMOL, the Young Communist League in 1938.[4] He registered in 1939 for Russian postsecondary education by enrolling at the Bauman Higher Technical Institute at Lenin University. This was short-lived, however, as the Soviets became engaged in the Great Patriotic War. He was eighteen years of age. It was November 1939, and Yevgeni was inducted into the Red Army.

During the initial stages of the war, Yevgeni was attached to the Search Light Corps of the Moscow Anti-Aircraft Defence System. He remained with this regiment until the end of December 1942 and attained the rank of sergeant. In early 1943 Yevgeni joined the CPSU and was subsequently transferred to an infantry division where he became a radio operator in a signals platoon. He was taught the craft of sending and receiving Russian Morse code messages. Yevgeni mastered the ability to rapidly send and receive messages using a series of on-off tones, lights, or clicks. He became so skilled at this that he remained with the signals platoon until the end of the war in May 1946.[5]

With the war over, Yevgeni remained in Moscow and found employment as a laborer working a daytime shift in a ball bearing plant. During the evenings he attended classes at Bauman Higher Technical Institute at Lenin University where he had been attending school prior to the commencement of war. Because of his fluency in English, he also earned income by translating American magazines and books for various schools and government organizations.

It was during this period shortly following the cessation of war that Yevgeni married his cousin, Antonina Ivanovna Lazareva. Antonina's mother and Yevgeni's mother were related, and both resided in Moscow where Yevgeni and Antonina met and fell in love. Marriage between cousins was not uncommon during this period.

Chapter Four

The KGB Beckons

Two years after the war Yevgeni was still employed at the ball bearing plant in Moscow and attending the Bauman Higher Technical Institute at night. One evening in March 1948, after classes were over, he returned to his apartment at 5 Kalisevsaya Street that he and his wife, Antonina, were sharing with Yevgeni's parents. Antonina handed him a card that had been delivered to their apartment earlier in the day. It was from the Soviet Bureau of Registration in Moscow and was formally addressed to him as Yevgeni Vladimirovich Brik.[1]

In essence, the card was an official government summons requiring Yevgeni's appearance at a meeting in a nondescript building the following week. Upon arrival he met a Soviet official who identified himself as Sergei Sergeyevich Sergeev. Sergeev's office, which was badly in need of paint, was barren save for his desk and chair, some filing cabinets, and a photograph of Stalin on the wall. The small office smelled heavily of stale cigarette smoke, and the ashtray on his desk was half filled with the remnants of his nasty habit. There was also an uncomfortable, stained guest chair that had seen much better days. Following his brief introduction, Sergeev began to question Yevgeni about his background. He described his early years in Novorossiysk and their sudden move to Moscow. He explained that his father had obtained employment with the Soviet Ministry of Foreign Trade and subsequently was posted to New York City. As he provided these details to Sergei Sergeev, Yevgeni began to suspect that Sergeev was already aware of everything he told him. Nevertheless, he continued with his narrative. Yevgeni explained that he and his mother sailed to New York almost a year after his father had settled in the city. As he described life in Brooklyn, Sergeev began posing questions to him in English. Surprised, Yevgeni responded in kind and the two talked of his experiences while attending school, his daily life in the

Brooklyn neighborhood, and family life in general. At the conclusion of their discussions, Sergeev commented that Yevgeni could easily pass for an American. In fact, he recognized that Yevgeni spoke English with a very distinct Brooklyn accent, just like a native.

Throughout the spring of 1948, Yevgeni was required to attend several similar meetings in this same building where Sergeev's office was located. The process was always the same; he was asked questions about his background, his philosophy, his commitment to the CPSU, his parents, and his friends. There were always forms to fill in, lots and lots of forms. As previously, he was questioned in both Russian and English. The only real change was that in addition to Sergei Sergeev, other officials periodically interviewed him. These additional interviewers placed emphasis on Yevgeni's period of residency in the United States, his military signals and Russian Morse code training, and his ability to use wireless radio communications equipment. And he was also questioned closely on his capacity to run a small, independent business in the United States.

When this process began in early March, Yevgeni had been tasked by Sergeev to begin cultivating relationships with students and former colleagues at the Anglo-American school where he had previously been a student. He was instructed to provide character assessments on these individuals. The KGB objective was twofold. They wanted to assess Yevgeni's ability to provide information on Western students, many of whom had parents working as diplomats in various embassies in Moscow. And the KGB wanted to obtain information about the possible recruitment vulnerabilities they could exploit. As the weeks progressed Yevgeni submitted written accounts to Sergeev providing the necessary details.

Several months after the interview process began, Yevgeni Brik and Sergei Sergeev were once again sitting alone in Sergeev's office discussing the long and arduous process. Brik sensed that the examination of his life was over. The interviewers were apparently satisfied. They appeared to have run out of questions to ask. And thankfully, there were no more forms to fill in. Sergeev complimented Brik and confided that he was pleased with the positive outcome of the investigation.

Seizing the moment, Brik surprised Sergeev by asking him pointedly if the Soviet government was assessing his character along with his ability and willingness to become a Soviet spy targeted against the United States.[2]

Uncharacteristic for Sergeev, he became very annoyed and made no effort to conceal his displeasure. Brik was reprimanded for using that terminology and was strongly counseled never to identify or refer to himself in that fashion ever again. He was told that it was the Soviet government's wish to induct Brik into the KGB and train him clandestinely as an intelligence officer. Sergeev informed Brik that the pay was much higher than most Russians earn annually and the benefits he and his family would receive were unattainable by average Russians. Brik recognized the opportunity that was being presented to him and readily accepted the offer.

Sergeev informed Yevgeni that arrangements would be made for him to leave his employment at the ball bearing plant in Moscow. He was also told that his KGB training would commence shortly. Most important of all, cautioned Sergeev, he was advised that he must maintain strict secrecy about his new employment with the KGB and was forbidden to tell anyone about these developments, including his wife and parents. Yevgeni assured Sergeev that he fully understood the importance of discretion and gave him a commitment not to divulge this information to anyone, including his immediate family. Yevgeni left the dingy, nondescript office of KGB officer Sergei Sergeev and returned home. In what can only be described as being a tell-tale sign of his character, he entered his apartment and promptly informed his wife and mother that he was about to become a Soviet spy. It was an early indication of his deeply flawed character that would come back to haunt the KGB in the years ahead.[3]

Chapter Five

KGB Directorate S,
Illegals Department

As instructed by Sergeev, newly inducted KGB officer Yevgeni Brik, carrying a single suitcase, arrived at the prearranged, designated meeting point in central Moscow and waited to be picked up. He had been told that one of the KGB officers who had previously conducted his background security investigation would show up at 0800 hours. Precisely at the appointed time a vehicle pulled up in front of Yevgeni. He immediately recognized the driver and climbed into the vehicle. They drove together for approximately thirty minutes and subsequently entered the garage of a nondescript building in an area of the city that was mostly unfamiliar to him. Yevgeni was taken to a safe-house apartment that would become his new home and primary training site for the next couple of years. It quickly became apparent to Yevgeni that he would only see his wife and parents sporadically during this period.

The training of deep-cover Illegals who were being prepared for overseas assignments was an arduous, lengthy, complicated, and expensive venture. It was also one of the closest guarded secrets of all KGB operations. The responsibility for these highly sensitive and covert operations fell to the KGB's S Directorate of the First Chief Directorate (Foreign Intelligence). Officers being trained for Illegals work were forbidden to visit any official KGB premise. Their training sessions were held in various safe houses around Moscow. Each officer received individualized training and did not know or have the support of other officers who were engaged in similar clandestine training programs. In recognition of operational security, prospective Illegals were not indoctrinated into broader KGB operations. In this manner, KGB headquarters ensured they would never be in a position to compromise KGB operations in the country they were targeted against if they were discovered and apprehended by host-country security services. Other than the specific

KGB officers who were directly involved with the training, the Illegals were never introduced to other KGB personnel.

Specialized training for Soviet Illegals typically lasted three to four years. In addition to traditional espionage tradecraft, there was a concentration on foreign language lessons. The Illegals had to become proficient, native speakers of the country or countries they would be targeted against. Many of the candidates had been selected by the KGB because they already possessed foreign language speaking capabilities. Most had been talent spotted by university professors or other educators who quietly passed their recommendations to the KGB for future consideration. If the candidates succeeded in passing the long security investigations of their past they would be invited to become members of the KGB themselves and enter espionage training.[1]

Yevgeni's proficiency with English was forged on the streets of Brooklyn and perfected in the schools he attended in New York and later at the Anglo-American school in Moscow. His established skill of sending and receiving Russian Morse code messages, which he learned as a signals officer during World War II in the Red Army, meant that there was no need to spend valuable time in this form of KGB training. As a result, his espionage training period was shortened to two years.

The KGB officer responsible for Yevgeni's training was introduced to him that first morning in the safe-house apartment. The man did not provide his family name. He simply indicated that he was Leonid Dmitrievich and that he would be handling his training course. He confided to Yevgeni that he would be assisted when necessary by other experienced officers from the Higher Intelligence School. He also told Yevgeni that all of his training would take place in this and various apartments around Moscow and that he should expect to go on training exercises to neighboring countries. The prospect of foreign travel intrigued and excited Yevgeni and stirred his imagination.

Yevgeni was a good student. During the next two years he learned, practiced, and perfected the espionage tradecraft that would allow him to work clandestinely overseas without being detected. He received extensive training in the art of finding and using "dead-letter boxes" or "dead drops," as his KGB instructors more commonly referred to them. Dead drops are concealment locations where films, reports, money, or other items could be hidden and retrieved later by a Soviet handler. Dead drops could be located in culverts, under a bridge, behind a loose brick in a wall, or any other similar location.[2] He also received training on the use of "live-letter boxes" or LLBs. These were highly trusted people who could be depended upon to pass a message, note, or letter to a Soviet handler on behalf of the Illegal. LLBs were frequently, but not exclusively, members of the host country's Communist Party who were sympathetically tied to Moscow.

KGB officers also provided training in talent spotting and the subsequent recruitment of agents. Yevgeni was given extensive training on how he should act in a target country so he could blend in with the local population and how he should act if he felt that he was under suspicion by local police authorities or security and intelligence officials. He was taught how to identify and secure a safe house, how to work with cipher messages, one-time pads, and how to lay a signal to request or abort a meeting or to advise that a DLB had been loaded or safely emptied. A significant portion of his technical training centered on photography. He learned about exposure, f-stops, depth of field, and taking photographs in different lighting conditions. Time was spent teaching him how to create a darkroom and how to develop photographic negatives. It was in the darkroom where he learned how to create microdots that would conceal documents from unwanted attention. He also learned how to use various forms of cameras from standard single-lens reflex cameras to mini, palm-sized cameras used for photographing documents clandestinely. Yevgeni became very proficient as a photographer.

Several months after he commenced espionage training, Leonid Dmitrievich informed Yevgeni that the KGB was going to dispatch him to Canada at the end of his training. From this point forward, Yevgeni's main task was to learn everything possible about the country. Special arrangements were made for him to spend time at a large public library where he studied everything he could find in relation to Canada's provinces and capitals, the country's politics, economics, social issues, and Canadian national, provincial, and municipal problems. He read statistics, health reports, and Canadian newspapers and magazines. When he was later informed that he would be setting up his operation in Montreal he switched his focus to learn all that he could about Montreal as a city and Quebec as a province. Week after week he spent time in the library poring over Montreal newspapers.[3]

The KGB advised Yevgeni that he would need to establish a small business in Montreal. It was decided that a watch repair shop would be suitable. Yevgeni spent several months in Moscow learning the intricate trade of a watch repairman from a professional in the craft. The watch repairman had no knowledge of Yevgeni's background or the reason why he was an understudy. He simply agreed to a request made of him by a local Soviet official to provide basic training.

Leonid Dmitrievich was pleased with Yevgeni's progress. He had a good understanding and firm grasp of the intelligence tradecraft that he had been taught. His knowledge of Canada was impressive when quizzed by a KGB officer who had previously been posted at the Soviet Embassy in Ottawa. The officer was amazed with the depth of his understanding of the political issues in Canada and his ability to easily debate them. His knowledge of Montreal in particular was exceptional. It was time to create his persona. Yevgeni was told that he would be assuming the name of a young Canadian man named David Soboloff. He was further surprised when told that his objective was to surface in Canada, establish himself in Montreal for a few years, and, at a time chosen by Moscow, immigrate to the United States. The KGB's ultimate objective was to have Yevgeni join established KGB Illegal Vilyam Genrikhovich Fisher, alias Emil Goldfus, alias Rudolf Abel, who was currently operating in New York City. The plan was for Yevgeni to become his radio and signals communications operator.[4]

According to his Canadian birth certificate, the real David Soboloff was born March 29, 1919, at Toronto General Hospital, Toronto, Ontario. His parents, Simon Soboloff and Ida Zaslaosky, resided at that time at 130 Humberside Avenue, Toronto, in the middle of the district bordered by High Park, The Junction, and the Junction Triangle. Both parents had immigrated to Canada from the Soviet Union several years previously. Like many other Canadians at the time, the Great Depression hit the family hard. Faced with economic difficulties and no support system, the Soboloff family returned permanently to Moscow in 1934. Young David Soboloff was fifteen years of age.

Leonid Dmitrievich provided Yevgeni with several authentic documents that had previously belonged to the real David Soboloff. He was also given a written history of the Soboloff family's time in Canada. However, he was never introduced to the real David Soboloff or to any member of his family. As the Soboloff family had left Canada permanently in 1934, Yevgeni had to create a believable legend covering the seventeen-year period from 1934 to 1951, the year Yevgeni would arrive in Canada. The legend was developed by Yevgeni and approved by his KGB instructors.

In the late winter of 1950, Leonid Dmitrievich informed Yevgeni that he was being sent to Poland and Czechoslovakia on a training exercise. He knew that his performance would be evaluated and that he would be the subject of intense surveillance by the KGB working in conjunction with their Polish and Czechoslovakian counterparts. He was given a basic objective and then left to his own devices to accomplish it. The KGB provided him with Western-style clothes as well as an authentic Canadian passport under the name Joseph Bugyi, which contained his photograph. It was up to Yevgeni to obtain the necessary visas for Poland and Czechoslovakia and to make all his own travel and hotel arrangements. At the expiration of the exercise, Yevgeni received a very favorable evaluation from the training staff. He had performed admirably. Of particular note, acting as a Canadian, he established contact with an Illegal in Warsaw. This Illegal operated a safe house that was used for receiving and forwarding coded KGB broadcast messages from Moscow.

Throughout his two years of training, Yevgeni was only exposed to a small number of KGB officers. Those he did meet rarely provided anything more than their first names. Nevertheless, one officer in particular stood out. His professional demeanor and attention to detail set him apart from the others. Nikolai Alekseyevich Korznikov was a man who was clearly in control of things. He was not a frequent visitor to Yevgeni's training sessions. But when he did make an appearance, others stood back and deferred completely to him. It was evident that Korznikov wielded a great deal of influence when it came to KGB Illegal operations. Yevgeni respected him but also feared him. On his last day of training, he wondered whether he would ever see him again.[5]

With his formal training complete, Yevgeni took a few days off and spent them with his wife, Antonina, and his parents at the family apartment. Yevgeni and Antonina's time together the past two years had been infrequent and often strained. They both knew that the years moving forward would be difficult as well.

In late October 1951, Yevgeni left Moscow and flew to Vienna using the same Josef Bugyi Canadian passport that had been given to him in training. Following procedures, Yevgeni signaled his arrival in Vienna and was subsequently met by a KGB officer who simply identified himself as Sasha. Yevgeni did not know if Sasha was a KGB officer from the Residency at the Soviet Embassy in Vienna or if he had been dispatched to Vienna specifically for this meeting. Sasha was accompanied by an individual named Ivan Vasilyevich Hladysh, a Soviet-born Canadian citizen who had been recruited by the KGB in July 1951. Hladysh had recently left Canada and was returning permanently to his former home in the Soviet Union via the United Kingdom and Europe. To facilitate Yevgeni's travel to and entry into Canada, Hladysh gave Yevgeni his Canadian passport along with other personal items from his wallet. Yevgeni reciprocated by handing over the Josef Bugyi passport to Sasha that he used when he exited Moscow. Yevgeni subsequently removed the Hladysh photograph from the passport and substituted his own. Yevgeni, alias Josef Bugyi, had just become Ivan Vasilyevich Hladysh.[6]

Hladysh, Sasha, and Yevgeni met in a Vienna hotel room for several hours over the next few days. Hladysh provided a full brief on his life in Canada, including personal details about his family, where he had lived, people he knew, and details about his community. He also outlined his recent departure from Canada and his travel to London, England, France, Germany, and finally to Vienna, Austria. These were all important details Yevgeni had to know in the event he was stopped and challenged by Canadian Immigration or customs officials when he entered Canada. Hladysh, on the other hand, was told absolutely nothing about Yevgeni; their conversation was a one-way street.

Several days later, traveling as Ivan Vasilyevich Hladysh, Yevgeni flew to Berne, Switzerland, and then on to Paris, where he remained for the next two weeks. Acting on instructions he received in Moscow prior to his departure, Yevgeni placed a mark on a certain park bench situated near a church, which was a signal to the Paris KGB Residency that he arrived safely. There was no intention for him to meet with anyone. However, he had been provided with an emergency Paris telephone number in the event he needed it. The original plan called for Yevgeni to go to the US Embassy and obtain a visa. The extra time in Paris would allow for the embassy to process the visa application. Upon receipt of the visa he would then sail from Paris to New York and then enter Canada directly from the United States. These plans fell through. Instead, Yevgeni took the train from Paris to the French port of Marseilles and purchased passage to Canada on the *Nea Hellas*, a Greek registered ship that carried a compliment of 318 passengers. On October 29, 1951, the *Nea Hellas* slipped its moorings and steamed west for Halifax, Nova Scotia. Yevgeni Vladimirovich Brik, alias Canadian resident Ivan Vasilyevich Hladysh, was safely ensconced in his cabin and looking forward to the voyage.[7]

Chapter Six

Dispatched to Canada

Yevgeni thoroughly enjoyed the North Atlantic crossing from France to Canada. His sense of freedom and adventure had been ignited. He relaxed during the day and walked the ship in the evenings trying to imagine what life in Canada would be like. He knew from his studies that Montreal was an exciting, cosmopolitan city. And he looked forward to experiencing Toronto, Ottawa, and Vancouver in the months ahead. But as the ship steamed closer to Canada he began to worry about immigration and customs procedures at the port of Halifax. Had he known how simple it was going to be, he need not have worried at all.

The *Nea Hellas* tied up on its port side adjacent to Pier 21 in Halifax, Nova Scotia, on Sunday, November 4, 1951. The large two-floor, red-brick build-ing with the white facade was an imposing sight. When working at capacity the grand hall could handle a maximum of 250 people at a time. Immigrants arriving in Canada for the first time were processed separately from Cana-dians who were returning home from overseas vacations and business trips.[1]

Yevgeni was functioning at a high state of alertness. His mind raced as he waited his turn to be processed through Immigration Services and Customs. He was thankful for the time he spent with the real Ivan Hladysh in Vienna as they reviewed immigration procedures until they all felt that Yevgeni could carry the ruse off without difficulty. Nevertheless, as he approached his turn at Immigration Services he began to harbor doubts.

Yevgeni produced the Ivan Hladysh Canadian passport that contained his own photograph and responded to a couple of innocuous questions about his travels in Europe. He cleared Immigration and then Customs Controls in less than three minutes. As he walked through the terminal and then up the ramp leading to the railway station, he clutched a hollowed-out penny in his pocket.

It contained two microfilms that outlined his various meeting arrangements that had been prepared for him by the KGB in Moscow.[2]

As he walked toward the railway station Yevgeni saw that vendors were selling food for passengers who would be boarding the trains. He purchased a few items and moved to the ticket counter and purchased a one-way ticket to Montreal. The train would not be leaving Halifax for over two hours, so he found an empty bench and settled in until the boarding announcement was made. Yevgeni followed the instructions he received in Moscow and made certain that he did not engage anyone in conversation. There was an abandoned newspaper on the adjacent bench, so he picked it up and buried himself in the articles.

The train trip from Halifax to Montreal was long but uneventful. Yevgeni gazed out the windows throughout the journey. He couldn't help but make comparisons between what he saw in eastern Canada and what he knew in Russia. Hours later, sitting in a small downtown Montreal hotel, Yevgeni found an address for an inexpensive rooming house. It was located at 8960 St. Laurent near the intersection of Beauharnois. Although the room was small and didn't contain much more than a single bed, a dresser, and a tiny closet, Yevgeni was satisfied with what he saw and moved into apartment #1. A washroom that was to be shared with other tenants was located directly across the hall.[3]

Several weeks earlier while still in Moscow, the KGB had made firm arrangements, which Yevgeni was to follow when he arrived in Montreal in order to meet his handler. It was agreed that Yevgeni would go to the Montreal Botanical Gardens on the 4th, 14th, or 24th day of any given month at 4:00 p.m. As Yevgeni arrived in Canada on November 4 and was in Halifax that day, he was naturally unable to meet his new handler in Montreal. Following the established meeting protocol, Yevgeni walked to the Botanical Gardens on November 14 and arrived at the designated time. He waited to see if anyone would show up or if he would have to repeat the operation on November 24. There was a cool breeze blowing. The flowerbeds were empty, anticipating the cold December winds and heavy snow that would follow. Yevgeni was shocked to see the Russian walking toward him on the pathway. He was wearing a black fedora and a long, dark trench coat with the collar turned up partially hiding his facial features. It was his old KGB trainer from Moscow, the man he knew as Leonid Dmitrievich.

As they shook hands and embraced in the park, Yevgeni learned that his former trainer's full name was Leonid Dmitrievich Abramov. Abramov, smiling broadly, told him that after Yevgeni left for Poland and Czechoslovakia on his training exercise that he had been posted to the KGB Residency at the Soviet Embassy, Ottawa. His official cover position at the embassy was Second Secretary of the Soviet Ministry of Foreign Affairs. Abramov explained that he arrived in Canada on November 11, 1950, from New York City having arrived in the United States as a passenger on the M.S. *Batory* four days previously.[4] Abramov's arrival in Canada preceded Yevgeni's by exactly one year.

Abramov had known throughout Yevgeni's training that he would be his handler in Canada but was not permitted to tell him. He certainly had a vested interest in ensuring that Yevgeni did well in all aspects of the KGB's espionage tradecraft training. During Yevgeni's final eleven months in Moscow, Abramov, who had simply vanished from Yevgeni's life without any explanation, was in Ottawa preparing the way for his espionage activities once he arrived.

Abramov and Yevgeni slipped away to an empty and fairly obscure coffee shop where they wouldn't be noticed. As soon as they settled into a booth that gave them a degree of privacy, Yevgeni handed Abramov the Ivan Vasilyevich Hladysh passport.[5] Abramov reciprocated and gave Yevgeni a cigarette case that contained the identity documents of David Semyonovich Soboloff, everything he needed with the exception of a Canadian passport. Yevgeni would have to apply for an authentic one in the months ahead. He also gave him $3,000 in Canadian $20 bills. Yevgeni's new life in Canada as David Soboloff had just begun.[6]

Chapter Seven

Becoming Established in the Canadian Shield

Prior to leaving Moscow the KGB instructed Yevgeni to take a familiarization trip across Canada shortly after his arrival to bolster his knowledge of the country. In spite of his extensive studies at the library in Moscow about Canadian life, the KGB wanted Yevgeni to personally experience it. He had to put himself in a position where he could confidently discuss aspects about Canada from his personal experiences. He would never achieve this level of self-assurance unless he walked the streets, ate in the restaurants, and spoke to everyday Canadians across the country. The real David Soboloff had lived in Toronto until 1934. Yevgeni had to acquire intimate knowledge of the area around 130 Humberside Avenue, Toronto, and the broad district of Old Toronto where the Soboloff family frequented.[1] When that was accomplished, he then had to travel west. According to his fictitious KGB legend, he had been residing in various cities in western Canada between 1934 and 1951 with his parents.

In December 1951, one month after settling into a Montreal rooming house, Yevgeni took the train to Toronto. He located a rooming house at 93 Elm Street near the intersection of Elizabeth and Elm Street and rented accommodations there for a couple of weeks. He walked miles around the city, became very familiar with the Humberside Avenue area, and frequented restaurants, bars, and other businesses in Old Toronto. In keeping with operational security Yevgeni did not have any clandestine meetings with Abramov but did respond to a signal directing him to a dead drop, which he safely emptied. He in turn left a signal marker indicating that he retrieved the instructions. As he had not been given specific or direct intelligence objectives by either Abramov or Moscow other than to become familiar with Toronto and the other western Canadian cities, Yevgeni was surprised with the message he found in the dead drop. He did not know if Abramov had traveled from Ottawa to load the dead drop or whether this was done by one of his agents. Heeding instructions, Yevgeni booked out of the Elm Street rooming house and took a bus to the northern mining town of Sudbury, Ontario, home to Inco and Falconbridge, two of the country's most important nickel mines.[2]

The following morning Yevgeni left his hotel and walked to the Banque Canadienne Nationale where he opened a bank account under the name David S. Soboloff and deposited several hundred dollars. Having accomplished what he had been tasked to do, Yevgeni walked around Sudbury, ate at a local public house, and returned to his hotel for the night. The following day he caught the early morning train to Fort William. He thoroughly enjoyed the trip around Lake Superior and was captivated by the Canadian wilderness. The journey took him past countless pristine lakes and miles of thick forests. The countryside made him think of his birth home in Novorossiysk and the wonderful hours he spent outdoors with his mother.

Yevgeni's time in Fort William was brief. He spent the day wandering around town, eating his meals at a local cafe and reading the local newspaper. Early the following morning he continued his journey west to Winnipeg, Manitoba. According to the carefully crafted KGB legend, David Soboloff lived in Winnipeg for an extended period of time. Knowing this was an important aspect of his cover story, Yevgeni stayed in Winnipeg for almost two weeks. He initially stayed at the Bell Hotel on Main Street West but moved to a less expensive rooming house as soon as he was able to find what suited him. Yevgeni frequented the men's-only beer parlor at the Jack's Hotel, often ate his meals at the Alexander Cafe, and spent his days becoming familiar with the area by walking around the city. The Royal Alexander Hotel, Winnipeg City Hall, the post office, Main Street, Portage Avenue, and the old residential district where he was supposed to have lived all became familiar to him.

Winnipeg was cold in December, and winter storms were frequent. Commercial businesses and private homes were brightly decorated for the Christmas season. This was something Yevgeni had not experienced since he was a child residing in the borough of Brooklyn in New York City so many years ago. It brought back many conflicting emotions and memories. His parents, devout communists, did not celebrate Christmas. Many of his neighbors and school friends did. It had been difficult for a young boy to understand.[3]

As Christmas drew near Yevgeni purchased a train ticket for Montreal and joined the large number of travelers who were moving across the country to be with family during the highly charged Christmas season. He settled back into the Montreal rooming house at 8960 St. Laurent. Yevgeni wrote a long and detailed report on his familiarization trip that had taken him to Toronto, Sudbury, Ft. William, and Winnipeg. He included details about having opened a bank account at the Banque Canadienne Nationale in Sudbury.

With the report buried deep in the pocket of his winter coat, Yevgeni left the rooming house and made his way to Montreal's famous Mount Royal where Abramov previously created a dead drop for Yevgeni's use. When he reached the site and was certain that he wasn't being watched, Yevgeni placed the report in the concealed dead drop and quickly departed. Later, in the privacy of his room, he wrote a brief coded note and mailed it to Abramov in Ottawa. Several days later, Abramov left a signal on a sign post in Montreal indicating that he had retrieved the report. At the same time, Abramov left another signal that instructed Yevgeni to go to a different location to retrieve new instructions. In addition to his new task, Yevgeni found that Abramov had left him $1,000 to cover his expenses. There was no personal contact of any kind between Abramov and Yevgeni during these exchanges. The security of their operation remained intact.

Yevgeni had been thinking about the watch repair courses he received in Moscow and the watch repair shop the KGB wanted him to establish in Montreal to serve as cover for his future espionage activities. Although he was not yet fully established in Montreal, he noticed that these shops were primarily owned and operated by European immigrants. He realized that a watch repair shop would not be the most effective way to establish his cover because he would be confined to his shop throughout the day. He knew there was a better way to establish the cover he needed.

Yevgeni wrote Leonid Abramov a report recommending that he forgo the watch repair business and instead capitalize on the photography training he received in Moscow. He explained to Abramov that a photographer worked outside of his studio a great deal and these absences would provide perfect cover for his espionage activities while being away from his business.

Yevgeni further explained to Abramov that he would also like to obtain permission to apply for a photography course that was being offered in the United States. He explained that this was a good strategy considering the KGB wanted him to relocate to New York in a couple of years to work with KGB Illegal Vilyam Genrikhovich Fisher. Fisher also used the pseudonyms Robert Callen, Emil Robert Goldfus, and Colonel Rudolf Abel. Yevgeni reasoned that entry into the United States to study at the photography school would provide him with a US immigration stamp in his passport. He believed this would make it easier for him to enter the United States in the future.

Yevgeni followed the established protocol for communicating with Abramov. Two weeks later a signal appeared instructing Yevgeni to retrieve something from another dead drop. What he found pleased him immensely. Yevgeni was astonished to learn that Moscow approved the change in operational plans. He was authorized to open a photography business rather than a watch repair shop. His reasoning and advice had been taken seriously at The

Centre. And surprisingly, Yevgeni's recommendation that he be permitted to apply to an American photography school and travel there if accepted was also approved by Moscow. Yevgeni began to make arrangements to move temporarily to Toronto.

In early January 1952, Yevgeni again checked out of the rooming house on St. Laurent and made his way to Central Station. The massive Montreal train station featuring art deco bas-relief friezes on its exterior and interior opened with great fanfare in 1943.[4] Once again Yevgeni purchased a one-way ticket and traveled back to Toronto. Not knowing if his application to study photography in the United States would be accepted, he decided to find something else while he waited. He had successfully applied for a student position at a welding school in Toronto and spent the cold, snowy months of January, February, and March living in a rooming house on Jarvis Street. The General Welding Works School of Instruction at 61 Jarvis Street was within easy walking distance from his new accommodations.

One afternoon after his welding instruction was finished for the day, Yevgeni paid a visit to the office of an elderly dentist with whom he had become acquainted. During conversation, Yevgeni produced a Canadian passport application and asked the kindly gentleman if he would consent to being a guarantor. The elderly and trusting dentist didn't hesitate. Two weeks later, Yevgeni held a genuine Canadian passport in his hand in the name of David Semyonovich Soboloff. The Soboloff passport contained Yevgeni's photograph. His Canadian documentation was now complete.[5]

In early April Yevgeni's application to study photography in the United States was accepted. He flew to New York City and used his new Canadian passport when he cleared US Immigration and Customs. Two days later he eagerly commenced the various courses at the Germain School of Photography in Manhattan. Yevgeni did well at the school. The practical and theoretical instructions he received in Moscow from the KGB photographic specialists gave him a strong base of knowledge. The instructors at the Germain School of Photography were impressed with Yevgeni's photographic achievements. They could see that he felt comfortable with a camera in his hands and that he understood the principles of angle, light, exposure, and depth of field. He also worked competently in the darkroom where he enjoyed seeing his images come to life in the acid baths. Yevgeni was liked by the other students, and his work was admired. He never hesitated to help someone understand the correct temperature of chemicals when developing images or how to manipulate a negative by dodging or burning them in the darkroom. However, Yevgeni's relationship with the other students was primarily contained within the confines of the school. It did not extend beyond those walls.

His evenings were spent in the bars and bawdy houses around his rooming house. On the weekends, he frequently wandered the streets and visited the district in Brooklyn where he previously lived with his parents and attended school as a child. He didn't try to connect with anyone from his past, but he felt the nostalgia all the same.[6]

Yevgeni enjoyed himself immensely during these weeks in New York. His time was his own. He had no direct or indirect contact with Abramov back in Canada, and he purposefully made no effort to try to connect with KGB Illegal Vilyam Fisher. To do so, without direct tasking from Moscow, would have been a serious breach of operational security for both himself and Fisher. Contact with him would come later when Moscow signaled that it was time to immigrate to the United States.

At the expiration of his course, Yevgeni received a professional certificate from the school and finished at the top of his class. Prior to leaving New York City he took one final stroll around his old Brooklyn neighborhood and then headed to the airport.

Yevgeni spent the next few nights in an inexpensive hotel when he arrived back in Toronto. He subsequently found accommodations at a Jarvis Street rooming house and began looking for employment. Abramov had been pressed by The Centre in Moscow to push Yevgeni to find a job in Toronto. He had been unsuccessful finding employment in the welding field. He continued to search for other opportunities but was not having much success. Yevgeni was unaware that the KGB was considering their options with respect to promoting him to the status of an Illegals Resident.[7] If they followed through with this, Yevgeni would assume responsibility for running agents that the KGB officers at the Soviet Embassy in Ottawa were currently running. The Soviets did not have a consulate in Toronto. With Yevgeni running the agents, it would remove the necessity of having an Ottawa-based KGB officer travel to Toronto to manage the risky operation. Moscow knew that detection by Canadian authorities of the clandestine agent operations would be less likely if they were handled by a deep-cover Illegal such as Yevgeni. But that was yet to come.

In July, on KGB instructions, Yevgeni boarded a bus at the Toronto Gray coach terminal and traveled to Buffalo, New York, where he opened a bank account under the name of David S. Soboloff. He deposited $1,200 of KGB operational money in the Erie County Savings Bank at Sheldon Square. His task completed, he returned to Toronto on the next available bus.[8]

Yevgeni knew that he had to find a more suitable place to live where he could receive encrypted Soviet Morse code communications from Moscow. He worried that other occupants in the rooming house would be able to hear the odd radio sounds at night. Following a brief search, Yevgeni rented a small, comfortably furnished apartment at 54 Maitland Street and moved into apartment #7. He was surprised and pleased that he did not have to sign or commit to a lease. He remained at this address until June 1953.

Although unemployed, Yevgeni lived comfortably in the Maitland Street apartment and added small pieces of furniture as he saw fit. He was not concerned about finances as he regularly received rent money and living expenses from Abramov. A Toronto-based intermediary, working in conjunction with Abramov, placed packages containing money and instructions in various dead drops throughout Toronto. Yevgeni would retrieve them after receiving a signal that the dead drop had been filled.

Cold winter winds gripped the city of Toronto in early December, but there was very little snow. Yevgeni had received instructions to travel to Chicago. The mid-morning flight was short, and he was riding in a taxi through the streets of Chicago shortly after noon. He advised a Chicago taxi driver that he wanted a very cheap hotel near some nighttime action. The driver took him to the West Loop and Chicago's Skid Row district. It was a depressing-looking area populated with boarded-up buildings, strip clubs, cheap hotels, and prostitutes. Yevgeni paid the driver, then booked a room for two nights at the New Norway, an inexpensive hotel near a number of cheap bars. Prostitutes worked the streets during the day and night, and winos were sleeping in door-ways and alleys. Yevgeni never felt the least bit threatened or intimidated. He loved that nobody knew who he was. He was free to play.

Yevgeni dropped his suitcase in his hotel room and took a taxi to William J. Halligan's radio manufacturing company on West 5th Avenue. As instructed by Moscow, he purchased a model SX-71 Hallicrafters shortwave radio. The SX-71 is a five-band communications receiver covering AM broadcast and shortwave from 538 KHz to 34 MHz in four overlapping bands. A fifth band covered 46 to 56 MHz directly on the band-spread dial, which was also cali-brated for the 80-, 40-, 20-, and 10-meter amateur radio bands.[9]

Yevgeni returned to the hotel and left the radio in his room. Back outside again, he got his bearings, then crossed the street and headed to a seedy-looking bar that featured strippers, dancers, and inexpensive beer. The bar was exactly how he liked it. Women were everywhere, cigarette smoke curled toward the ceiling, and the music was loud. Yevgeni removed his winter coat and hat and settled in for a night of entertainment. He slept later than normal the following morning. When he awoke his head was throbbing from the consumption of too many Bismarck beers, and his throat and eyes were burning from cigarette smoke. Although he was unable to recall details, he had a foggy recollection of a blonde-haired woman leaving his bed sometime in the night.

Yevgeni's eyes scanned the room. He felt immense relief when he saw that the unopened box that contained the Hallicrafters SX-71 was still there. His wallet was open on the dresser. It appeared that money had been removed. Or had he spent more than he realized at the last strip club he patronized?[10]

After he arrived back to his Maitland Street apartment in Toronto, Yevgeni informed the Soviet embassy that he had returned from Chicago and, as instructed, he had acquired the SX-71 radio. Within weeks, he began receiving regular Russian Morse code transmissions in the middle of the night from Moscow. Decrypting these messages was a long and arduous task. They were transmitted in five number groups. A typical message would contain thirty-five to fifty groups. Once Yevgeni had the numbered groups copied he would then use a one-time pad, the key for decrypting the message. Each page on the one-time pad would only be used once and destroyed. After hours of painstaking work the message revealed might be an operational task, be simply birthday wishes, or some other message of little importance. Minor messages were deliberately transmitted by Moscow to keep Yevgeni familiar with the code and the state of his equipment. Occasionally it would contain greetings from his wife. Decrypting the messages was frustrating for Yevgeni. He begrudged the time and effort it took to decrypt each and every message received.

Chapter Eight

Rocky Mountains and Love in the Prairies

In early June 1953, Yevgeni placed a letter in a Toronto dead drop asking for a meeting with Vasili Shitarev, KGB Resident at the Soviet Embassy in Ottawa.[1] Yevgeni explained in his letter that he had had a disagreement with Leonid Abramov and that he was unhappy with the outcome. He wished to discuss the matter with Abramov's superior. When approval for the meeting arrived several days later, Yevgeni made arrangements to travel once again.

Two days later, Yevgeni was standing in Union Station, Toronto's magnificent Front Street railway terminal in the center of the city. Construction began in 1914 but faltered during the Great War due to a dire shortage of building materials. Canada's war effort consumed raw materials at an enormous pace, which had a direct impact on building projects across Canada. Construction picked up again following the war, and Union Station, the pride of Canada, was opened with great fanfare on August 6, 1927. His Royal Highness, Edward, Prince of Wales, officiated at the opening and was accompanied by the duke and duchess of York, British prime minister Stanley Baldwin and Canadian prime minister William Lyon Mackenzie King. It was a grand occasion.[2]

Yevgeni had been told that upon arrival in Ottawa he was to take a taxi from the railway station across from the Château Laurier and direct the driver to take him to the British Hotel, 71 rue Principale, Aylmer, Quebec.

The Soviet official who picked him up in front of the British Hotel identified himself as Sergey Aleksandrovich. In spite of the fact that he was meeting Yevgeni, the KGB officer used an alias. There was no individual within the Soviet establishment in Canada, neither KGB intelligence officer nor legitimate diplomat, with the name Sergey Aleksandrovich. Nevertheless, the two men drove around the Aylmer area for three hours while Yevgeni explained the problem he was having with Abramov. Whether he assessed

Yevgeni's concern to be frivolous or serious, Sergey convinced him that the issue would be taken care of and that the problem would disappear. He also took time to pass along news from Moscow. Yevgeni happily received Sergey's comments that Moscow was pleased with his progress in Canada and that they wanted him to leave Toronto and continue his familiarization trip across western Canada. He was to travel to Vancouver and find employment. Sergey Aleksandrovich also informed him that Moscow wanted him to return to Montreal following his western Canadian trip and find more permanent accommodations. They also wanted him to begin preliminary research for what would be required for him to eventually relocate to the United States.

Back in Toronto the following day, Yevgeni made arrangements to vacate his Maitland Street apartment and travel to British Columbia. He had read a great deal about Vancouver, Victoria, and other cities in the province while at the Moscow library during his intelligence training days. He knew about their reliance on the lumber industry, the abundance of sea life in the Pacific, and the natural beauty of the Rocky Mountains. He was anxious to see it all.

The flight to Vancouver was long due to stops in Winnipeg and Edmonton. Nevertheless, it was enjoyable. Yevgeni was reminded of Russia when he saw the flat wheat fields of Manitoba and Saskatchewan, which seemed to go on forever. But it was the grandeur of the Rocky Mountains in Alberta and British Columbia that excited him the most.

Upon arrival in Vancouver, Yevgeni took a taxi to the Hotel Langham, 1115 Nelson Street, where he booked a room for the entire month. He often ate his early morning breakfast at the hotel but would explore the local streets in the evening to find a reasonably priced restaurant to have his dinner. As directed, Yevgeni obtained employment as a general laborer at a small construction company that worked on various jobs in the downtown core. He worked hard every day and received a fair salary for his labor. Life in Vancouver appealed to him. However, he knew without asking he would never get permission from Moscow to relocate permanently there. The Soviet Union did not have a consulate in Vancouver, and the embassy in Ottawa was simply too far away and would not be able to support Yevgeni's intelligence needs. Nevertheless, he liked the people of Vancouver, their way of life, and what he read and heard about their milder climate. Most of all, he enjoyed the spectacular scenery and proximity of the snow-capped mountains to the east. In spite of his feelings for Vancouver, Yevgeni knew he had to continue the course that had been laid out for him by Moscow. His legend required that he continue his journey and become familiar with other western Canadian cities. Four weeks after arriving in Vancouver, Yevgeni quit his job and flew to Edmonton, Alberta.

According to his legend David Soboloff had lived and worked in Edmonton. Yevgeni needed to spend time there and get to know the city. He knew his legend would collapse if he was unable to speak knowledgeably about the city as a former resident could. Yevgeni spent an uneventful month working once again as a general laborer on projects that required physical exertion. He stayed at a downtown rooming house that did not give him the same feeling of independence he felt while staying at Vancouver's Hotel Langham. Yevgeni missed Vancouver and the beauty of the west coast city. Edmonton was hot, dry, and dusty. He was unhappy and wished that he had remained longer in British Columbia. He walked all over town, became familiar with the main stores, and read the Edmonton newspaper every day. Nevertheless, he found the days long and the nights longer. He entertained himself by frequenting various bars but was unable to bring women back to the rooming house. At the end of four weeks he took a taxi to the airport and flew to Winnipeg, Manitoba. Although he had spent time in Winnipeg during his initial Western Canadian familiarization trip, little did he realize that the next several weeks would fundamentally change his life in ways he had never imagined.

Similar to Edmonton, Yevgeni found Winnipeg to be another sweltering prairie city that fell far short of the natural beauty of Vancouver. Once again, he had to familiarize himself with another city where, according to his legend, David Soboloff had lived and worked.

Yevgeni obtained a room at the Windsor Hotel, at 187 Garry Street, and immediately began searching for employment as a photographer or studio assistant. He didn't want to spend another month working as a laborer. He simultaneously began looking for alternative housing as his funds were running low. There was of course no way of obtaining additional travel funds from Leonid Abramov in Ottawa. Three days later Yevgeni moved into a rooming house on Carlton Street and struck up a conversation with Larissa Cunningham,[3] the married daughter of Andrei and Yeva Tarasov who owned the home. Larissa had traveled to Winnipeg with her two young children to visit her parents. Her husband, Barry Cunningham,[4] a corporal in the Canadian Army, was away on extended military maneuvers from his home base at Camp Barriefield near Kingston, Ontario. Yevgeni was smitten by Larissa from the very beginning.

At twenty-seven years of age Larissa was a slim, attractive blonde with shoulder-length wavy hair. At five-foot, seven inches, she maintained an appealing figure. Larissa smiled easily and often. She especially enjoyed having the opportunity to engage in adult conversations whenever she could. Having two young children at home made her world seem small and her conversations juvenile. Most people would characterize Larissa as being a warm, charming, and happy soul. However, it was all a facade. Lurking just below the surface was a very unhappy young lady. Her marriage was in trouble. Her husband was frequently away on military exercises or attending courses at bases in Petawawa, Barrie, or Gagetown, New Brunswick. The sudden appearance of the handsome, single young man at her parents' rooming house caught Larissa's attention. She immediately seized the opportunity to talk with Yevgeni. She felt comfortable around him and could discuss things that she would never speak about with her parents.

Yevgeni and Larissa's relationship developed quickly and soon blossomed into an illicit affair. As frequently as she could arrange it, Larissa left her children in the care of her parents while she escaped for a few hours of quiet happiness with Yevgeni. She feared doing or saying anything that would tip off her parents about the affair. Yevgeni would leave the rooming house early in the morning as if he was going to work as a hired laborer in the city. When the amorous relationship began, Yevgeni quit looking for any form of employment. Larissa would join him in the early afternoon and stay with him until she returned to her parents' home just before dinner. Yevgeni was smitten. Larissa was different from all the women he encountered across the country in bars and dance halls. And she was certainly nothing like the prostitutes he paid by the hour. In spite of being married with a wife back in Moscow, Yevgeni came to the conclusion that he wanted to spend the rest of his life with Larissa. He began to plot how he could convince her to leave her military husband and move to Quebec and live with him.[5]

As quickly as the affair began Larissa informed Yevgeni that she and the children had to return to their home at Camp Barriefield in Kingston. Not wanting to lose her, Yevgeni purchased a train ticket for Montreal, which passed through Toronto and Kingston. He convinced Larissa to allow him to travel back to Ontario with her and the children. They both knew that it would be a delicate matter to negotiate with both of Larissa's children beside them on the train. Yevgeni had his own sleeping compartment apart from Larissa and the children. It was a bold, some might say reckless, move. Yevgeni knew the KGB was tolerant with respect to extramarital relationships. In fact, it was expected that KGB Illegals would develop relationships and affairs with women while they were working in foreign countries. However, he and others were under instructions to report the names and biographic information of all the women with whom they developed liaisons. Yevgeni also knew the KGB would not tolerate the nature and extent of the relationship he was having with Larissa. This kind of behavior had the potential of quickly leading to serious trouble. When they finally reached Toronto, Yevgeni left Larissa and her children at Union Station on Front Street and told them he would return within a few hours. Their connecting train to Kingston and Montreal was not scheduled to leave for several hours. Yevgeni switched to operational mode and left them at Union Station as he had business to attend.

During his three months in Western Canada, Yevgeni maintained a progressive trip report commencing with his tenure and employment in Vancouver. The report included details of his time in Edmonton and Winnipeg. In direct violation of instructions from Moscow, Yevgeni failed to tell Moscow about his relationship with Larissa and chose to leave out all mention of their journey from Winnipeg to Toronto. Yevgeni took the trip report and concealed it in a designated Toronto dead drop and left a signal at a separate location indicating it had been filled. With this job completed, Yevgeni returned to Union Station and joined Larissa and the children on the next train east to Kingston. With the children present they were unable to say good-bye in the manner they desired. Within ten minutes the train began pulling away from the station and Yevgeni continued his journey to Montreal. Three days later he was back in Kingston asking Larissa to leave her husband.[6]

Chapter Nine

A Change of HART

Yevgeni and Larissa's adulterous affair was passionate, complicated, and based on a series of lies. Yevgeni led her to believe that he was an eligible bachelor. He had charisma, a wonderful sense of humor, and an aura of mystery about him. She was completely unaware of his background, knew nothing about his true identity, and of course, possessed no knowledge about his wife living in Moscow.

Larissa felt trapped in a loveless marriage and recognized that she would not be able to raise and support her two children if she were on her own. Life with Barry was difficult. The pay of an army corporal was insufficient for the needs of a family of four. There were frequent arguments, and the family bills often went unpaid. Their debt was spiraling out of control. Barry's frequent drunkenness and the family's lack of money dominated their ever-increasing arguments. Their only reprieve from squabbling was when he was away on military exercises. Larissa was lonely and vulnerable. Yevgeni filled the void in her life. But she was tormented, and felt guilty and conflicted. She worried about the uncertain future with Barry.

Nevertheless, Larissa recognized there likely was no future with Yevgeni. In spite of the passion she felt for him, she was confused and uncertain whether he was being honest with her. He talked about living in Montreal, but she knew he had just traveled across western Canada working at jobs in Vancouver, Edmonton, and Winnipeg. He sounded sincere, but his stories often contradicted one another. Larissa had trouble reconciling why at times he seemed uncertain, confused, or outright ignorant of simple things that most people would know as a matter of course. She certainly did not suspect him of anything nefarious, she just found the situation a little odd.

Yevgeni spent the summer and autumn of 1953 traveling back and forth between his new home and the city of Kingston several hours to the west. He had recently established himself in a ground-floor apartment at 5381 Bannantyne Avenue in Verdun, Quebec. His home was situated in a distinctly working-class neighborhood in this blue-collar municipality adjacent to Montreal.

He and Larissa would meet in local hotels for hours at a time. Yevgeni continued to encourage her to leave her husband while Larissa tried fervently to make Yevgeni understand how difficult it would be for her to end her marriage. In spite of her decision not to leave her husband, she continued to see Yevgeni each time he took the train to Kingston.

Leonid Abramov and the KGB in Moscow were still unaware of Yevgeni's love affair with Larissa.[1] Yevgeni knew that he was taking a huge risk with the KGB by concealing this relationship. He had no doubt that he would be summoned back to Moscow if the KGB discovered that Yevgeni was deceiving them. He wanted to prevent this at all costs.

In late November 1953, when Yevgeni arrived once again in Kingston to see Larissa, he was shocked to learn that she had indeed left her husband. It was what Yevgeni wanted all along. Having gone over this scenario in his head hundreds of times during the summer, he now understood that he had to be honest and truthful to Larissa about who he really was and what he was doing in Canada. It was Larissa's turn to be shocked.

Yevgeni sat Larissa down and explained that he was a Russian citizen and a KGB agent who had been dispatched to Canada as a deep-cover spy, known in the business as an Illegal. He told her that his true name was not David Soboloff and that he was living a lie. Yevgeni stated that he reported clandestinely to a KGB officer in the Soviet Embassy, Ottawa, through the use of dead drops as well as through coded letters posted in the mail. In response to her questions he told her that he was married and that his wife lived in Moscow but that he did not want to return to the Soviet Union.[2]

Larissa was shaken by Yevgeni's revelations. She now understood the reasons why he had puzzling gaps of knowledge about Canada and Canadian life and why he was unable to answer many elementary questions that most schoolchildren knew instinctively. She was not a political person and had no idea what the KGB was or what it represented. Larissa loved David Soboloff. She had no idea who Yevgeni Brik was.

Larissa was anxious and feared what would happen to her now that she left her husband. At the same time, she felt liberated for having the courage to stand up to him and his angry tantrums. Nevertheless, she now knew that she could not run away with Yevgeni. Their dreams of running off together and living quietly in western Canada were simply that, dreams. Rather than lash out at him, Larissa began to talk to Yevgeni about turning himself in to the RCMP. She told him that the RCMP would protect him and keep him safe from the long reach of the KGB in Canada and internationally. She spoke convincingly that the RCMP and the government of Canada would allow him to stay in Canada in the same way they did when Igor Gouzenko, a cipher clerk from the Glavnoye Razvedyvatelnoye Upravleniye (GRU, Soviet Military Intelligence), defected from the Soviet Embassy, Ottawa, in September 1945.

On November 25, 1953,[3] Yevgeni, accompanied by Larissa, took the train to Ottawa. When they arrived at the Ottawa train station across the road from the Château Laurier Hotel, they hired a taxi that took them away from the city core and out to the west end. At Yevgeni's request, they were dropped at a pay telephone booth on Richmond Road. Yevgeni placed a telephone call to RCMP A Division Headquarters. He told the Mountie who answered that he wished to meet an RCMP officer at the corner of Winston Street and Madison Avenue in the West Ottawa community of Westboro. Without revealing the specific reason for requesting a meeting of this nature, Yevgeni convinced the officer on the telephone that it was important that they meet. After the call was terminated, Larissa returned to the train station and arrived back in Kingston a few hours later.

Fifteen minutes later, RCMP corporal Melvin E. Linden[4] arrived at the designated intersection, but nobody was there. It was a bitter cold morning. Unable to remain warm, Yevgeni had gone for a brief walk to get his blood circulating and to calm his nerves. Within a few short minutes, Yevgeni returned to the designated street corner and climbed into the unmarked RCMP car with Linden. His life was about to take another dramatic turn. Yevgeni gathered his courage and blurted out to an astonished Linden, "I am another Gouzenko."

During the next hour, Yevgeni provided Corporal Linden with sufficient details of his KGB background, intelligence training, and dispatch to Canada to convince him that he was telling the truth. He advised Linden that he had taken familiarization trips across Canada and that he had been to the United States on more than one occasion during the past two years. He carefully explained that he had not yet begun to conduct espionage within Canada but that he had been communicating clandestinely with Ottawa-based KGB officer Leonid Abramov. And he advised Linden that he was receiving encrypted Russian Morse code communications directly from Moscow and deciphering them at his home in Verdun, Quebec. As a show of good faith and to give credibility to his story, he provided Linden with an Ottawa address, #1 Hawthorne Street, and told him that this was a clandestine accommodation address that Abramov used to channel letters between himself and Yevgeni. The purpose of the accommodation address was to conceal from Canadian authorities all communications between KGB officer Leonid Abramov and himself.

Yevgeni directed Linden to drive down the east side of the Rideau Canal along The Driveway and showed him a spot where a concealed DLB was situated near Hogs Back Falls. Most importantly, Yevgeni informed Linden that he had a meeting scheduled with Abramov that very evening at 9:00 p.m. at the Montcalm Theatre in Hull, Quebec, directly across the river from Ottawa.

The Igor Gouzenko defection and the espionage cases that sprang from it was still fresh in the minds of the small Security Service branch as it existed within the RCMP in 1953. The initial information Yevgeni provided to RCMP corporal Linden was sufficient to convince his senior officers within the A Division regional office to take this matter very seriously. RCMP officers Corporal Lloyd Culbert and Constable Murray Cottell, two plainclothes officers of the Security Service, were immediately dispatched to the Albion Hotel, at #1 Daly Avenue, to secure proper accommodations where a more comprehensive interview could be conducted in strict privacy. They secured a room under the fictitious name of M. Swartz, leaving no identifiable connection to the RCMP Security Service or to Yevgeni.[5]

After Corporal Linden was advised that secure arrangements had been arranged for them at the Albion Hotel, he took Yevgeni to Room #37. Linden introduced Yevgeni to his supervisor, RCMP sergeant Mitch Hanna, who was waiting for them in the room. The two officers thoroughly debriefed Yevgeni for several hours but were very careful to ensure that he left the hotel in sufficient time to get to the Montcalm Theatre across the Ottawa River in Hull. They wanted Yevgeni to keep his scheduled clandestine rendezvous with Abramov. Prior to departing the Albion Hotel, the officers made arrangements to meet Yevgeni the following day and to drive him to the more secluded Maple Leaf Tourist Hotel. It was situated south of Ottawa city limits, on Highway #16. The officers wanted to get him out of the downtown core area and away from the proximity of the Soviet Embassy.

After Yevgeni left the Albion Hotel, the A Division Security Service officers returned to their regional office and briefed their senior cadre, who in turn contacted their counterparts at RCMP HQ. By the end of the afternoon, all senior officers at A Division and RCMP HQ were aware of the extraordinary circumstances of the day. The information Yevgeni provided convinced everyone that they did in fact have another Gouzenko. However, one very important figure was out of the loop.

RCMP inspector Terence (Terry) M. Guernsey, officer in charge of the force's HQ's Counter Intelligence Operations, known as B Operations, was, at that moment, a patient at the Ottawa Civic Hospital. When word of Yevgeni's apparent defection to the RCMP was communicated to him, Guernsey immediately recognized the tremendous potential of the case. He knew that much more would be gained by running Yevgeni as a double agent back against the KGB as opposed to simply debriefing him as a defector.

In spite of being incapacitated in his hospital room, Inspector Guernsey took immediate control of the situation. He told his briefers from HQ Security Service that Yevgeni must be informed, when seen the following morning at the Maple Leaf Tourist Hotel, that the RCMP no longer handles national security matters. He would also be told that representatives from another Canadian government department, who had taken over responsibility for national security investigations, would contact him in Verdun within the next few days. The decision to follow this strategy was made in the event Yevgeni was in fact a "triple" agent whose intent was to penetrate the RCMP Security Service to determine the identity of their officers and discover their sources and methods of operations. No other officer had considered this. Guernsey believed that if Yevgeni was a triple agent, news that another Canadian government department was now responsible for conducting national security investigations would confuse the Soviets and cause them to question what other changes had taken place within the government following the defection of Igor Gouzenko.

Guernsey, from his hospital bed, formally transferred the case from RCMP A Division to HQ Security Service. He knew that HQ employed more experienced and knowledgeable investigators in counterespionage operations than their regional counterparts. He informed his briefers that the case would formally be named KEYSTONE, gave it a top-secret classification, and strictly compartmentalized who would have access to and knowledge of this very sensitive operation. To protect the name of Yevgeni from being exposed, he assigned him the codename GIDEON.[6]

Guernsey's next move was surprising and perhaps a little controversial at the time. Rather than assign Operation KEYSTONE to RCMP corporal Henry P. Tadeson, who handled the Russian Desk responsibilities, he turned it over to thirty-seven-year-old RCMP corporal Charles J. Sweeny. At the time, Sweeny was working in B Operations, Satellite Operations concentrating on the intelligence services of East European embassies other than Soviet. Czechoslovakia, Poland, East Germany, Romania, and Hungary all had intelligence services operating clandestinely from their Ottawa embassies.

Sweeny was considered a rising star among his peers. A short, slim man with dark hair combed back over his head, he sported a trimmed, military moustache, and his civilian dress was always impeccable. The Security Service officers, of course, did not wear RCMP uniforms. Sweeny enjoyed a solid reputation as a very competent, professional investigator with a proven track record running counterintelligence operations. He could be a little officious at times, and it was accepted that he did not have the broad picture of espionage that characterized Guernsey. However, he enjoyed the confidence of Inspector Guernsey, his superior officer. Sweeny was so well regarded by the RCMP hierarchy that he was regularly appointed to assume responsibility for B Operations during those occasions when Inspector Guernsey was away.

In spite of his slightly formal nature, Sweeny was well regarded by others and was considered to be an easy person to work with. On April 18, 1940, at the age of twenty-five, he joined the RCMP in Montreal and was posted to Newfoundland following his recruit training in Regina, Saskatchewan. However, like many others during the war years, he purchased his discharge from the force on May 31, 1944, and joined the Canadian army. He was posted to continental Europe during the latter stage of World War II. Following the termination of hostilities, Sweeny reengaged in the RCMP on October 12, 1945, and served in the Maritimes until being transferred to Ottawa in 1948.[7]

Although Guernsey and Sweeny recognized they had an extraordinary double-agent case in their hands, neither could have imagined the roller coaster ride they were about to begin. Or for that matter, where the journey would take them. The only thing predictable about Yevgeni was that he was highly unpredictable.

Chapter Ten

GIDEON and
Operation KEYSTONE

In the very early morning hours of November 26, prior to the scheduled meeting of RCMP sergeant Hanna and Corporal Linden with Yevgeni at the Maple Leaf Hotel, a very serious meeting was underway at RCMP HQ. The top officers of the Security Service gathered to discuss developments and plan strategy in relation to Operation KEYSTONE. The meeting was chaired by Superintendent James Lemieux, the officer in charge of HQ Security Service. His counterpart in the Regional Office, Superintendent Joseph H. T. Poudrette, was also there. Joining them was Inspector Terry Guernsey who, remarkably, had signed himself out of the hospital hours earlier so he could attend this key meeting. Everyone in attendance acknowledged, without explicitly saying so, that nobody was as well equipped to manage Operation KEYSTONE than Terry Guernsey. Officers Hanna and Linden were there to get final instructions before they departed for the Maple Leaf Tourist Hotel. And Corporal Charles Sweeny, the officer who would be responsible for the day-to-day running of the operation, was seated at the table.[1] The meeting itself was an affirmation of the decisions made the previous evening at the hospital bedside of Terry Guernsey. Lemieux was only too happy to allow Guernsey to run with it. Poudrette was already aware that the operation had been transferred from his A Division Office to HQ Security Service. All that remained was to convince Yevgeni to return to Montreal and await a meeting with the agent from the fictitious Canadian Security Agency (CSA).

Later that morning, while being debriefed at the Maple Leaf Tourist Hotel, Yevgeni informed the officers that he was on time for his meeting the previous night with Abramov at the Montcalm Theatre in Hull, Quebec. He was playing a dangerous game of duplicity, and he knew it. He worried that the Soviets had discovered that he did not return to Montreal following his late-night rendezvous with Abramov. He was anxious that he may have been the subject of Soviet surveillance, and they may have observed him being picked up by the RCMP and driven to the Maple Leaf Tourist Hotel. Nobody knew or understood better than Yevgeni the consequences his wife and family would face in Moscow if the Soviets discovered he was double dealing them and cooperating with the RCMP as a recruited double agent.

Yevgeni told the officers that he was tired from his late-night session with Abramov. Privately, he was also nervous about meeting Sgt. Hanna once again. He knew he had completely compromised his position with the KGB and that there was no turning back. He also knew the KGB would be ruthless if they discovered his treachery.

Sensing Yevgeni's level of anxiety, Sgt. Hanna did his best to calm him down and reassure him about his personal safety. Hanna followed Inspector Guernsey's instructions explicitly and informed Yevgeni that the RCMP no longer had authority or responsibility for investigating Canadian national security matters. Yevgeni was shocked and confused by this revelation. He was further astounded to learn that an organization called the CSA had the mandate to investigate all matters related to Canada's national security interests, especially espionage.

Yevgeni couldn't understand how his KGB trainers in Moscow could have been so misinformed. They stressed that his main enemy in Canada would be the RCMP. There was never any mention of an organization called the CSA. There were no references to the CSA in the Canadian books, magazines, or newspapers he was devouring in the library in Moscow. Nonetheless, Hanna assured him the agency did in fact exist and was a closely guarded secret.

Thrusting his hand into his pocket, Hanna retrieved a $1 bill that had been torn in half and informed Yevgeni that he should take it and return to Montreal immediately. He was advised that someone from the CSA would meet him in Montreal. He was given instructions to be present at a designated telephone booth on St. Catherine Street in downtown Montreal at a specific time and that he would receive a call. Yevgeni would know he was meeting the right man when the individual showed him the matching half of the torn $1 bill. Hanna provided the particulars of the Montreal rendezvous site, drove him back downtown, and let him out in a quiet area. Yevgeni walked to the bus station, purchased a ticket, and left for Montreal. Operation KEYSTONE was now the sole responsibility of RCMP HQ Security Service, B Operations Branch.

The following morning, Yevgeni was standing beside the designated telephone booth on St. Catherine's Street when the telephone rang. Responding to instructions he received during that call, Yevgeni walked to another telephone booth a block away. The pay telephone booth was empty, and the phone was ringing as he arrived. The male caller instructed Yevgeni to walk to the Mount Royal Hotel, enter the foyer, and take the elevator to the fifth floor and exit into the hallway. When he arrived on the fifth floor he saw a man walking toward him. It was RCMP corporal Charles Sweeny wearing civilian clothes. With little fanfare Sweeny produced his half of the previously torn dollar bill, and Yevgeni matched it. Sweeny turned and led Yevgeni down to the fourth floor where they entered a room that Sweeny had obtained earlier.

Sweeny introduced himself as Eugene Walker. He explained that he was from the CSA and would be responsible for Yevgeni's welfare. Sweeny spoke confidently in a professional voice that exhibited no trace of arrogance. He quickly eliminated Yevgeni's doubts about the existence of the CSA. Sweeny convinced him that the RCMP was responsible for federal policing in Ontario and Quebec and for provincial police work in many of the other Canadian provinces. He explained that the Canadian government lost confidence in the RCMP's ability to investigate sophisticated national security investigations following the Gouzenko revelations of Soviet spying in Canada. As a consequence, they removed those responsibilities from the RCMP, created the CSA, and entrusted national security matters to this new agency. He further stated that this was all accomplished in the greatest of secrecy by Canadian prime minister Louis St. Laurent and his cabinet colleagues. Yevgeni accepted Sweeny's explanation with little argument and agreed right then and there to work for the CSA as a double agent against the KGB.

Sweeny, a man with a serious demeanor, methodically established operational protocols and explained that it was critical that Yevgeni adhere to them for his own personal safety. He was told that if he deviated from them the KGB would easily discover his treachery. Sweeny also informed Yevgeni that they would have regular meetings in his Bannantyne Street photographic studio in Verdun. Yevgeni learned that Sweeny would pose as a photographic supplies representative who makes regular business calls to clients in the greater Montreal region. To ensure that there would be no difficulties with this cover story, Sweeny had already formally registered as a photographic sales supplier in the Province of Quebec.

Sweeny's protocol procedures included an emergency contact process. In any case of emergency, or if needed for operational assistance, Yevgeni was instructed to call a certain Ottawa telephone number that was registered to an established city dentist. When the call was connected he was to simply ask to speak to Mr. Walker. He was admonished not to leave a message of any kind. The dentist would promptly telephone Sweeny, who in turn would immediately contact Yevgeni. The dental clinic was located on O'Connor Street in downtown Ottawa. The dentist, a long-time personal friend of Sweeny, lived in the upscale Alta Vista Drive area of the city.

Yevgeni immediately felt comfortable and confident in Sweeny's presence. He recognized that Sweeny was a professional intelligence officer who was credible, knowledgeable, and appeared to have the requisite authority to make important operational decisions. He respected Sweeny's "take charge" attitude.[2] He may have felt differently had he known that he was being duped by Sweeny and that neither Eugene Walker nor the CSA actually existed.

During the months that followed, Sweeny debriefed Yevgeni about his entire life. Yevgeni confided everything to Sweeny. He told him of his early life in Novorossiysk, Moscow, Brooklyn, and the family's return to Moscow once again. He described his wartime service and how he was recruited into the KGB in Moscow. Yevgeni described his intelligence training in full and provided as much detail as he could remember about his various instructors. He explained that he was taught the tradecraft of a Soviet Illegal, including the art of intelligence collection; running agents; how to use dead-letter boxes, also known as dead drops; surreptitious photography; Russian Morse code; and how to function undetected in a foreign country.

Yevgeni described his practical training exercises in Poland and Czechoslovakia and his dispatch to Canada via Western Europe. He informed Sweeny that in spite of his face-to-face meeting with Abramov at the Botanical Gardens in Montreal and his cross-Canada familiarization trips, he had not conducted any espionage since his arrival in Canada in November 1951. He described his method of communication with Abramov through letters sent to an LLB and through dead drops as well as personal meetings with him once or twice per year. Yevgeni identified the locations and details of the various dead drops and LLB connections and turned over copies of letters he had received from Abramov.

Most significantly, Yevgeni provided Sweeny with the precise radio frequencies and KGB transmission schedule that they were using to send him encrypted messages. He also gave Sweeny the vitally important one-time pads that were essential for decrypting these messages.[3] Without the one-time pads, the KGB communications would have remained unbroken and therefore, unreadable. With the pads, frequencies, and schedule, the Security Service was able to read all of the KGB's encrypted messages and establish the identities of individuals and Canadian companies that the KGB had an interest in. As time progressed, the messages and assignments became more and more frequent, causing Yevgeni a great deal of personal anguish. He was unable to keep up with Moscow's demanding schedule.

Sweeny became increasingly aware that Yevgeni was a very difficult person to control. He experienced wild mood swings, engaged in binge drinking, was prone to fits of anger, and would willfully neglect to monitor the scheduled Moscow Centre broadcasts, thereby missing several of his KGB assignments. Sweeny recognized that Yevgeni's romantic entanglement with Larissa in Kingston had exacerbated everything else in their operation. In fact, it had the potential of derailing Operation KEYSTONE completely. Could the situation become more precarious? The answer was yes; and it did.

Chapter Eleven

Trouble in Paradise

Yevgeni's erratic behavior caused great consternation within RCMP HQ Security Service. Inspector Guernsey was deeply concerned that their double-agent operation against the KGB was in danger of imploding if Yevgeni did not end the affair with Larissa. Although she had recently left her husband, Larissa reconsidered that decision and returned to the family home. She had quickly recognized that she did not have the courage to dissolve their unhappy marriage. Nor did she possess the financial means to support herself and her two boys.

Guernsey agonized over the tangled affair and considered various options on how to end it. He finally arrived at the only solution he believed would work. Guernsey picked up the telephone and hastily arranged an unofficial meeting, "off the books," with a senior officer in the Canadian army. When they sat down together, Guernsey selected his words carefully. Without compromising his counterintelligence operation, he confided the briefest of details of the KEYSTONE operation and explained how vitally important it was in terms of Canadian national security. He disclosed his deep concern that Yevgeni's affair with the wife of Corporal Barry Cunningham could compromise the most promising counterintelligence operation in Canada if it did not stop. Guernsey boldly and bluntly asked the senior military officer if he would transfer Cunningham out of the Kingston area, thereby placing Larissa out of Yevgeni's reach. Within days, the military response surpassed Guernsey's expectations. Cunningham received orders transferring him forthwith from the Kingston area army base at Camp Barriefield to a remote base in the Yukon Territory in Canada's far north. The affair was over. Yevgeni never saw or spoke with Larissa again.[1]

Although the affair ended, serious problems remained. Yevgeni was grief stricken over the military transfer that resulted in the loss of his friend and lover. He was convinced that Sweeny was behind the move and was furious. Considering this situation to be of such import, Yevgeni invoked the emergency protocol measures and telephoned the dentist's office in Ottawa. Following procedures, the dentist contacted Sweeny. When Sweeny arrived at Yevgeni's Verdun apartment, he found him in a fit of rage. Yevgeni lashed into Sweeny, accusing him of engineering Cunningham's transfer, thereby destroying any chance Yevgeni had in convincing Larissa to establish a life with him. Sweeny's denials were to no avail. Yevgeni did not believe him and was inconsolable. He firmly stated that his relationship with the CSA was over and asked Sweeny to leave. Sweeny tried to reason with him and finally convinced Yevgeni to travel to Ottawa the following week. He argued that it was essential that Yevgeni submit his normal operational report to Leonid Abramov through the designated dead drop. Yevgeni agreed, knowing that he had to placate the KGB while maintaining the illusion that all was well and that his cover was secure. Sweeny achieved an additional concession by artfully convincing Yevgeni to meet his boss while he was in Ottawa submitting his report to Abramov. Having achieved what he could, Sweeny left Yevgeni's apartment and returned to Ottawa.

The following week, Sweeny introduced Yevgeni to Inspector Terry Guernsey, who was posing as Mr. Henderson, head of the fictitious CSA. Within the RCMP, Guernsey was well known as a deep-thinking, quiet-spoken individual who rarely, if ever, raised his voice or became ruffled. He was a very serious-minded officer who some would describe as being a little distant from his men in a social context. Nevertheless, he was deeply respected and completely dedicated to the field of counterintelligence work.

Terry Guernsey had been posted to the Canadian High Commission in London, England, where he initially worked on the second floor of Canada House in the Visa Control Section at Trafalgar Square. He, and fellow RCMP officers Bruce James, Chuck Smith, and Steve Dalton, were among the first RCMP officers to be given this opportunity. In 1958 Guernsey left the Visa Control Section and became the first representative of the RCMP Security Service to become a security liaison officer, where he worked directly with the British Security Service. He was highly regarded by the British, who recognized his unique talent as a first-rate intelligence professional. Those who knew him well on both sides of the Atlantic recognized that Guernsey was more suited to intelligence work than to police duties.[2]

Upon meeting the notional head of the CSA, Yevgeni turned his back on Sweeny and directed his full attention and anger toward Guernsey. He wasted no time in commencing his rant indicating that his future had been destroyed by Sweeny's intervention with the military that resulted in his lover and her husband being transferred to northern Canada. He, of course, had no knowledge that it was Guernsey who approached the army in this regard. He told Guernsey that he was through. He would no longer cooperate with the CSA and, incredibly and certainly naively, that he was going to quit working for the KGB as well. He screamed that all he wanted was to live his life in peace and harmony in Canada with his lover, Larissa Cunningham. The angrier he became the more he lost control. He yelled blasphemies, cried, and literally lay down on the floor and acted like a petulant child. Guernsey sat quietly and watched the spectacle without reacting or responding.[3]

Emotionally and physically drained, Yevgeni sat up but remained on the floor. Silence enveloped the room. Speaking softly at first, Guernsey began speaking of Yevgeni's wife and parents who were waiting for his eventual return to Moscow. He spoke of their obvious love for him and their increasing loneliness the longer he was away. He spoke of his wife being alone day after day without the company of her husband to talk about the future with. He mentioned that his parents were growing older and that health issues were always a complication. And he reminded Yevgeni that their lives would be turned upside down by the KGB if he ever attempted to sever his relationship with them. Guernsey's calm demeanor and fatherly influence hit a nerve with Yevgeni. In spite of his outrageous behavior since his arrival in Canada in November 1951—consorting with prostitutes, meeting women in bars, drinking heavily, and carrying on an adulterous affair with Larissa Cunningham—deep within himself, he remained in love with his wife, Antonina.

As Guernsey spoke about his family, Yevgeni began to see the situation in a different light. He recognized the truth and wise counsel and stopped his childish behavior. The crisis had been averted, and Yevgeni returned to his Verdun apartment with a renewed commitment to continue working with the man he knew as Walker and the shadowy CSA.

Chapter Twelve

Brik's Advancement to Active Espionage

Vladimir Pavlovich Bourdine was a young, ambitious KGB officer. His posting to the Soviet Embassy, Ottawa, on May 21, 1949, predated Yevgeni's surreptitious arrival in Canada by almost two years.[1] Previously, Bourdine had gained valuable experience and confidence as an agent-running officer during an earlier posting to Washington, DC. He spent the war and postwar years of 1944 to 1946 becoming familiar with what he believed to be the excesses of Western society, failed capitalism, and a flawed democracy. The interval between his Washington and Ottawa postings had been spent back at The Centre in Moscow.[2]

Yevgeni did not know it yet, but he would never see Leonid Abramov again. His old mentor and trainer in Moscow and his first operational handler, or Illegal Support Officer, in Canada had been recalled several months previously to The Centre. He had not taken the time to inform Yevgeni of his recall or advise him that someone else from the embassy would become his new handler. Abramov never bid him farewell.

Nor did Yevgeni know that back in his earlier Moscow training days in 1950 to 1951 Abramov had also been mentoring and coordinating the training of another KGB Illegal by the name of Reino Hayhanen. Like Yevgeni, his training was conducted in a restricted area of Moscow where citizens could not enter. However, his training was held in a separate suite of safe houses from that of Yevgeni. The KGB demanded and practiced stringent compartmentalization protocols in an effort to safeguard and protect the identities of other Soviet Illegals in training. This assured the KGB that a defecting Soviet Illegal in one country could not compromise operations elsewhere.

The Centre dispatched Hayhanen to New York City to work under the supervision of KGB Illegal Vilyam Fisher. He arrived in New York in October 1952, eleven months after Yevgeni's ship docked in Halifax. Hayhanen

filled the position that the KGB originally planned to give to Yevgeni after
he had sufficiently established himself and his cover in Canada. Hayhanen's
dispatch to New York effectively guaranteed that Yevgeni would remain
in Canada rather than relocate to the United States. Hayhanen had sailed to
North America on board the RMS *Queen Mary* using documentation that
identified him as Eugene Nikolai Maki.[3]

With the departure of Abramov, Bourdine was assigned to take over the
operational running of Yevgeni in Canada. When Abramov was his Illegals
Support Officer, face-to-face meetings were very rare. Yevgeni and Abramov
would have personal, direct contact once or twice a year. Operational security
was paramount. There was always a risk that the RCMP Security Service
would discover Yevgeni by placing surveillance on Abramov whenever he
left the embassy or his home. Their primary vehicle for communication with
one another was through the surreptitious use of dead drops or coded letters
sent to LLBs.

Yevgeni's relationship with Abramov was, for the most part, fairly good.
This was about to change under Bourdine. Vladimir Bourdine was a hard-
nosed KGB officer who expected results and adherence to The Centre's
operational requirements. Bourdine would not accept lackadaisical effort on
Yevgeni's part. He was ambitious and wanted to show Moscow that he was
a rising star in the KGB. He devised a new strategy with respect to Yevgeni
with the aim of bringing him under control. It included an increase in the
number of potentially clandestine personal meetings with Yevgeni. He also
set about to step up his operational activity level. However, at this juncture,
Yevgeni was blissfully unaware of Bourdine or the added stress his life was
about to experience.

Months earlier when The Centre decided that Yevgeni would remain in
Canada rather than follow through with the original plan of sending him
to New York, they increased his operational responsibilities in Canada.
He had been elevated to the important position of Illegal Resident, which
meant he would no longer be working entirely on his own. This change in
status was important to both the KGB and, ironically, the RCMP Security
Service. It provided protection to the KGB officers at the Soviet Embassy
because it insulated them from the agents and greatly reduced the chances
that they would be compromised by the Security Service. However, Yevgeni
was a double agent cooperating with the "CSA" and was providing Charles
Sweeny with the names and details of the KGB's agents that he had become
responsible for.

As Yevgeni became more settled in Canada, The Centre increased the
number and frequency of encrypted messages to him. This resulted in an
ever-increasing number of assignments for him to complete. Most requests

dealt with open information that could be found in public libraries, newspapers, and business journals. The sheer number of assignments was overwhelming, and Yevgeni had great difficulty meeting his deadlines. It was a labor-intensive exercise to decrypt each message using his one-time pads, conduct the necessary research in the city, and write reports back to The Centre that he would leave in dead drops. All the while, he had to maintain the cover of running his photography business as well as meet with Sweeny on a regular basis.

Yevgeni detested the time and effort it took to tune in and listen to the transmissions on his SX-71 shortwave radio in his apartment late at night. To complicate matters, many of the transmitted messages were double and sometimes triple encrypted. On numerous occasions, Yevgeni would miss coded transmissions from The Centre. More frequently than not, he would blame adverse atmospheric conditions for the reason he missed them. When this occurred he would send a meaningless letter to the proprietor of an Ottawa appliance store on Rideau Street. The proprietor in turn would place a plain card in the window of his store. Abramov, and later Bourdine, would walk past the store and see the card, which was a signal to them indicating that Yevgeni had missed the latest transmission. They in turn would notify The Centre, who would retransmit the message on the next scheduled cycle. The proprietor of the Ottawa appliance store was a member of the Communist Party of Canada and a recruited KGB live-letter box with the KGB codename POMOSHCHNIK.[4]

Yevgeni was not the only one receiving and decrypting the messages from The Centre. He had given Charles Sweeny the one-time pads and the key for breaking the Russian Morse code. After copying them, Sweeny returned the one-time pads to Yevgeni so he could continue to decrypt the coded messages as they were being communicated to him according to the transmission schedule devised by The Centre. Yevgeni knew that the CSA was decrypting and reading the messages, thereby discovering the tasks he was receiving. These messages identified the KGB's interest in various Canadian companies, individuals, and government policies. Yevgeni knew that if Sweeny were able to receive the messages, perhaps someone inside the Soviet Embassy in Ottawa was receiving and decrypting the messages too. Telling his Illegals Support Officer that he missed a message because of adverse atmospheric conditions was a foolhardy thing to do as he would immediately know that Yevgeni was lying. As he was about to find out, Vladimir Bourdine would not tolerate this.

Chapter Thirteen

Shades of Gouzenko

The KGB Residency in Ottawa had been deeply criticized by The Centre in the years following the defection of GRU cipher clerk Igor Gouzenko in September 1945. His revelations of Soviet military intelligence spying caused a sensation that resulted in the conviction of Communist Party of Canada and Labour Progressive Party member of parliament Fred Rose, and others, on espionage charges. Canadian prime minister William Lyon Mackenzie King established a Royal Commission on Espionage and appointed Supreme Court justices Roy Kellock and Robert Taschereau to head the inquiry.

The Gouzenko revelations and the conclusions of the Kellock-Taschereau hearings clearly established that the vast majority of recruited Soviet agents in Canada were those who were chosen from the ranks of the Communist Party of Canada. Others were recruited from within small Communist study groups that were, in effect, embryo spy units. The Soviet agents who Gouzenko identified had almost all attended Marxist-Leninist study sessions. The Communist Party of Canada, which was relied upon to assist the KGB whenever required, kept a watch for potential candidates for possible KGB recruitment. They concentrated on individuals who were sympathetic toward and admirers of the Soviet Union, those who embraced the Soviet philosophy of world peace, and those who occupied sensitive government jobs.

Most of the recruited agents were considered intellectuals and were highly educated. Many were senior officials of the Communist Party of Canada whose services as talent spotters were indispensable to the KGB. Others were support agents of lesser importance who made themselves available to assist espionage operations in any way possible, such as serving as LLBs relaying instructions to other agents on behalf of the KGB. There were, of course, those agents working within the government of Canada who had access to classified information and made it available to their Soviet handlers. And

54

there were incidental contacts that provided special services to the KGB, such as the procurement of passports, birth certificates, driver's licences, and other similar government-produced documents.

In the wake of the Gouzenko-inspired espionage trials and the Royal Commission on Espionage, the KGB Residency in Ottawa all but ceased operations. Half a dozen years after the Gouzenko defection, the KGB still had not recruited agents with access to information of value to The Centre.[1]

In response to heavy criticism from The Centre, the KGB Residency began a renewed recruitment campaign in the early 1950s. Sergei Leontyevich Rudchenko, the KGB Resident from 1951 to 1953, and his successor, Vasili Nikolayevich Shitarev, who was Resident from 1953 to 1956, each pushed an agenda of agent recruitments. However, with the exception of a few successes, the officers achieved only limited results.[2]

One of the exceptions was the recruitment of Canadian citizen Hugh George Hambleton in 1952 by Vladimir Bourdine, the officer who succeeded Abramov as Yevgeni's Illegals Support officer. Hambleton went on to spy for the KGB for over twenty years, including five years while working at NATO headquarters. A committed communist, who was recruited with the help of the Communist Party of Canada, Hambleton had been assigned the KGB codename RIMEN. It was later changed to RADOV. A few years following his recruitment, while employed at NATO headquarters, Hambleton compromised thousands of classified documents that ranged from NATO, British, and Canadian defense and military-spending plans as well as economic forecasts. Hambleton had been engaged in clandestine meetings with his handler, Aleksey Fyodorovich Trishin. Famed KGB defector Oleg Gordievsky, who had defected to Britain's Secret Intelligence Service in 1985 after having worked in place as a double agent for them since 1972, collaborated with distinguished British author and historian Christopher Andrew. He reported in his book *KGB: The Inside Story* that Hambleton compromised so many NATO sensitive documents that the KGB Resident in Paris, Mikhail Stepanovich Tsymbal, had to establish a special unit to deal with them. Hambleton was arrested in the United Kingdom in 1981. He was charged and convicted under the Official Secrets Act and sentenced to ten years imprisonment. Hambleton has been characterized as being the most important recruited KGB agent in Canada during the Cold War. In spite of the fact that he was the newly promoted KGB Illegals Resident, Yevgeni was not provided any information about the recruitment or handling of Hambleton. Had Bourdine confided this information to him, it can be argued that Hambleton's espionage career would have ended abruptly in 1953, when Yevgeni began to work with Sweeny and the RCMP Security Service as a double agent against the KGB.

Having been promoted to the position of Illegals Resident by decree of The Centre, KGB Resident Vasili Shitarev instructed Bourdine to brief Yevgeni on his new responsibilities. He was appointed to be the controller of five of the Residency's eleven recruited agents. Having Yevgeni manage and service the agents rather than KGB officers from the Residency would insulate and protect the officers and agents from being detected by the RCMP Security Service. It marked the first time that he actually began to engage in espionage since his arrival in Canada in November 1951. Sweeny of course learned directly from Yevgeni the details of his new assignments and the identities of his newly assigned, unsuspecting agents.

In addition to POMOSHCHNIK in Ottawa, Yevgeni became responsible for LIND, a Toronto member of the Communist Party of Canada who was employed at the A. V. Roe Company in Malton.[3]

A. V. Roe, formerly known as Victory Aircraft, was developing the CF-105 Avro Arrow. At the time, it was considered the most advanced fighter aircraft under development in the world. The company, owned by British aviation magnate Sir Roy Dobson, became known as Avro Canada. It designed, built, and put the aircraft through test trials from their facility in Malton. LIND did not have access to all the classified reports pertaining to the development of the CF-105. However, he was able to provide the KGB with engineering schematics of the aircraft and data for the CF-105's powerful Orenda jet engines. LIND also compromised the Sparrow II missile system that was also under development at the time. The Sparrow II was being designed and tested for use as the Avro Arrow's advanced weapons system.

Yevgeni also became responsible for managing and handling LISTER, a thirty-five-year-old Canadian of Ukrainian heritage and a member of the Communist Party of Canada. LISTER provided logistical assistance to the Ottawa KGB Residency by loading and unloading dead drops in the Toronto area as well as performing other functions on behalf of the KGB.

Two other agents, EMMA and MARA, were two committed Communists who functioned as LLBs. Talent spotted and recruited while studying at the Sorbonne in Paris, The Centre's long-range plans for EMMA were dashed when she later failed the qualifying examinations required to obtain a job at the Canadian Department of External Affairs in Ottawa. The KGB had hoped she might eventually attain a position of some importance or work in an area of sensitivity where she would have access to classified government documents. At the very least, she would have been well positioned to provide character assessments of External Affairs officers who may be susceptible to recruitment. Having failed the entrance exams, EMMA went on to establish a small arts and crafts business in Quebec with the result that the KGB later lost interest in her.

MARA was a co-owner of an upscale furniture store in Paris and a well-known fashion designer. She discreetly functioned as an LLB for the KGB where she forwarded letters and other communications to The Centre in Moscow that had originated in Canada. Although she fell under the responsibility of Yevgeni, in actual fact, he had little to do with her.[4]

At about the same time that Yevgeni was taking over operational responsibility for the KGB agents assigned to him, he received coded instructions to travel to Ottawa to attend another rare face-to-face meeting with his handler. Upon his arrival at the rendezvous site, Yevgeni was surprised to see someone new appear on the scene. He was of course expecting to see Leonid Abramov. The unfamiliar visitor introduced himself as Vladimir Bourdine. Bourdine informed Yevgeni that Abramov had been recalled to The Centre several months previously and was now back in Moscow. He bluntly informed Yevgeni that he was his new handler.

Bourdine displayed none of the charismatic personality that characterized Abramov. He showed no warmth and offered no hand of friendship. Bourdine was aggressive and direct and demanded to know why Yevgeni was not completing the work assignments The Centre had been sending him or why he was missing so many broadcasts. Yevgeni immediately felt uncomfortable in Bourdine's presence. He felt threatened and wanted desperately to get back to his apartment in Verdun. He could not understand why Abramov left without sending word of his departure. Yevgeni immediately recognized that Bourdine would be a very difficult person to work with. He would no longer be able to get away with performing as little work as possible. He knew he would now have to spend longer hours at night receiving and decrypting message traffic from The Centre and then complete the new assignments during the day.

Yevgeni was nauseated as he rode the train back to Montreal this cold February night in 1954. He vowed he would quit working for both the KGB and the CSA. He was fed up with both organizations and their demanding ways. Back in his Verdun apartment, Yevgeni slipped into depression and began drinking heavily. He was angry that Abramov had left without any word. He disliked the cold, frightening Bourdine and was heartbroken and lonely over the loss of Larissa Cunningham. He was exhausted and suffering severe stress from staying up late at night monitoring coded messages from The Centre. And he was angry with Eugene Walker and Mr. Henderson from the CSA. Yevgeni's drinking intensified as he brooded over the horrible events that beset him.[5]

Unaware that Sweeny had previously arranged to have all his telephone calls monitored by the RCMP Security Service, Yevgeni pulled his telephone book out of a drawer and looked up the number for the Night News Desk at the *Montreal Gazette*. Moments later he spoke to a news editor and informed him that he was a Soviet spy. He explained that, in fact, he was a KGB Illegal who had been sent to Canada several years previously. Incredibly, he continued his story by telling the skeptical editor that he recently defected to the RCMP Security Service in Ottawa. Continuing his drunken tirade, Yevgeni advised the editor that the RCMP Security Service turned him over to the CSA and that he was now being run back against the KGB as a double agent.[6]

The busy editor was trying to meet the *Montreal Gazette*'s filing deadline and did not have time for the distraction that Yevgeni was creating. It was painfully obvious to him that the caller was quite inebriated and was speaking English with a distinctive Brooklyn accent. There was no trace of a Russian accent in his voice. The editor knew there was no such government organization called the CSA. He dismissed Yevgeni as being a drunk and a "nut case," and he quickly hung up on him. With the notable exception of the abuse of alcohol, the entire scene was remarkably similar to circumstances that unfolded in September 1945. On that unfortunate occasion, it was Soviet cypher clerk Igor Gouzenko who was turned away by a busy news editor who was facing a filing deadline at the *Ottawa Journal*. Gouzenko was dismissed by him the night he defected from the Soviet embassy. He had 109 classified Soviet documents with him that described Soviet military espionage operations in Canada, including the identities of the Soviet agents.

The RCMP Security Service was not about to let Yevgeni off as easily as the *Montreal Gazette*. The Security Service employee who listened to the intercepted telephone call recognized the seriousness of the situation and immediately advised Sweeny. When Sweeny listened to the astonishing call, he was horrified and furious. He quickly devised a plan and contacted his RCMP colleagues in Montreal. Sweeny knew the elaborate ruse, which he was putting in place, would terrify Yevgeni. If it worked, it would bring him back under control. But Sweeny also knew there was no guarantee it would be successful. In spite of the very late hour, he set the plan in motion that very night.

A couple of hours after Yevgeni spoke to the news editor, two Montreal-based uniformed RCMP officers showed up at his Bannantyne Street apartment in Verdun. Yevgeni, who was still drunk, was firmly told that a *Montreal Gazette* news editor had called them and repeated Yevgeni's admission of being a Soviet spy operating clandestinely in Canada. He was unceremoniously arrested, removed from his home, and immediately driven to RCMP HQ in Ottawa. Neither officer spoke with Yevgeni during the two-hour drive nor acknowledged anything he said. Yevgeni quickly began to sober up and was terrified over the predicament that he had created for himself.

He was placed in a holding room, similar to a cell, inside RCMP HQ where he remained for two and a half days. He was intermittently interrogated by uniformed RCMP officers. Yevgeni was accused of various indictable offenses against Canada and threatened with a long prison sentence. During his interrogation on the third day, an unfamiliar officer entered the room, walked over to the others, and whispered something to the senior investigator. The two interrogating officers immediately looked upset, turned and faced Yevgeni without speaking, and then all three police officers left him in the room alone.

Several minutes later the door opened and a somber-looking Charles Sweeny entered the room alone. He acted officious and displayed a stern demeanor. He advised Yevgeni that the RCMP had notified the CSA of his arrest and that "Mr. Henderson," the head of CSA, had sent him to RCMP HQ to investigate the circumstances that led to Yevgeni's arrest and interrogation. Sweeny angrily served notice that the RCMP intended to charge him with various serious indictable offenses, including espionage against Canada, and would seek to send him to prison for a considerable period of time. Yevgeni was visibly distraught and sat with his head down, shaking in the chair. Sweeny angrily exclaimed that it took a great deal of persuasion as well as some heated arguing, but he successfully convinced the RCMP that matters of national security were at risk. The officers were highly annoyed but reluctantly agreed to stop their investigation and drop any notion of charging Yevgeni with espionage offenses. Sweeny then explained to Yevgeni that he convinced the RCMP to release him and allow the CSA to look after this unpleasant matter. Yevgeni was greatly relieved and grateful for Sweeny's intervention. It was all a wonderful display of theater at Yevgeni's expense.[7]

At that moment, neither Sweeny nor Yevgeni knew that circumstances beyond their control, which would unfold shortly, would adversely alter Operation KEYSTONE and their lives forever.

Chapter Fourteen

For the Sake of a
Smoked Meat Sandwich

James R. (Jim) Lemieux was a respected and experienced officer of the RCMP. In 1938 he received the RCMP Commissioner's Commendation for successfully concluding a difficult Canada Excise Act investigation in St. Anselm, Quebec.[1]

He distinguished himself in the 1940s as an astute and tenacious investigator who brought counterfeiters and narcotics traffickers before the courts.

The son of Wilfred Lemieux, a former municipal police chief, Jim Lemieux was born and brought up in Valleyfield, Quebec. He joined the RCMP in 1932 and worked in various locations in the province known within the RCMP as C Division. While serving in Montreal in 1940, the successful Detective Sergeant Lemieux was commissioned as an officer with the rank of subinspector and became head of the Criminal Investigation Bureau. He was promoted to full Inspector in 1945 and took command of C Division's Montreal Subdivision. Other honors followed. Inspector Lemieux was selected by RCMP commissioner Leonard H. Nicholson to attend the prestigious National Defence College in Kingston, Ontario, in 1951. Upon completion of the one-year course, he was transferred to RCMP HQ, Ottawa, where he assumed command of the RCMP Security Service.[2]

Jim Lemieux was acknowledged as a thoroughly professional policeman. It was a world he thrived in and was completely comfortable with. The Criminal Code, the paramilitary bearing of the force, and the immaculate uniforms of his officers was the domain in which he lived. The Security Service was a world apart from this. Nobody wore police uniforms, first names were often used as opposed to someone's rank within the organization, and the rules of the game were completely different from those in the police world. Many within the force looked down on those serving in the Security Service as men who were not performing "real" police work. They did not understand the intricacies of the intelligence world or the potential international repercussions for Canada if an intelligence operation against a target country went wrong.

Promoted to full inspector,[3] Lemieux moved from what he knew and did well to a position that was completely unfamiliar to him. Like many of his police colleagues, he did not see the value in having a Security Service. He desperately wanted to return to the world of active police work where the rules of engagement were black and white. He was a cop, not a spy. There were many within the RCMP who saw Lemieux as an outstanding policeman but an ineffectual Head of the Security Service.

On February 18, 1954, Lemieux made a terrible, impromptu, and clearly wrong decision. The impact of this, unknown at the time, would cause the intelligence services and the governments of Canada, the Soviet Union, and even Great Britain to stumble and scramble on the world stage, albeit very quietly. Without knowing it, and certainly in the absence of any ill intent, Lemieux's action changed the course of history and the lives of many people.

As the officer in charge of the Security Service, Lemieux was fully aware of the ruse being perpetrated against Yevgeni that had been unfolding the past few days inside RCMP HQ. To make this deception work, Terry Guernsey and Charles Sweeny had to remain well out of sight of the interrogation area. This ploy to wrestle Yevgeni back into control and save their operation would fail if he discovered that they were in fact RCMP officers and not representatives of the fictitious CSA.

When Lemieux learned that the charade was over and that Yevgeni was going to require transportation back to Montreal, he picked up the telephone and called RCMP corporal James Morrison and asked that he report to his office. Neither Guernsey nor Sweeny were privy to that request. Lemieux's decision to summon Morrison was a colossal mistake and displayed bad judgment.

To support their counterintelligence initiatives, the RCMP Security Service created a clandestine physical surveillance unit that internally was known as the Watcher Service. The team operated from a covert site on Somerset Street that had no markings or other identifying characteristics associated with the RCMP or any other government entity.

This nascent team of watchers was developed as a strategy to conduct discreet surveillance of Security Service targets. Known and suspected Soviet and other East European intelligence officers was the primary focus of this team. The Watcher Service was very small, consisting of only a handful of men, all of whom were members of the RCMP. They wore civilian clothes, grew their hair a little longer than their police colleagues, and were not permitted to enter RCMP premises.

In truth, the Watcher Service was not very good in its formative years. It certainly was no match for the professionally trained KGB officers who frequently, and without difficulty, identified the surveillance team members.

Guernsey, who was in charge of counterintelligence known within the RCMP Security Service as B Ops. Branch, had little confidence in the Watcher Service. He was very selective with respect to their use and refused to include or indoctrinate them on very sensitive operations. Guernsey and Sweeny made certain that their exclusion applied particularly to the Operation KEYSTONE and GIDEON cases.

Jim Lemieux, on the other hand, enjoyed the luxury of having the Watcher Service under his command. He frequently misused the Watcher Service for his own personal convenience. He had befriended Corporal James Morrison and often dispatched him, without advising Guernsey, to run personal errands that had nothing remotely to do with his official duties. This mismanagement of resources annoyed Guernsey tremendously. Although he had little use for the Watcher Service as it currently existed, he had work assignments for Morrison that were not being attended to on those occasions when Lemieux had him run errands. Morrison, who had long abandoned the Watcher Service rule of not entering RCMP buildings or property, would meet privately with Lemieux in his office and then leave the building without checking in with Guernsey or Sweeny.

When Morrison arrived at Lemieux's office, he was pleasantly surprised to learn that Lemieux wanted him to drive an individual to Montreal. Unconscionably, and without any operational reason for doing so, Lemieux briefed Morrison on the very sensitive Operation KEYSTONE case as well as details about Yevgeni. The briefing violated all precepts of operational security and the "need to know" principle. When they later found out, Guernsey and Sweeny were visibly exasperated. Not because they had any reason to distrust Morrison. Rather, this unfathomable breach of security, by the head of the Security Service, widened the circle of people who were now aware of this very important, but troubled, double-agent case.

Operational matters aside, Lemieux had an ulterior motive for sending Morrison to Montreal. It was not on official business and had nothing to do with Yevgeni. He was simply the convenient excuse. What Lemieux really wanted was for Morrison to run a personal errand in Montreal. Unbelievably, he instructed Morrison to go to the internationally known and hugely popular Dunn's Restaurant and Deli. He wanted Morrison to bring back a quantity of his beloved Montreal smoked meat. Morrison, who also loved and frequented this very popular establishment, was only too happy to oblige. This selfish personal request and the unconscionable breach of security that accompanied it set the stage for what would later become a devastating and life-altering event for many people.

Inside RCMP headquarters, James Morrison was introduced to Yevgeni. The two of them, accompanied by RCMP sergeant Barrett and Special Constable Mervyn Black, immediately departed for Montreal.[4] Morrison enjoyed the opportunity of getting out of Ottawa, and Yevgeni was happy to get away from the RCMP interrogation. During their drive to Montreal, Morrison probed deeper into who Yevgeni was but made little headway. Yevgeni chose to keep his answers short and vague. A couple of hours later Morrison dropped Yevgeni several blocks away from his Verdun apartment. Twenty minutes later, he, Barrett, and Black walked into Dunn's Restaurant and Deli where they enjoyed a huge Montreal smoked meat sandwich that they washed down with cold beer. As Morrison and the others were leaving Dunn's, he fulfilled Lemieux's request and purchased a quantity of smoked meat. Before leaving the city Morrison made a brief stop to see his father and then drove back to Ottawa. The damage Jimmy Lemieux created by having Morrison drive Yevgeni back to Montreal could not be undone.

Chapter Fifteen

The Mountie Who
Became LONG KNIFE

James Douglas Finley Morrison was born March 16, 1916, in Chatham, New Brunswick. The son of Angus Morrison and Ellen Gilmour, he was one of several children.[1] Life for the large Morrison family was not particularly easy. Angus Morrison worked as a general laborer. He was not always an easy person to live with or be around.

At the age of twenty-one, Morrison joined the RCMP as a Reserve Constable (R44) in Montreal on July 1, 1937.[2] For reasons that remain unknown, he was discharged two months later for being medically unfit. Upon his release, Morrison joined the Canadian Grenadier Guards. For some inexplicable reason, when he filled out the Attestation document for the army he identified himself as Douglas Morrison. Although technically correct, Douglas was his second name. But it was a sequence of names that he seldom if ever used. He indicated he was single, that he resided at 2225 Wildon Avenue, Montreal, and that he previously worked at the T. Eaton Company Ltd., in the Notre-Dame-de-Grace region of Montreal. There was no indication that he had previously been engaged with the RCMP as a Reserve Officer. Was he trying to mask that he had been dismissed from the RCMP as being medically unfit? Or was it simply that the Grenadier Guards needed men and the tall, physically fit Morrison was eager to join?

Two years later, Morrison's parents separated. Morrison chose to move in with his father at 2320 Belgrove Avenue. His short time there was influenced by world events and the hostile activities of Adolf Hitler.

Nazi Germany invaded Poland on September 1, 1939, which plunged Great Britain and Europe into war against Adolph Hitler. Canada, a strong member of the British Commonwealth, followed suit nine days later. On September 13, RCMP commissioner Stuart Taylor Wood petitioned the Rt. Hon. Ian Alistair Mackenzie, minister of defence in Prime Minister William Lyon Mackenzie

King's government, to form a military Provost Company made up of volunteer RCMP officers. The petition was quickly accepted, and No. 1, Provost Company (RCMP) of the Canadian army, was immediately established.[3]

With war drums beating, Morrison packed his clothes and moved to Ottawa where he reengaged in the RCMP at N Division, Rockcliffe. Whatever the reason for his medical discharge in 1937, it was no longer considered an issue in 1939. He was sworn in as a Regular Member of the RCMP on December 1, 1939, and assigned Regimental No. 13251. His Warrant of Appointment states, "Pursuant to the Statutory authority vested in me as Commissioner of the Royal Canadian Mounted Police, I have this day appointed, and do appoint, James Douglas Finley Morrison a Constable in the Royal Canadian Mounted Police, subject to the provisions of the said Statutes, for duty within the Dominion of Canada. Given under my hand and seal at the City of Ottawa, this first day of December in the year of Our Lord, one thousand nine hundred and thirty-nine." The Warrant of Appointment was signed by Commissioner S. T. Wood, Royal Canadian Mounted Police.[4]

Morrison also signed an Oath of Allegiance and an Oath of Office swearing that he would "faithfully, diligently and impartially execute and perform the duties required of me as a member of the Royal Canadian Mounted Police, and will well and truly obey and perform all lawful orders and instructions which I shall receive as such, without fear, favour or affection of or towards any person. So help me God."

Morrison, like most men his age, wanted to do his patriotic duty and contribute to the war effort. He would get his chance.

The RCMP volunteers who signed up to become members of No. 1, Provost Corps began basic military training at N Division, Rockcliffe. Constable Morrison did not hesitate to volunteer for this duty. Similar to his troop mates, he immediately transitioned from being an RCMP officer and became a private in the Canadian army. The newly established military police unit took form within days.

In early December, Private Morrison shipped out for the United Kingdom along with his Provost Corps comrades. He and his fellow former RCMP officers were sent to the British army base at Camp Aldershot to assist in the establishment of the Canadian Provost Corps Depot. RCMP officers, now serving as military police, became members of the training staff and provided instruction to those from other corps who had been sent to Camp Aldershot for six weeks of training. The curriculum included instruction in motorcycle operations and training, military law, report writing, traffic control, map reading, police procedures, and close-order drill and weapons firing.

The following year, now a lance corporal and based at British army base Camp Borden, Morrison broke his ankle in a motorcycle accident and was hospitalized. The Canadian army had taken over the local Butlin's Holiday Camp and turned it into a convalescent facility for its military personnel. As a convalescing patient, Morrison, along with five other injured Canadian soldiers, had the good fortune to be invited to a garden party at the home of British World War I veteran Lieutenant Commander (RNVR) Gerrard Laurie Vidian Jones. His wife, Mrs. Mabel Annie Vidian Jones, was head of the local Women's Voluntary Service. It was a position she handled with class and pride. To show appreciation to the injured Canadian soldiers, she hosted a garden party every Sunday afternoon at their home in Brixham, Devon, and treated the Canadians with food, beer, and hard cider. Also attending the garden party that day was their attractive daughter, Gwynneth, and their son, Ryan, a midshipman in the Royal Naval Reserve who was home on leave from Greenwich Royal Naval College.[5]

Both Gerrard and Mabel Vidian Jones came from privileged backgrounds. Gerrard's father was a surgeon who descended from British shipping owners. Gerrard's mother came from an extended family of coal mine owners. Her father was Colonel in Chief of the Middlesex Regiment. He was the owner and publisher of the respected British magazine *Engineering*. Gerrard and Mable, or Maylar as the family affectionately called her, had high expectations for their children.

Gwynneth, eight years senior to her brother, was a quiet, attractive, and unassuming person. She was a good and gracious hostess who enjoyed meeting the injured Canadian soldiers who attended the Sunday garden parties. Gwynneth was well educated, having attended the right schools for someone of her family's station in life. She attended "finishing school" near Bournemouth, Hampshire, in southwest England, where she learned all the social graces that were expected of a gentle lady.

Gwynneth made friends easily and had numerous casual boyfriends, many of whom were cadets at the Royal Naval College in Dartmouth near where the Vidian Jones family lived. Several of these fine young cadets also came from Britain's privileged families. Her parents liked these young cadets and had high hopes that Gwynneth would make a "good marriage" within her own social and economic circle. They had not accounted for their daughter's subsequent involvement and developing romantic relationship with James Morrison after she met him at the garden party that Sunday afternoon in the summer of 1941.

James Morrison was a great disappointment to Gwynneth's parents. Her mother never openly showed her displeasure for him. But she had high hopes that her daughter would be able to smooth some of his rough edges and teach him how to become a gentleman. Her father openly disliked him and did not approve of his daughter's selection of a mate. It was with a heavy heart that he learned his daughter accepted James Morrison's marriage proposal and that they would marry ten months after they initially met at her parents' garden party. Morrison followed military requirements and formally requested, and received, permission from his commanding officer to marry Gwynneth. He never extended the same courtesy to her father. Their marriage took place on February 25, 1942, in Saint Mary's Church in Upper Brixham, Devon, a short walk from Gwynneth's home. As he threatened to do, Lt. Commander Vidian Jones did not attend their wedding. A military friend of the family, Captain Broadbent, stood up with Gwynneth, taking the place of her very unhappy father who was conveniently out of town for the day. Gwynneth's brother, Ryan, was absent as well. He was a seventeen-year-old midshipman on a British troop ship sailing to India where he was being transferred to the Royal Indian navy.[6]

The newlywed couple moved into #10 Harrington Villas, Brighton, Sussex, where Gwynneth obtained wartime employment assembling British-manufactured Bren Guns at a nearby factory. It was a critical job for the Allied war effort and part of her war service to Britain. The following year they moved to White Cottage, Milton Street, South Devon.[7] It was a good year for the Morrisons. Gwynneth gave birth to the couple's first son. James was promoted to the rank of lieutenant. Gwynneth was fortunate to have the assistance of her mother, who looked after the baby much of the time. Lt. Commander Vidian Jones remained distant and cool toward Morrison. He held strong convictions that he was not good enough for his young daughter, and he plainly didn't like him.[8]

James Morrison's star continued to rise. He received another promotion in March 1944 to the rank of acting captain and was given command of the Canadian Provost Corps, Special Investigation Section. It was a well-earned field promotion to a position of importance. Three weeks after D-Day, Morrison landed in France, and twelve weeks later his promotion to the rank of captain was formalized and he was sent to the Netherlands. As the officer in charge of the Special Investigation Section, Morrison was responsible for investigating German wartime atrocities against the Dutch population. Working with senior officials within the Dutch government, he became acquainted with members of the Dutch Royal Family. Prince Bernhardt of the Netherlands was impressed with the tall, handsome Canadian who was determined to capture fleeing Nazi officers and others who committed war crimes against the Dutch. The prince's admiration and respect for him was so high that he convinced the Canadian army to appoint Morrison to be his aide-de-camp. The prince then arranged to have Morrison's wife Gwynneth travel from England and join them in The Hague. But most astonishing of all, Prince Bernhardt invited James and Gwynneth Morrison to live in a private apartment situated within the Royal Palace. During this period, Gwynneth's parents in England looked after their young grandson.[9]

In May 1945, at the end of World War II, Morrison remained in Europe and continued to hunt German war criminals. His father in Montreal received a letter written April 16, 1946, from Colonel C. L. Laurin, director of records, who was writing on behalf of the adjutant-general, Canadian army. The letter stated,

Dear Sir,

Ref. Captain James Douglas Finley Morrison

It is with much pleasure that I write you on behalf of the Minister of National Defence and Members of the Army Council to congratulate you and the members of your family on the honour and distinction which has come to your son the marginally named, through his being Mentioned in Despatches in recognition of gallant and distinguished services.

The King's Certificate in connection with this award will be forwarded in due course. Present indications are that some time will elapse before the Certificate is available.

Yours very truly,
C. L. Laurin, Colonel[10]

James Morrison's World War II service saw him rise from the rank of private to captain. He was employed in general provost duties for twelve months and then on Special Investigations for twenty months as a noncommissioned officer. Following his commission he became Provost Company platoon commander for six months followed by officer in charge of special investigations for thirty-six months. In total, he served eighty months in the United Kingdom, France, Belgium, the Netherlands, and Germany. He received the 1939 to 1945 Star, France and Germany Star, Defence Medal, War Medal 1939 to 1945, Canadian Volunteer Medal and Clasp, and Mentioned in Despatches (MID).

Captain James Morrison, in the company of other Canadian soldiers, sailed home to Canada on June 21, 1946, on the RMS *Queen Mary*. Functioning as a wartime troop carrier, many Canadian soldiers crossed the Atlantic on the majestic *Queen Mary*. It was one of many converted civilian ships that made similar voyages carrying soldiers and equipment. Gwynneth left the Netherlands and returned to her parents' home in the United Kingdom where her son was staying with his grandparents.

Upon landing back in Canada, Morrison took the train to Regina where he signed his military release documents from the Canadian Provost Corps on August 6, 1946. He immediately signed back on as an RCMP officer. At the stroke of a pen and after signing oaths to king and country, Captain Morrison reverted to being Constable Morrison. As far as the RCMP was concerned, the previous rank, honor, and prestige of his army commission did not account for anything now that he was a Mountie once again. He had gone from being a commissioned officer responsible for Special Investigations and living in the Royal Palace in the company of the Royal Family to the lowest rank in the RCMP.

Much to the disappointment of Gerrard and Mabel Vidian Jones, Gwynneth and her young toddler left England and followed her husband to Canada. Mother and son set sail aboard the RMS *Mauretania* for Halifax. It was the same ship that had its first dedicated sailing in February 1946 carrying English war brides and their children as they immigrated to Canada to join their husbands and fathers. Gwynneth too was a war bride setting out to establish a new life for herself and her family in Regina. She was seven months pregnant and more than a little frightened.

Back in the fold of the RCMP, Morrison was posted to Depot Division, Regina, where he underwent RCMP refresher training. For him and Gwynneth the contrast could not have been more dramatic or traumatic. They had transitioned from living in relative luxury within the Dutch Royal Palace in The Hague to their dreadful new accommodations in Regina. They were living in appalling conditions in a converted garage that had a dirt floor and an outside toilet. It was under these conditions that their second son was born.

Three months later, Morrison was sent back to RCMP N Division, Rockcliffe, located in Ottawa, for an additional twelve weeks of training. It was a very difficult time for Gwynneth. She was new to Canada, unfamiliar with Regina, and had no friends to support her. She had two small boys to look after, and her husband was back in Eastern Canada.

James Morrison had plunged his family into serious indebtedness, and Gwynneth was having difficulty coping. He had fallen into a pattern of living well beyond his means and spending money he simply did not have. With Gwynneth in Regina and James in Ottawa, their expenses ballooned. Her parents were deeply concerned about her welfare and that of their grandchildren. Gerrard and Mabel Vidian Jones made a life-altering decision. They dissolved their considerable assets in the United Kingdom and moved to Regina where they could provide love and material support to Gwynneth and her young children.[11]

When his training was completed at N Division, Rockcliffe, Morrison was posted to RCMP Regina Town Station Detachment. It was a normal procedure where newly trained officers were sent to their local subdivision headquarters before being selected for a smaller rural detachment. Eight weeks later on April 16, 1947, he was posted 117 miles southwest of Regina to the small RCMP detachment in the French-speaking community of Gravelbourg, Saskatchewan. There was only one other RCMP officer stationed at the detachment. Twenty-one-year-old Constable Alexander McCallum, affectionately known as Sandy, was a single, popular, hard-as-nails young Mountie who was born in Kirkland Lake, Ontario. James Morrison was his detachment commander.[12]

James and Gwynneth and their two sons lived in the RCMP detachment in the small Saskatchewan town. RCMP detachment commanders throughout the province were respected pillars in the community. They kept the towns safe, settled disputes, and participated in community events. Townspeople looked up to the RCMP officers and were proud to have them in their community. Constable McCallum was worried. He very quickly recognized that Morrison was a dramatically different person than what others in the town saw.

Professionally, McCallum saw an officer who looked good in uniform, had a gift for speaking easily with people, but privately was a poor manager and a very bad role model. He did as little as he could get away with in the office. Worse, McCallum witnessed his deceitful ways and worried that the townspeople saw it too. His police investigations were far below the standards taught to RCMP officers. He made poor and unprofessional judgments with respect to criminal investigations and often ignored what he considered nuisance calls from the public.[13]

On the personal side, McCallum witnessed much worse. He knew that Morrison was a serial adulterer. He engaged in extramarital relationships and regularly had trysts in the general detachment region they worked as well as in Regina. McCallum knew, as did many in the community, that Morrison was constantly unfaithful to Gwynneth and their children. Morrison frequently asked McCallum to cover for him while he was out with another woman. He tried to persuade McCallum to lie to Gwynneth and convince her that Morrison was out on an investigation or police interview. McCallum was very fond of Gwynneth and her two sons. He knew that Gwynneth was fully aware that her husband was being unfaithful to her but kept that information from her children and never discussed the problem. McCallum had no respect for Morrison and found it very difficult working for him. In the frequent absences of their father, McCallum tried to spend time with Morrison's two young sons. The children called him Uncle Sandy. The eldest of the two boys used to hug McCallum and tell him, "I wish you were our daddy." McCallum characterized Morrison as being a self-serving "son-of-a-bitch" who cared about nothing or nobody except himself. They worked together for a little over a year. Their careers would later converge again in Ottawa in the Security Service.[14]

Thirteen months later Morrison was transferred again. This time it was to the small farming community of Moosomin, twelve miles west of the Saskatchewan-Manitoba border. Morrison was placed in charge of the three-man detachment. Recognizing that Gwynneth required help and support, Gerrard and Mabel Vidian Jones moved from Regina to be close to her and the grandchildren. In what can only be described as awkward, they too resided in the large detachment residence.

In June 1948, the Vidian Jones family was overjoyed to learn that their son, Ryan, had also immigrated to Canada. He visited his parents and sister in Moosomin. During that short stay, Ryan had the opportunity to go out on a rural police patrol with Morrison. He saw this as an opportunity to get to know his brother-in-law a little better as the war years had kept them apart. As always, Morrison's uniform was immaculate. His high brown boots, worn with the riding breeches the Mounties were so proud of, were highly polished. He was a handsome and impressive-looking officer. It was a quiet night on the prairie with clear skies and a full moon. There had been no vehicle or farm accidents and no police calls over the police radio for them to respond to.

Morrison drove the marked police car into a local farm yard and established that nobody was at home. Ryan was quite taken aback and momentarily speechless when he witnessed Morrison enter an unoccupied smokehouse on the property and emerge moments later with objects in his hands. Ryan quickly recognized that Morrison had stolen a couple of smoked hams from the absent farmer's smokehouse. Ryan challenged Morrison about the impropriety and illegality of his actions. Morrison arrogantly responded by saying he would return to the farm later and pay the farmer. Ryan was stunned by Morrison's actions and was skeptical that the farmer would ever be paid for the two smoked hams. He characterized Morrison as being a thief and a liar and a disgrace to the uniform of the RCMP.[15]

In October 1949, Ryan engaged in the RCMP at Depot Division, Regina, with Regimental Number 15666 and completed Part I and Part II training as a member of A Squad. His formal training included equitation and the care and grooming of the force's beautiful horses under the watchful eye of Staff Sergeant Cecil Walker, the disciplined Riding Master at Depot for seventeen years. Many young RCMP officers who graduated from the equestrian training program in Regina went on to become members of the world-famous RCMP Musical Ride, which thrilled admirers around the world.

Ryan was initially posted to K Division Headquarters in Edmonton, Alberta, which was the norm for a new officer straight out of training. Within a short period of time, after senior officers had an opportunity to evaluate him as a police officer, he was posted to a smaller detachment at Medicine Hat, where he served under RCMP sergeant Stephen (Mickey) Slinn. After proving himself as a proficient and resourceful police officer, Ryan was moved to the Criminal Investigations Division (CID) in Lethbridge. Inspector "Black Jack" Mcdonnell, the officer in charge of the CID, selected only the best officers to work in this unit. Ryan thoroughly enjoyed the scope of the work and the unique challenges that CID offered. He and his colleagues investigated serious criminal cases as plainclothes detectives. However, his tenure in the RCMP was short-lived. He resigned in 1951 due to the archaic and restrictive rules related to marriage restrictions. The force's marriage policy at the time forbade officers to marry within the first seven years of their police service. Ryan had other ideas.

The most significant change in the lives of James Morrison and his small family came on May 30, 1950. Former soldier Colonel Len Nicholson, wartime Army Provost Martial, 2nd Corps, knew Morrison to be an accomplished, competent, and decorated military officer in Europe when he had been Morrison's commanding officer. With the war and his military service behind him, Nicholson, like so many former RCMP officers, rejoined the RCMP and became an assistant commissioner. With Morrison's solid military reputation in mind, Nicholson selected him for sensitive, undercover duties in the fledgling Security Service and transferred him to Ottawa. In a memorandum found on Morrison's RCMP service file, RCMP commissioner Nicholson wrote, "The transfer of Morrison would be in line with the planned expansion of the Special Branch. Constable Morrison's posting would not be a replacement of any of the present staff. The matter has already been discussed with the Commissioner and he has given tentative approval."[16] Nicholson would later rue the day he made that decision.

Chapter Sixteen

A Life in Transition

The Morrison family's transfer to Ottawa was seen as a new beginning for Gwynneth. They were in a new, modern city that enjoyed culture, upscale shopping from what they had in small-town Saskatchewan, a theater, a great variety of restaurants, and what she saw as endless opportunities for her children in education and sporting activities. She was also happy to move away from small-town living where the wife of the RCMP detachment commander was always under the watchful eyes of everyone in the community. Although she had established some good relationships, there were others who remained distant due to her husband's extracurricular activities and personality. Gwynneth's parents had followed them to Ottawa and were looking forward to living in the nation's capital. Lt. Commander Vidian Jones enjoyed being close to the political pulse of the country and the daily machinations of political parties. His wife, Mabel, doted on her two grandsons.

James Morrison's life changed in more fundamental ways. He no longer wore a police uniform to work. Nor did he have a police vehicle at his disposal to be used as he saw fit. He knew, however, that he would enjoy the anonymity that wearing plainclothes would give him. After all, he was now employed in a newly established surveillance unit where plainclothes were a requirement. He wasted little time finding exclusive men's stores where he purchased expensive made-to-measure suits. He had a penchant for spending other people's money, money he did not have of his own.

Morrison's biggest change, at least in the beginning, was the rule that members of the Watcher Service were not permitted to go to, or enter, RCMP facilities. Their effectiveness as surveillance operators would be destroyed if representatives from the Soviet or People's Republic of China embassies saw them enter or depart RCMP headquarters. The Watcher Service operated from a nondescript building on Somerset Street in downtown Ottawa.

Because of this arrangement, members of the Watcher Service did not have detailed access to operational case files. They knew that the Security Service was interested in Soviet KGB officers such as Leonid Abramov, Vladimir Bourdine, Nikolai Ostrovskiy, and others, but they didn't always know why they were placing these Soviets under surveillance. The only time they would learn something was when they received an operational briefing because they needed to perform a specific job.

But in time, Morrison came to view the requirement to stay away from publicly identified RCMP buildings as being for everyone else but him. He gradually came to ignore this regulation and did as he wished.

As an undercover operative, Morrison used his personal car while working on RCMP surveillance operations. In fact, it was a vehicle that his mother-in-law purchased and paid for. It was not the first car that she purchased, nor would it be the last. But Morrison would never divulge this kind of information to his work colleagues. He was too vain for that. Nor would he mention that Mabel Vidian Jones was also paying the rent on his comfortable home at 1449 Portal Street in the Pleasant Park area of Ottawa. He was content to allow others to think that he was providing for his family. His debts were accumulating, and he was having difficulty meeting normal household expenses. Gwynneth's brother Ryan characterized James by stating, "Jim fancied himself as a big time operator. He wore expensive clothing, smoked big cigars but was forever broke. He conned my mother into buying expensive cars and other things. She acquiesced in order to keep their marriage together."

Ryan and his wife, Dorothy, calculated that Morrison took advantage of his mother-in-law's generosity to such an extent that it cost their estate well in excess of $200,000 in 1950s money. It was a considerable fortune at that time. Ryan declared that Morrison was "a liar, a cheat, a con-man and a thief. In retrospect, he was the most despicable man I ever met."[1]

James Morrison's daughter-in-law,[2] the wife of James Morrison's oldest son, stated that her father-in-law was always in debt. At the same time, he tried to give the impression that he was an important figure.

Working undercover in a surveillance team such as the RCMP Security Service's nascent Watcher Service demanded discipline, self-confidence, and an ability to work well with others. Team members worked long and, sometimes, unusual hours in close proximity to one another. The officers got to know each other intimately and became aware of their problems, strengths, successes, and family life. In most cases, the operatives became as close as brothers and fiercely protected each other. At this time in their early history, there were no female members on the Watcher Service.

Team members became closer than family and frequently spent more time with one another than they did with their own family members. On occasion, a team member simply could not fit in. Most often it was because the officer was disliked because of a prickly personality, moodiness, or he simply could not work well with a team. James Morrison possessed all the necessary abilities to be a good operative. But his arrogance and conceit separated him from the others. He was generally disliked and seen as a boisterous loud mouth who considered himself to be much more clever and important than his peers. Nevertheless, he worked with the team as they covered their primary KGB and GRU military targets from the Soviet Embassy as well as the other known and suspected clandestine intelligence officers from the Chinese and East European embassies in Ottawa.

Nobody knows with any certainty when it was that Morrison began to cultivate thoughts about approaching the Soviets with the view of selling them classified information. Between 1952 and 1954 his personal debts began to accumulate at an alarming rate. He knew that he could not manage his own financial affairs. The problem was compounded by the fact that his surveillance expenses were limited to $40 per month, which was insufficient for the duties he had to perform. By late 1954 he recognized that he was in deep financial trouble. By the spring of 1955, having exhausted every avenue there was for borrowing money, including banks, credit unions, finance companies, friends, and family, he made a terrible decision.

In April 1955, Morrison misappropriated RCMP operational funds that he had been entrusted with.[3] The money, $700 in cash, was payment for legitimate operations for which he was assigned to deliver to their primary contact at the local telephone company. He misappropriated the same $700 of operational funds for the month of May as well. In June 1955, he took the operational funds to the telephone company contact and informed him that it was payment for their April account. By the end of June, Morrison was still $1,400 in arrears of RCMP operational funds.[4] That represented a significant amount of money at the time. He was desperate and knew full well that he could not hide what he had done forever. He had to find a way to replace this money at all costs.

Chapter Seventeen

Establishing the Framework for Treason

Treason, like infidelity, is committed in the mind before the actual deed is consummated. RCMP corporal James Morrison knew this firsthand. He was already known to be a Lothario, but now he was about to plunge headfirst into the treachery of treason.

Morrison was a vain, handsome man. He stood in excess of six feet in height, had broad shoulders and a fit, trim build. He was heavy in the chest and possessed the physique of a man that signaled that he could take care of himself if ever challenged. James Morrison walked tall, displaying self-confidence combined with a heavy measure of arrogance. An expensive cigar was seldom far from his mouth. His suits were stylish, extravagant, and hand tailored. They came from the best clothiers available in Montreal and Ottawa. Many of his RCMP colleagues admired his late-model car while simultaneously they envied him and wondered how he could afford such things. There were whispers that the money came from Gwynneth's parents, his British war bride. Her family was known to have been wealthy. Little did his colleagues know how much of a sham his life really was or how heavily he was indebted to the banks, family, and friends. Nor were they aware that he was also a thief, stealing money from the very organization that employed him.[1]

It was late June 1955, and Ottawa was experiencing higher-than-normal temperatures. Summer was less than a week old, but Ottawa was already sweating under 81 degree Fahrenheit temperatures and oppressive humidity. Underneath his suit jacket, Morrison's freshly ironed shirt was sticking to his back as rivulets of perspiration trickled down his spine. His arrival at the Grand Hotel on Sussex Drive had less to do with cooling off over a cold beer as it did to finding Nikolai Ostrovskiy. If he was honest with himself, and he rarely was, he would admit to having some level of anxiety and even an unsettled stomach. But he was determined to follow through with his ill-conceived plan. A quick scan of the beer parlor established that Ostrovskiy was not sitting at his usual table in the "men's only" establishment. Nevertheless, Morrison pulled up a chair, ordered a beer, lit his cigar, and waited. He was confident that the unsuspecting Ostrovskiy would walk into the beverage room, make himself comfortable, and order a beer. Morrison wouldn't have to wait long.

Nikolai Pavlovich Ostrovskiy arrived in Canada on June 19, 1954,[2] and took up post as Second Secretary at the Embassy of the Union of Soviet Socialist Republics (USSR) on Charlotte Street, Ottawa. In spite of his diplomatic designation, Ostrovskiy was a clandestine intelligence officer of the KGB. Ostrovskiy was well trained, astute, and a good agent-running officer. He arrived at the Grand Hotel's beer parlor alone. He was in no particular hurry to leave.

Five years earlier, RCMP corporal James Morrison had been transferred from general-duty policing in Moosomin, Saskatchewan, to Ottawa. He was assigned to a sensitive, undercover position in the fledgling Watcher Service that had the responsibility of conducting surveillance operations on targets identified by the RCMP Security Service. Known and suspected intelligence officers of the KGB were their top priority. As a member of the small Watcher Service, Morrison knew when the various KGB officers were under surveillance and when they were not. It was an advantage that he was about to capitalize on.

Morrison sat at his table and watched Ostrovskiy settle in with his beer. Ostrovskiy dressed differently from most of his colleagues at the embassy. He was more urbane and in tune with Western fashion then most of his Soviet and East European colleagues. And his comportment was a refreshing change from many of the other Soviets who had been his predecessors over the years. Ostrovskiy spoke good English, smiled easily, and liked to wear a fedora at a jaunty angle. It suggested an air of fun, or mischievousness, which set him apart from others. People liked him, and he used that to his advantage. His suits were stylish but certainly not in the same league as those worn by Morrison. For that matter, few in the RCMP wore suits that would compare in value to anything that Morrison wore.

Ostrovskiy was fond of the Grand Hotel's beer parlor. He especially liked that it was for male patrons only. The Grand Hotel was a short drive from the Soviet Embassy, and from his home as well. In spite of his approachable and extroverted nature, Ostrovskiy normally went to the beer parlor unaccompanied and rarely engaged in conversation with the other patrons. He considered it a refuge from the pressures of the embassy and an opportunity to distance himself from some of the people he worked with. He particularly enjoyed the relaxed atmosphere where he could sit quietly, consume his beer, and observe the mannerisms of Westerners.

But on this day, his usual routine was altered as he watched a tall, good-looking gentleman with military bearing move across the room and occupy a chair at a table beside him. Nobody knew it then, but the groundwork was being laid that would transform the lives of many people and destroy what was, at the time, considered the most important counterespionage operation in Canada.

Morrison took a drink of his beer, shifted slightly, and angled his body toward Ostrovskiy. Addressing him, he asked, "How are you today?" Ostrovskiy hesitated, searched the man's face for some form of recognition, and then simply replied, "I'm fine. How do you feel?"[3]

Morrison never equivocated. He maintained direct eye contact with Ostrovskiy and exclaimed, "I would like to see you privately. Is there any place I can meet you later today?"

"What do you want to see me about?" inquired Ostrovskiy.

Morrison replied, "Well . . . we can't talk about that here."

Still maintaining direct eye contact, Ostrovskiy told Morrison that he would be going out to the west end of Ottawa later that evening. Speaking clearly and deliberately, Ostrovskiy told Morrison that he would be at the Champlain Café at 11:30 p.m. and if Morrison wished to see him, they could meet there. The café was just off Island Park Drive close to the Champlain Bridge on the Ontario side of the Ottawa River. It was well known to the Watcher Service.

Years later, Morrison related this sequence of events somewhat differently. On March 31, 1971, RCMP Security Service sergeants James (Jim) S. Warren and Randall (Randy) B. Claxton interrogated Morrison at the RCMP Detachment in Prince Rupert, British Columbia, over a period of four days. The interview sessions and polygraph examinations total twenty-three-and-a-half hours of investigation. On that occasion, Morrison confirmed the details of his meeting with Ostrovskiy at the Grand Hotel in Ottawa. However, he stated that, rather than speaking to Ostrovskiy in the hotel beverage room, he wrote a note to him on the inside of an empty cigar package. The note said something to the effect that he wanted to meet Ostrovskiy at the Champlain Café later that day. He stated that when Ostrovskiy got up to leave the bar he followed him to his car, which was parked on Besserer Street. As Ostrovskiy settled into his car seat, Morrison stated he walked past the open window and dropped the cigar package onto his lap. As he walked in front of the car, Morrison stated that he glanced sideways at Ostrovskiy so that the KGB officer could see his face and get a good look at him.[4] Whichever scenario is true, Morrison admitted making contact with a known clandestine intelligence officer of the KGB with the intent of committing treason. Morrison also agreed that in the course of his surveillance duties with the Watcher Service, the

Soviets had very likely identified him as a member of the RCMP and that Ostrovskiy probably knew who he was when he dropped the note through the window.

Late that evening, Morrison pulled into the small parking lot next to the Champlain Café. He immediately observed Ostrovskiy standing beside his car, smoking a cigarette near the bridge. Using his countersurveillance training, Morrison quickly established there were no other embassy cars in the area that might be providing cover for Ostrovskiy. Nor did he see any familiar unmarked Security Service cars.

Morrison pulled up beside him, rolled down his window, and invited Ostrovskiy to get into his car. Ostrovskiy hesitated and suggested that Morrison join him. It was a minor standoff that was settled quickly, with Ostrovskiy acquiescing. As soon as Ostrovskiy closed the door, Morrison pulled out of the lot and drove across the Champlain Bridge and into the Province of Quebec. He pulled his car into the vacant parking lot of the Royal Ottawa Golf Club. It was dark, and the two would easily be able to discern if anyone approached the area.

As soon as they were stopped, Ostrovskiy seized the moment and exerted control. He demanded, "Who are you, and what is it that you want to talk about?" Although Morrison had practiced how he would respond to just such a question, he initially faltered and then nervously pulled out his RCMP identification. He responded, "My name is Jim Morrison. I am a member of the Royal Canadian Mounted Police."

Ostrovskiy studied Morrison's warrant card and pointedly asked, "What department are you with and what is the nature of your duties?"

Morrison replied, "I am in the Security Service. I conduct surveillance operations as well as other security investigations."

Ostrovskiy knew precisely what Morrison was talking about but pressed him to reveal more. "Well, just what do you mean by surveillance and security work?"

Morrison responded, "It is carrying out certain observations of your people . . . the embassy staff."

In a strong, steady voice and maintaining control of their meeting, Ostrovskiy persisted, "What do you particularly want to talk about?"

Jim Morrison, the officer who had sworn an oath to the RCMP and the Canadian government that he could be trusted to maintain sacred the secrets of his profession, stared at Ostrovskiy and replied, "I have some information that I will give you, for which I want to receive $3,000."[5] This represented more money than Morrison earned in a year.

Ostrovskiy remained stone faced. He neither reacted, nor displayed, any emotion at the mention of that princely sum. When he asked Morrison the nature of the information, Morrison told him, "You are going to have to produce the $3,000, in order to receive that intelligence. We will then be able to discuss it. But first, you will have to pay."

Every foreign intelligence officer in the world dreams of recruiting someone within a host country intelligence service. The RCMP Security Service was Ostrovskiy's primary target. And here was one of its officers, voluntarily, sitting in the dark parking lot of a remote golf course on the verge of committing treason. It would be a significant coup for the KGB and Ostrovskiy specifically if he could successfully recruit one of the RCMP Security Service officers. Obtaining detailed information about a KGB adversary including names of officers, details of their counterespionage operations, the location of covert Security Service premises, and the names of agents dispatched to the Soviet Union had Ostrovskiy's imagination dancing. He did not wish to lose this opportunity. At the same time, Ostrovskiy recognized that he would have to be on the alert for an intelligence trap. Was the RCMP setting him up? He would have to wait and see.

Ostrovskiy softened his stance and agreed with Morrison that perhaps they could work together. It was, after all, Morrison who had approached him. Not wanting to lose a potential spy within the heart of the RCMP Security Service, Ostrovskiy offered encouragement, with the objective of securing another clandestine meeting. "Well, perhaps I can meet you again and we can discuss this further,"[6] Ostrovskiy replied. With this agreement in mind, they established a date and time for their next clandestine rendezvous. They agreed to meet late in the evening at the Glenlea Golf Club on Aylmer Road, in Aylmer, Quebec. It would be a meeting that would lead to terrible consequences in the weeks ahead, perhaps even to the execution of another unsuspecting spy.

Chapter Eighteen

Betrayal

Nikolai Ostrovskiy spent the entire afternoon conducting countersurveillance measures in an effort to determine whether he was being followed by the RCMP Watcher Service. To a casual observer, Ostrovskiy appeared to be spending the day aimlessly driving around Ottawa, randomly stopping at shopping areas and visiting cafés. In truth, he was executing a carefully predetermined route that was designed in such a manner to establish whether he was being followed. He shouldn't have worried. Unknown to Ostrovskiy, the RCMP Security Service, including all the members of the Watcher Service, had taken the night off. They were attending an annual RCMP summer barbeque at Long Island. This beautiful, secluded forested property, nestled by the Rideau River, was an exclusive RCMP recreational camping ground. It was a favorite RCMP retreat that was loved by the families who used it. Situated several miles south of Ottawa, the property was donated to the RCMP by a wealthy benefactor who loved the force and the romantic stories associated with it. Besides swimming in the river, the camp offered fire pits, a play area for children, and a number of intimate cabins that could be rented far below market price. In fact, Morrison, his wife, Gwynneth, and their two boys were staying in one of the cabins for the summer. It was idyllic.

Ostrovskiy was totally focused on tonight's meeting. Was Jim Morrison a potential spy for the KGB, or was he the key player in an elaborate Security Service trap? Would he show up at the rendezvous site? If so, would he divulge the classified information that he alluded to during their last meeting? Would he agree to future meetings? As a recruited agent within the Security Service, Morrison could provide invaluable intelligence for which the KGB would reward him substantially. Ostrovskiy had been thinking of little else since they met at the Royal Ottawa Golf Club the previous week.

In the days following that initial late-night meeting, there had been a great deal of activity and consternation inside the Ottawa KGB Residency and at Moscow Centre as well. Ostrovskiy had briefed Vasili Nikolayevich Shitarev, the KGB Resident, on every aspect of Morrison's approach. No detail was omitted. No point was considered unimportant. He described their brief conversation inside the beverage room in the Grand Hotel, Morrison's request to meet privately, their quick rendezvous at the Champlain Café, and their subsequent late-night, clandestine meeting at the Royal Ottawa Golf Club across the river in Quebec. As the case officer directly involved with Morrison, he knew he was in the best position to offer an opinion on whether Morrison was a legitimate intelligence volunteer or an agent provocateur. Ostrovskiy had studied Morrison closely looking for some indication that the man was setting up an elaborate trap. Ostrovskiy believed he was staring into the eyes of a desperate man, a man who was consumed by demons and other unstated problems. He believed Morrison had important intelligence to impart and that he could be a valuable spy for the KGB. He instinctively knew that Morrison's motivation was centered on money. He was no ideologue. Moscow Centre urged caution but agreed with the recommendation Shitarev had furnished. He had convincingly articulated that he had confidence in Ostrovskiy and expressed the notion that the risk was worth the reward. Shitarev was banking on the fact that Morrison was a legitimate intelligence "walk-in."

Ten days after their initial meeting and mere hours before the commencement of the RCMP Long Island barbeque, Ostrovskiy was conducting his premeeting countersurveillance run and Morrison was at RCMP Headquarters in a state of shock. He had just been formally advised that RCMP assistant commissioner Clifford Harvison signed documentation transferring Morrison back to Western Canada. His orders stipulated that he was being posted to D Division, Winnipeg, Manitoba.[1] While Ostrovskiy, Shitarev, and Moscow Centre were scheming and preparing for intelligence coups to come, Morrison recognized immediately that his access to classified intelligence was about to end abruptly. More frightening to him was the realization that his conduit to badly needed funds was about to end as well.

At precisely 10:30 p.m., Morrison watched Ostrovskiy arrive at the Glenlea Golf Course. He drove over to the west side of the deserted parking lot and pulled up beside Morrison's car. Ostrovskiy exited his vehicle and walked around to the passenger side and joined Morrison. Not wanting to be seen together in the area, they quickly left the golf course and drove in darkness along the Aylmer-Hull Road. Other than exchanging a few rudimentary greetings, they never said a word to each other about their pending business. Morrison eventually pulled off on to a seldom-used driveway that led to a vacant farmhouse a mile north of the golf course.

Morrison's car was practically invisible in the remote, abandoned farmyard. Nor were there any lights illuminating the yard from any of the adjacent farm buildings. Morrison suspected that the electricity for the farm had been turned off by the municipality months previously.

Ostrovskiy examined the car closely, then asked Morrison if there was a police radio concealed somewhere in the vehicle. Did Ostrovskiy suspect that perhaps a microphone had been installed in such a manner that would allow their conversation to be broadcast to someone else close at hand? Morrison assured him that there was no microphone or radio in the car. Abandoning any suggestion of casual or friendly small talk, Ostrovskiy pointedly stated, "You said at the last meeting that you had information for me."

Without hesitating, Morrison responded, "Yes, I have information. Have you got your end of the bargain with you?" When Ostrovskiy confirmed that he had, Morrison didn't waver. In an act of egregious treachery, he turned toward Ostrovskiy and said, "You have an agent operating in Montreal. This man has been in touch with us. I suggest that you get him out of the country soon."

"Who is this man?" Ostrovskiy questioned.

Morrison responded, "I don't know the man's name, so I can't tell you. But he lives in the north end of Montreal and operates some kind of shop."

Unsatisfied, Ostrovskiy pressed for more information. "Why can't you tell me his name? Have you ever seen this man?"

"I don't know the man's name," Morrison repeated. "I only met him once when I was asked to drive him to Montreal."

"What was he doing here in Ottawa?" demanded Ostrovskiy.

Again, Morrison did not hesitate, "I don't really know. I think he was down here on some business with us."

Ostrovskiy prodded deeper, "Where did you take him in Montreal?"

"I took him some place close to the corner of Coté-de-Liesse in St. Laurent," Morrison told him.

Internally, Ostrovskiy was deeply concerned but did not wish to signal this emotion to Morrison. "What did this man look like?"

"I would say that he is possibly twenty-seven to thirty years of age. He was much shorter than me. I don't know. He was perhaps five feet seven or eight but he could have been shorter. His hair was dark brown and had waves. I would say that he was of medium build."

Ostrovskiy sat quietly for a moment. It was evident he was deep in thought. He had never had to deal with one of his own who had committed treachery against the KGB. He knew Shitarev would be furious. He also knew that they would have to inform The Centre so that a plan to get him back to Moscow could be hastily arranged. He knew he had to remain calm and not overreact in front of Morrison.

He looked at Morrison and stated, "I think I know what you are talking about."[2] Ostrovskiy slowly and deliberately removed a bulky envelope from the inside pocket of his suit jacket and handed it to Morrison. He also passed him a receipt and instructed Morrison to sign for the cash using a fictitious name. Ostrovskiy lectured him that he must protect his identity from being exposed and that it was essential that he must never sign a receipt in his own personal name.[3]

Ostrovskiy decided to probe further. "I am interested in the structure and organization of the Security Service. We will pay you well for this," he explained.

Morrison hesitated. He had not planned for this. He was quite prepared to provide additional information for money, but he had to get to the Long Island summer party. It was already late and he did not want his colleagues to start asking his wife where he might be at this late hour. "Not this evening. There is someplace I have to be." Ostrovskiy reluctantly accepted this but instructed Morrison to purchase a coil notebook and write down everything he knew about the man in Montreal and the structure and organization of the Security Service before their next meeting.

In spite of the fact that he would be moving to Winnipeg in the weeks ahead, Morrison agreed to meet Ostrovskiy again on the Friday night of July 29 in Templeton, Quebec. He did not divulge to Ostrovskiy that he had, just hours before, been told of his transfer to Winnipeg. Morrison wasn't about to cut off the KGB funds now that he had received payment for classified RCMP intelligence. He returned to the Long Island camp and concealed the cash in his rented cabin.

His treachery wasn't over. It was just beginning.

Chapter Nineteen

Reluctant Guest of Lubyanka

Nikolai Alekseyevich Korznikov, reputedly one of the most important and influential KGB officials in the First Chief Directorate's Department S, the Illegals Directorate, motioned for Yevgeni to get into the black ZIS 110 limousine. The ZIS was developed by the Soviets by reverse engineering an American 1942 Packard Super Eight, which had been given to Josef Stalin as a gift by US president Franklin D. Roosevelt in 1945. Stalin had presented a number of ZIS limousines to various Communist leaders as gifts, including Mao Zedong, Kim Il Sung, and Enver Hoxha.[1]

Korznikov was responsible for KGB Illegals operations worldwide. The two men sat in silence as the limousine left the tarmac of Moscow's Sheremetyevo Airport and headed into the center of the city. Yevgeni did not know and didn't even want to think of where they might be headed. There was little conversation in the car between them. Breaking the silence, Korznikov inquired into Yevgeni's health and asked him if anything in particular happened in Canada. Yevgeni responded quietly, saying that he was fine. As calmly as he could under the circumstances, he stated that nothing special or out of the ordinary had occurred. Their vehicle continued through Moscow's broad streets as the two men sat in awkward silence. Almost as an afterthought, Korznikov mentioned that the chief wanted to see him right away because there was something he wanted to get straight.

The chief was General Aleksandr Semyonovich Panyushkin, the overall head of the First Chief Directorate (Foreign Intelligence) of the KGB. As such, he held a very senior executive position and was responsible for all foreign intelligence operations worldwide.

As the limousine approached Dzerzhinsky Square, Yevgeni began to feel increasingly more uncomfortable. Throughout his intelligence training four years previously, Yevgeni, like all other KGB Illegals in training, had never been permitted to enter any identified KGB building. Now here he was, an operational Illegal, sitting in an official KGB limousine pulling into an inner courtyard at Lubyanka, the dreaded main headquarters of the KGB in Moscow. Every Muscovite knew the terrifying history and reputation that this building harbored. And Yevgeni knew that this meeting with Panyushkin could, and probably would, end very badly for him.

By the time that Yevgeni and Korznikov had shown their identification and cleared the various guard posts inside Lubyanka, Yevgeni's discomfort level had escalated to an emotion of abject fear. Korznikov led Yevgeni into Panyushkin's spacious office on the third floor of the infamous and feared old building. The statue of Felix Dzerzhinsky, the "father" of the Soviet secret police, the Cheka, stood tall below his windows.

Panyushkin sat in a heavily padded chair behind a large wooden desk. Yevgeni felt vulnerable as images of Soviet premier Nikita Khrushchev and Ivan Aleksandrovich Serov, chairman of the Committee for State Security, stared down at him. Prior to becoming chief of the First Chief Directorate, Panyushkin had been the Soviet ambassador respectively to the United States and China. While in Washington, he also occupied the position of KGB Resident.

Korznikov made no effort to introduce Panyushkin to Yevgeni. General Panyushkin spoke first and calmly asked Yevgeni how things had gone in Canada and if he noticed anything untoward that might have caused him to suspect that things were not good. It was the second time he had been asked this question since his arrival in Moscow a short time earlier. He told General Panyushkin that everything was normal and that from his perspective, there were no signs of trouble that he detected.

Panyushkin then surprised him by asking why the photographs of the CF-105 Avro Arrow were out of focus. He told Yevgeni that the photographs could not be seen clearly.[2]

Working under Charles Sweeny's direction and control, Yevgeni had purposefully photographed the CF-105 advanced fighter aircraft designs out of focus before he placed the films in a drop box for his KGB Illegal Support Officer to retrieve. As calmly as possible, Yevgeni responded to Panyushkin that he was not aware that the photographs were out of focus. Panyushkin paused momentarily and asked if everything in Canada was okay. Was his operation secure? Yevgeni indicated that all was good. He had no problems.

Panyushkin remained silent for a moment and then stared intently at Yevgeni, who was sitting directly in front of him. The next words out of his mouth shook Yevgeni to the core. He coldly asked Yevgeni to explain to him the circumstances of how it was he had become a traitor to his country and when it was that he started to betray the interests of the KGB. Yevgeni struggled to maintain his composure. He denied any knowledge of what Panyushkin had just accused him of and tried to defend himself. But his efforts were in vain.

Panyushkin pushed a button that was installed on his desk. It was a signal for the two uniformed guards who were waiting in the hall outside of Panyushkin's office to enter. Before they did so, Panyushkin warned Yevgeni not to reveal his true name to anybody, even the Lubyanka guards. He told him that until further notice he would be known by the name Eugene Ivanov. With the Igor Gouzenko defection, trials, media attention, and the Royal Commission on Espionage in Ottawa still in their minds, the KGB knew full well that their political masters in the Politburo would be furious about another intelligence failure. Insofar as Yevgeni's case was concerned, the KGB had already begun to restrict knowledge of it and establish early damage control.[3]

The guards escorted Yevgeni down a series of corridors and placed him in a dreary, small, and brightly illuminated prison cell. He realized immediately he was in solitary confinement. He had not seen or heard any other prisoners as he was being led to his cell. Upon entering the cell, he was required to strip completely and was provided with prison clothing. The guards were unaccustomed to seeing good-quality Western-styled clothing on the prisoners being held in Lubyanka.

Yevgeni took stock of his surroundings and felt vulnerable, isolated, and frightened. His imagination was conjuring up endless scenarios as to what his fate might be. He harbored a glimmer of hope that perhaps Panyushkin and the KGB were testing him. No evidence was offered to support Panyushkin's accusation that he had become a traitor. Perhaps they had suspicions but no actual proof. Providing him with another alias seemed to support this theory.

Yevgeni was left alone in the tiny cell for almost three days. His only human contact was with the guards who brought him his meals. But there was no interaction between them. The guards never acknowledged or spoke to Yevgeni.

His isolation changed on the third day when a guard entered his cell, handcuffed his hands behind his back, and led him down the same corridor that he had walked through three days previously. Yevgeni feared that this was a death march. Surely someone will step out from a dark alcove, put a gun to the back of his head, and execute him. He began to perspire heavily, and his heart and respiration began to race.

Moments later, they heard others some distance down the long corridor walking toward them. There was a tall, upright wooden box in the passageway that had a functional, makeshift door. The guard pushed Yevgeni into the wooden box and closed the doorway so the others could not see who he was or what he looked like. Yevgeni was terrified as he stood in the narrow, dark, and dank-smelling box. He imagined that he was in an upright coffin and that this is where he would die. But then he was able to discern the receding footsteps as the others continued on down the corridor. Moments later he was released from the box and taken further down the corridor to a small interrogation room where Nikolai Korznikov was waiting for him.[4]

The room was barren save for two ancient chairs and an old rusted metal table. The walls were cinderblock and unpainted, and there was a dank smell of sweat, nicotine, and urine permeating the air. Yevgeni did not want to think about what fate may have become former prisoners in this room over the years. The chair that Yevgeni was directed to was bolted firmly to the unpainted concrete floor. The three windows in the room were covered with a heavy-gauge metal mesh. And there was an armed guard posted outside the interrogation room door. If Korznikov required anything, there was a button with which he could summon a guard. There was no water, food, or toilet in the room. The thought of escaping never entered Yevgeni's mind.

During his incarceration in the isolation cell, Yevgeni's mind and imagination ran amok. How much did Korznikov and the KGB already know about his cooperation with the Royal Canadian Mounted Police, or that they turned him over to the notional Canadian Security Agency? Did they know anything, or were they simply acting on a tip, an allegation from someone in Canada? Had they discovered something about his secret relationship with Larissa Cunningham and her encouragement to turn himself in to the RCMP? Had Larissa confessed her love affair to her husband, including details of Yevgeni's espionage role in Canada? Was it possible that her husband contacted the Soviet embassy and told them everything? His mind was racing.

Yevgeni knew and was obsessed with the knowledge that the KGB was known to hunt down and assassinate defectors and Soviet dissidents living overseas. And he knew how ruthless they could be. Sitting in his prison cell, he knew he would be interrogated in order to get an admission of guilt from him along with full details of his treachery. When the interrogation was over, he knew that he would be summarily executed with a bullet to the back of the head or perhaps by a firing squad.

Sitting handcuffed and across the table from Korznikov in the interrogation room, Yevgeni hoped he had the courage and fortitude to follow the plan he worked out while alone in his cell. He would make no admissions and reveal as little as possible in the hope of gauging how much Korznikov knew. He believed he would be able to discern this knowledge based upon the questions Korznikov asked him. It was a wholly inadequate plan that contained neither depth nor substance. Nevertheless, this was the approach he decided upon. He knew it would not stand up to any form of interrogation under physical abuse. But he did not think that Korznikov was this type of person. What he feared most was that someone else, someone from the feared Second Chief Directorate responsible for domestic intelligence and crushing internal dissent, would take over the questioning. He had no illusion about what that would mean for him.

As the interrogation began, Yevgeni quickly learned the extent of Korznikov's knowledge about his treachery in Canada. He was shocked and felt doomed.

Yevgeni Brik at his Portraits by Soboloff studio in Verdun, Quebec, 1953.

Brik's birth certificate. He was born in Novorossiysk, USSR, November 25, 1921.

Nikolai Alekseyevich Korznikov, KGB First Chief Directorate, Directorate S, Illegals Department. Photo courtesy of CSIS.

Leonid Dmitrievich Abramov was Brik's initial KGB trainer and first Illegal Support Officer in Ottawa. Photo courtesy of CSIS.

Brik's home and photo studio at 5381 Bannantyne Avenue, Verdun, Quebec.

KGB officer Vladimir Pavlovich Bourdine, Canadian prime minister Louis St. Laurent, and Soviet military attaché P. Komin at Soviet embassy reception. Material republished with the express permission of Ottawa Citizen, a division of Postmedia Network Inc.

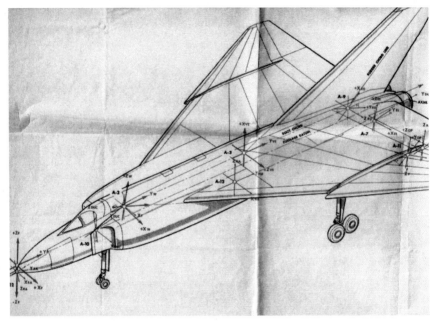

One of Brik's agents provided classified reports on the CF-105 Avro Arrow.

KGB officer Nikolai Pavlovich Ostrovskiy was Brik's third Illegal Support Officer. He also ran RCMP corporal James Douglas Finley Morrison. Photo courtesy of CSIS.

James Morrison was a member of #1 Canadian Provost Corps (RCMP), for which he served with distinction during World War II. The Brechin Group Inc.

James Morrison and his son at RCMP Detachment, Moosomin, Saskatchewan. Photo courtesy of the late Ryan Vidian-Jones.

Gwynneth Morrison (nee Vidian-Jones) met Morrison in the UK at her parents' home during World War II. Photo courtesy of the late Ryan Vidian-Jones.

James Morrison approached KGB officer Ostrovskiy at the Grand Hotel, Ottawa. City of Ottawa Archives. MG011-CA023160.

Brik was taken to the Albion Hotel, Ottawa, when he defected to the RCMP in 1953. City of Ottawa Archives. MGO11-CA025236-Ron Rosidi.

Inspector Terry Guernsey was the head of the RCMP SS Counter Intelligence Branch. Photo courtesy of RCMP Historical Branch.

RCMP corporal Charles Sweeny was responsible for Operation KEYSTONE and was Brik's handler. Photo courtesy of RCMP Historical Branch.

Brik was initially debriefed at the Maple Leaf Tourist Hotel on Highway 16, south of Ottawa.

RCMP Superintendent J. R. Lemieux was the head of the Security Service in 1955. Photo courtesy of RCMP Historical Branch.

The author standing in front of Lubyanka in 2008, former KGB HQ in Moscow.

Daphne Margaret Sybil Desirée Park, Baroness of Monmouth. © Rob Judges. Telegraph Media Group Limited, 2003.

Soviet Embassy fire aftermath, January 2, 1956. City of Ottawa Archives. MG393-CA025226-Newton.

James Morrison met KGB officers Ostrovskiy, Krasilnikov, and Aksenov at the Orléans Hotel east of Ottawa. Photo courtesy of Colette Coté and Louis V. Patry, SFOPHO.

Morrison in disguise for CBC TV's Fifth Estate, November 9, 1982. CBC Licensing.

James Morrison in Ottawa during his trial for espionage. The Canadian Press. Chris Schwartz.

Brik served eight years in notorious Vladimir Central Prison, Vladimir, Russia. Photo courtesy of Marvin W. Makinen.

Francis Gary Powers Jr. visited the cell at Vladimir Central Prison where his father, a CIA U-2 pilot, was held prisoner. From the private collection of Francis Gary Powers Jr.

СССР
МИНИСТЕРСТВО
ВНУТРЕННИХ ДЕЛ
Мордовской АССР СПРАВКА № 057181
Учреждение
ЖХ-385/3
19 августа 70.
СЕРИЯ АС
Выдан гражданину-ке Брик
Евгению Владимировичу
год рождения 1921 национальность русский
уроженцу-ке г. Новороссийск.

осужденному-ой Военной Коллегией Верховного
суда СССР
4 сентября 1956 г. по ст.ст. 58-1г рсфср
к 15 годам лишения свободы с конф. имущество
имеющему-ей в прошлом судимости не судим.

в том, что он-а отбывал-а наказание в местах заключения
с 19 августа 1955 г. по 19 августа 1970 г.
откуда освобожден-а по Отбытию срока наказ.

Начальник подразделения
подпись
Начальник части
Печать
подпись

Brik spent seven years incarcerated in the Temnikovskiy Labor Camp.

Mrs. Carol Anne Mahar provided logistical support to the exfiltration operation.

Brik in Vilnius, Lithuania, on the eve of his exfiltration. Photo courtesy of Gordon Gramlick.

Brik and CSIS officer Gordon Gramlick at the Sheraton Hotel, Stockholm, Sweden, after a successful exfiltration.

Brik and CSIS officer Donald G. Mahar at the Sheraton Hotel, Stockholm, Sweden, ordering a celebration dinner. Photo courtesy of Gordon Gramlick.

Brik on the flight deck of the Canadian Airlines 747 returning to Canada.

This unmarked ossuary of disgraced RCMP officer James Douglas Finley Morrison is his final resting place.

Chapter Twenty

The Treachery Continues

On July 4, 1955, the RCMP Security Service discovered that Corporal James Morrison had misappropriated RCMP funds. He had stolen money that was owed to the local telephone company for service they provided to the force.[1] Morrison used the stolen funds to pay off debts he owed. Constable Burton E. Flumerfelt, a work colleague, informed him that Inspector Terry Guernsey wanted to see him. Morrison felt nauseated and knew precisely what Guernsey wanted to see him about.

That evening Morrison drove over to Terry and Dorothy Guernsey's home at 2264 Prospect Avenue, Ottawa, and had a private conversation with his superior officer. He immediately took responsibility for the missing funds and admitted his guilt. He promised to make full restitution by midday on July 6. Morrison informed Guernsey that he planned to sell his late model 1954 Buick and use the proceeds of the sale to pay back the missing RCMP funds. Morrison did sell the car. But he hadn't bargained on having to give the proceeds of the sale to his mother-in-law, who was the legal owner of the car.

On the morning of July 6, Morrison repaid the money he owed the RCMP with cash he had received from Ostrovskiy a few nights earlier. The irony could not have escaped Morrison that he used KGB funds to repay money owed to the telephone company for service they provided to intercept KGB telephone communications.

Nevertheless, Morrison was still deeply in debt, and to exacerbate matters, he was now without a car. In spite of his pending transfer to Winnipeg, he made up his mind that he would maintain contact with the Soviets. He desperately needed the money that the KGB, through Ostrovskiy, could provide. However, in order to receive more KGB funds, he would have to be able to provide the Soviets with additional intelligence that they deemed valuable. This prospect became more difficult on July 6 when Terry Guernsey removed

Morrison from all access to Security Service files, records, and documentation. He was summarily kicked out of the Security Service, but not the RCMP itself.[2]

Working behind the scenes, RCMP Superintendent Lloyd Bingham, the RCMP Commissioner's Adjutant, sent a confidential memorandum to Assistant Commissioner Samuel Bullard, the Officer Commanding D Division, Winnipeg, Manitoba, officially transferring Morrison. He wrote,

> This non-commissioned officer has been employed in Security Service work at this Headquarters for several years and is being returned to uniform duty for cause. He is to be employed in the Winnipeg area but is not to be used for plain clothes duty. Please advise the point to which this member is being transferred, after which the Officer Commanding "HQ" Division will advise you direct of his time of arrival. For your information, Corporal Morrison has good background of police experience, is considered to be a good investigator and should be suitable for any type of general police duty. You will find particulars of his past service upon receipt of his service file.[3]

In a follow-up memorandum dated July 25, 1955, Assistant Commissioner Bullard concurred with the transfer of Morrison to Winnipeg and ordered that he fill the position being made vacant through the retirement of Corporal Wallace S. (Stu) Lavers.

Morrison's final meeting with Ostrovskiy prior to leaving for Winnipeg was on July 29 in the small village of Templeton on the north shore of the Ottawa River. Situated in the Province of Quebec, Templeton is eleven kilometers northeast of Ottawa and an easy drive. It removed both Ostrovskiy and Morrison from the city and lessened the possibility that they would be seen together.

Ostrovskiy, notebook in hand, questioned Morrison on the size and makeup of the Security Service. In a written confession dated February 4, 1958, and witnessed by RCMP Security Service inspectors Charles Sweeny and Leslie Higgitt, Morrison spoke about the intelligence he furnished Ostrovskiy at their meeting in Templeton twenty-seven months earlier. Morrison's statement says, inter alia, "I gave him the names of the four officers who were in charge of the Security Service. They were Assistant Commissioner Clifford W. Harvison (Head of the Branch), Inspector Guernsey (Head of Counter Espionage), Inspector Charles Sweeny (works with Guernsey in Counter Espionage) and Inspector Norm Jones (Head of Communist Party of Canada investigations)."

Morrison also confessed that he provided Ostrovskiy with identifications of several members of the Watcher Service, including Sergeant Phil Keeler; constables Hank Robichaud, George Campbell, Clement Despins; and Special Constable Harry Hurd. He told Ostrovskiy that there were normally seven or eight members of the Watcher Service depending upon transfers in and out of the unit. Ostrovskiy asked him if he could obtain photographs of the Watcher Service members. He also asked if Morrison could provide him with the work schedule of the team members. And Morrison confessed that he also compromised the descriptions of the covert cars they used on surveillance duty.

In his long, written confession, Morrison stated that he identified the techniques that the Watcher Service employed while keeping targets under surveillance. Ostrovskiy asked him about details of the classified Watcher Service radio frequencies, but Morrison told him that he did not know them and that it would be next to impossible for him to obtain that kind of information. He was also asked about Security Service technical operations against the Soviets. And Ostrovskiy inquired about Security Service telephones and telegraph machines, but Morrison told him that this was not in his area of responsibility and that he could not help him.

On a subsequent occasion, Morrison stated that he also provided character profiles on RCMP commissioner Leonard H. Nicholson, Deputy Commissioner Jimmy Lemieux, Superintendent Ken Hall, Inspector Terry Guernsey, and noncommissioned officers Hank Tadeson and Murray Sexsmith, all of whom later became senior officers of the RCMP Security Service.[4]

During his 1971 interrogation by Warren and Claxton, Morrison stated that he answered all of Ostrovskiy's questions "to the best of my ability." But he was adamant that Ostrovskiy never pushed him for detailed biographies on the rank and file of the Security Service members. He commiserated that he certainly had this detailed information that he would have shared, if asked, but Ostrovskiy never pressed him for it. Morrison suggested to Warren and Claxton that perhaps the Soviets did not require this level of detail because they were already in possession of it. The implication was that perhaps there was some other inside source who had provided these biographies.

Near the end of their meeting in Templeton, Quebec, on July 29, 1955, Ostrovskiy instructed Morrison to write him a personal letter whenever he wished to signal meetings in the future. He instructed Morrison to send letters to his home at 247 Goulburn Avenue, Ottawa. He was cautioned to write only about normal, everyday things and to indicate in the letter a rendezvous date three days ahead of the actual date that they should meet. And finally, he informed Morrison to sign his letters using the name "Pete."

Before their meeting ended, Morrison advised Ostrovskiy that he had been transferred to Winnipeg and that he would be leaving for Manitoba the following day. He did not tell Ostrovskiy that his access to classified information had been removed or that he had been kicked out of the Security Service. In spite of his imminent move to western Canada, Ostrovskiy and Morrison discussed future meetings in Ottawa. The following day, July 30, 1955, Morrison departed for his new posting at RCMP Winnipeg Town Station.

Chapter Twenty-One

Peeling Back the Onion of Deceit

Yevgeni Brik sat manacled to the interrogation table across from Nikolai Korznikov. A consummate professional, Korznikov was organized, always well prepared for the task at hand, and prone to thinking before he spoke. He was respected by his peers in Directorate S, and was known to be a man of conviction and principles. He was not the type of person who would pound the table and scream at his subordinates or those in perilous positions such as Yevgeni. There were of course others within the Directorate who were jealous of his successes and those who considered him soft when it came to corporal punishment of those held in custody. But nobody questioned his experience or superior knowledge with respect to Soviet Illegals operations around the world.

In his book, *Inside the KGB, My Life in Soviet Espionage*, the late KGB defector Vladimir Kuzichkin described his first meeting inside Lubyanka when he was being assessed for possible deployment in the KGB. He did not know it at the time, but he was about to be interviewed by Korznikov and two others for a position as an Illegals Support Officer in the First Chief Directorate (Foreign Intelligence), Directorate S, the Illegals Department. The distinction was that, if successful at this interview, he would work under suitable cover at a Soviet Embassy or Trade Office in a foreign country. He would be responsible for servicing the needs of the Illegals Department at The Centre and the needs of those Soviet Illegals in the country he was serving in. In Kuzichkin's case, it was in Iran.

That meeting was held in the office of Nikolai Korznikov, which was located on the sixth floor of Lubyanka. Kuzichkin described Korznikov as being approximately sixty years of age, with a noble face and intelligent eyes. It was evident that he was in control of the meeting.[1]

In spite of his initial, ill-conceived plan to admit nothing during his inter-rogation, Yevgeni began to respond to Korznikov's questions by admitting to minor transgressions. Over the days that followed, he quickly realized that it was pointless to deny everything. Korznikov was armed with knowledge that had to come from an insider. Who that person was haunted Yevgeni when he was alone in his cell between interrogation sessions.

Each interrogation was conducted in the same room by Korznikov with-out any other KGB official present. Knowing the history of the KGB and the sordid past of Lubyanka, one would have thought that Yevgeni's inter-rogation would be marked with violence and inhumane treatment because of the treachery he committed against the USSR in general and the KGB in particular. However, this was not the case. Korznikov was never aggressive. He never treated Yevgeni in a harsh or violent manner. He never needed to. His level of preparation and knowledge convinced Yevgeni that Korznikov already knew the answers to the questions he was asking.[2]

But Yevgeni did hold back information that he believed would place him in even greater peril with the KGB than he was already in. One of his most significant concerns related to a meeting he had at the Queen Elizabeth Hotel in Montreal on May 20, 1955.[3] That meeting was set up by Charles Sweeny. The objective was to fully discuss all aspects of Yevgeni's scheduled return to Moscow for what they believed was for administrative leave, additional espionage training, and for family reunification. At that point, there was no indication that Yevgeni was in immediate danger. RCMP corporal James Morrison had not yet met with Nikolai Ostrovskiy or betrayed Yevgeni to the Soviets. Yevgeni's recall to Moscow had been discussed with him prior to his initial dispatch to Canada in November 1951. The recall was in fact a normal operational procedure afforded to Soviet Illegals who had been operating for long periods of time overseas. Yevgeni fully expected to return to Canada at the expiration of his leave period.

In consideration of his return to Moscow, Terry Guernsey and Charles Sweeny knew they had to plan for all contingencies. It was not uncommon for The Centre to change its mind and keep their agents in Moscow for longer periods of time than initially planned. Nor was it uncommon for them to can-cel their return altogether. Under these circumstances, Guernsey and Sweeny knew they had to have options.

One such option was to inform Yevgeni that he did not have to return to Moscow at all. If he chose to, he could defect and remain in Canada. The RCMP Security Service would provide the appropriate level of protection and financial support for him if this was his choice.

Guernsey and Sweeny both knew that they could not provide any level of support for Yevgeni if he chose to return to Moscow, and, for whatever reason, was unable to leave the country again. In order to communicate with him, they would have to deploy intelligence tradecraft. They would have to make use of dead drops and brush contacts, where Yevgeni would be exposed to someone for merely a matter of seconds, in order to pass something to or from him. Guernsey and Sweeny knew they would require help from Canada's allies. Yevgeni was a functioning double agent and an important penetration of the KGB in both Canada and Moscow. Guernsey had worked in London with the British intelligence services. He had confidence and trust in them and knew they had the experience to help. Terry Guernsey had initially informed the British Secret Intelligence Service (SIS) about the double-agent operation against the KGB on December 8, 1953, thirteen days following Yevgeni's initial contact with the RCMP Security Service on November 25, 1953. Guernsey decided he would turn to the SIS and seek their assistance in maintaining contact with Yevgeni in Moscow.[4]

British SIS officer, the late Mr. Leslie Mitchell, flew to Ottawa from Washington, DC, where he was a member of the British Embassy diplomatic staff.[5] Although posted to the United States, he was also accredited to Canada where he functioned as a liaison officer with the RCMP Security Service in Ottawa. Guernsey, Sweeny, and Mitchell established an operational plan that would be presented to Yevgeni at an upcoming meeting at the Queen Elizabeth Hotel in Montreal.

Sitting at the interrogation table in Lubyanka, Yevgeni hoped that Korznikov had no knowledge of that meeting or the nature and extent of the operational plan that had been presented to him.

At the Montreal meeting on May 20, Sweeny, who Yevgeni knew as Eugene Walker, discussed the various options open to him. He could return to Moscow as directed by The Centre, travel to Europe on his way back to Moscow, and, if he changed his mind, he could return to Canada, or he could simply remain in Canada and defect. There was no doubt in Yevgeni's mind that he intended to go back to Moscow, visit his wife and parents, undergo the additional espionage training, and return to Canada in several weeks' time.

With the decision made, Sweeny provided Yevgeni with instructions and guidance on how he should handle any problems or concerns he might encounter during his return. To begin with, he identified an Ottawa mailing address that Yevgeni had to commit to memory. He was told that it was an accommodation address where he could write to Sweeny to advise him of his travel and safety status. The address was the home of the same Ottawa dentist who Yevgeni used to call in cases of emergency or if he needed to set up a meeting with Sweeny. He was instructed to write a postcard to this address and, using agreed-upon innocuous language, to provide situation reports and details of his voyage back to Moscow.

At this same time, Sweeny introduced SIS officer Leslie Mitchell to Yevgeni under the alias of Leslie Laird. Mitchell instructed Yevgeni on operational security in Moscow and made him memorize the location of four "iron meet" sites in Moscow. These were specific locations where Yevgeni could be seen in Moscow on a predetermined date and time. No contact whatsoever was to be made with him. Nor would Yevgeni know the identity of the SIS person or persons who would be monitoring that specific location on the appointed date and time. An iron meet site is designed specifically to show that the subject is alive and well. Along with the location of the iron meet sites, Yevgeni was instructed by Mitchell on specific signals he was to use when out walking on the appointed day; signals such as carrying a parcel with a specific colored ribbon, having a newspaper in the pocket of his suit jacket, or wiping his hand through his hair as he walked by the site all had specific meanings. It could mean he was in distress, that he was under suspicion by the KGB, or that he was out on the street and under the control of the Soviets. However, a certain signal could also indicate to the SIS that he was not under suspicion and that he was in good health.

Sitting in the interrogation cell with Korznikov, Yevgeni did not wish to reveal any of this sensitive intelligence information. And he most certainly did not want to tell Korznikov that Mitchell had identified an SIS dead drop location in Moscow for his use. During the Montreal meeting, Mitchell had told him that someone from the SIS station in Moscow would place a loaded revolver and silencer, a suicide capsule, an escape plan and map, and a sophisticated British transmitter that Yevgeni could use during any attempt he might make to escape. The escape plan was mapped out for him and contained mileage distances, the location of railroad lines, instructions on how to purify water, and the identification of edible plants and berries. The map directed him to a specific area on the Soviet border with Norway. This area was sparsely populated and, due to its isolation, not patroled by the Soviets. It was a place where Yevgeni would be able to cross the shallow river safely into Norway. If successful, he would be safely out of the Soviet Union.

Korznikov's interrogation over the next several weeks was methodical. He covered Yevgeni's entire time in Canada, the trips he made to the United States, and the names and identities of the people he met. He never revealed how the KGB had learned of Yevgeni's treachery. For his part, Yevgeni watched Korznikov for any clue that he might drop as to the identity of the KGB source. But this, of course, never happened. Night after night as Yevgeni sat in solitary confinement, the identity of the KGB's source haunted him.

In the end, Yevgeni was no match for Korznikov's experience, knowledge, and superior interrogation skills. Yevgeni knew his only hope was to try to provide selective, partial truths. He also knew that he must not volunteer any information about issues not directly asked of him. Yevgeni calculated that, in order to give the appearance that he was fully cooperating, he had to reveal details of his cooperation with Eugene Walker (Charles Sweeny) and Mr. Henderson (Terry Guernsey). In doing so, he held back as much as he felt he could get away with. He informed Korznikov about the existence of the CSA, and that the CSA had assumed full responsibility for national security investigations from the RCMP Security Service following the defection of Igor Gouzenko. Going on the offensive briefly, Yevgeni angrily questioned Korznikov about why his KGB trainers had not known about this new Canadian counterespionage organization. Why, he asked, were they not better informed? Of course, Korznikov knew the difference. He was fully aware that Yevgeni had been fooled by the RCMP Security Service into believing that there was an entity in Canada called the CSA. Korznikov knew this because he was fully cognizant of the recruitment of RCMP Security Service corporal James Morrison, who had volunteered his services to Nikolai Ostrovskiy in exchange for money. Korznikov did not react to Yevgeni's outburst. Rather, he allowed him to prattle on and get things off his chest. In doing so, he judged that Yevgeni would reveal more than he intended. At the same time, Korznikov used the intelligence from Ostrovskiy's operational reports to The Centre to gage the honesty of Yevgeni's responses during the interrogation.

Yevgeni wasn't certain how long he could play this dangerous game of cat and mouse with Korznikov by admitting to some activities while, simultaneously, withholding other sensitive matters. He knew it was dangerous because he judged correctly that there were others within the KGB's Directorate S, Illegals Department who wished to see him executed. Had they known about his British connection, he believed his execution would be swift and that his wife and parents would never know what happened to him. What was most troubling to him was that he did not know how much actual knowledge Korznikov and the KGB already were aware of.

Chapter Twenty-Two

Back in the Game

One of the consequences of James Morrison's transfer to Winnipeg, Manitoba, was that he returned to general police duties and the wearing of an RCMP uniform. More troubling to him, he was no longer in the Security Service and, therefore, did not have direct access to current classified information that he could exploit and sell to the Soviets. However, he was resourceful, and that was not about to stop him. He needed KGB funds now more than ever to help him get out of serious, spiraling, personal debt. In spite of his loss of access to classified intelligence, he was confident that he could still provide information to the KGB and that they would be prepared to compensate him well for it. He had amassed a great deal of information during the previous five years while working in the Watcher Service. He had not shared most of this intelligence with Ostrovskiy. And he was certain that if he acted judiciously, he would be able to obtain useful intelligence from his unsuspecting friends in the Security Service in Ottawa, through supposedly innocuous conversations with them. But that of course meant he would have to return there.

A few weeks after he arrived in Manitoba, Morrison received a personal letter from a Mr. J. Peterson of Ottawa, which had been mailed to RCMP D Division Headquarters in Winnipeg. The writer asked Morrison to meet with him the next time he would be in Ottawa. Although Morrison already had the means to reach the writer, the note also contained a backup telephone number that could be used if necessary. Morrison knew, in fact, that the letter writer was KGB officer Nikolai Ostrovskiy using a pseudonym. After noting the alternative telephone number, he destroyed the letter.[1]

Several weeks later, an opportunity arose for Morrison to return to Eastern Canada. The RCMP in Winnipeg needed one of their officers to perform prisoner escort duties. It was necessary for someone to fly to Ottawa in order to take custody of a prisoner in Hull, Quebec, and return him to Winnipeg. This type of duty is not uncommon for RCMP officers, particularly if the fugitive in question is wanted on a Canada wide warrant. This situation was perfect for Morrison's needs. It is unknown whether Morrison volunteered for this escort duty or whether his staff sergeant, knowing he had family living in Montreal, offered it to him.

On October 28, 1955, Morrison arrived at Ottawa's Uplands Airport at 10:25 p.m. He rented a car and drove downtown to Union Station, which was situated directly across the street from the magnificent Château Laurier Hotel. Morrison entered the concourse of Union Station and walked to the station master's office, where he wrote a hasty note to Nikolai Ostrovskiy and mailed it to his home address at 247 Goulburn Street, Ottawa. The note informed Ostrovskiy that he had arrived in Ottawa and that he would be meeting some friends the next few days. It also confirmed to Ostrovskiy that he would meet him, as scheduled, at 7:30 p.m. on October 30 at the Orleans Hotel. As instructed previously, Morrison signed the note with the false Christian name of "Pete."

With those details completed, Morrison walked to a public telephone booth inside Union Station and made calls to two of his former Security Service friends and made arrangements to see them. One of those calls was to Shirley Droughan, a friendly and popular secretary who worked for the Security Service at RCMP Headquarters. The other was to his close friend, Leslie James (Jim) Bennett, the civilian employee of the Security Service who, later, would erroneously be suspected of being a Soviet KGB mole. Bennett worked in B Operations, the RCMP Security Service Counter Espionage Branch, and rose to the position of head of the Russian Desk. Following years of suspicion, investigation, and interrogations, Bennett, who had left the service a broken man in 1992, was completely exonerated. He subsequently received an official apology from the Hon. Doug Lewis, Solicitor General of Canada, in 1993 from the floor of the House of Commons in Canada's Parliament. He stated, "I want to assure Mr. Bennett and the House, that the Government of Canada believes that Mr. Bennett was never a KGB mole."[2]

Jim Bennett received approximately $150,000 in compensation from the government of Canada. But no amount of financial consideration would ever compensate the man for the trauma and suspicion he endured for decades, the loss of his wife and family life, the destruction of his career, nor the severe damage that had been caused to his reputation. Jim Bennett's complete and unconditional exoneration came twenty-one years after he had been dismissed from the RCMP.

After Morrison completed his telephone calls, he drove his car across Elgin Street and entered the regal Lord Elgin Hotel. He did not wish to needlessly publicize his presence in Ottawa, which was somewhat odd considering he was sent to the city on RCMP business. Nevertheless, when he arrived at the front desk reception area, Morrison registered under the false name of Mr. J. Harvey of Calgary, Alberta. After he deposited his suitcase in his room, Morrison left the Lord Elgin Hotel and drove to the home of Jim Bennett, where he spent several hours socializing.[3]

The following day, Morrison met with a Mr. Burden, one of his long-suffering creditors, and promised he would settle what seemed to be a never-ending outstanding debt. Later that evening, Morrison picked up Shirley Droughan, and they drove to the Bennetts' home. Shortly thereafter, they all attended a house party on Frank Street where a number of Security Service personnel were enjoying an evening of drinks and cigars. In the very late hours after the party, Morrison, Droughan, and the Bennetts drove to Montreal where they socialized with Morrison's father and mother for several more hours. The party left Montreal mid-morning on Sunday and returned to Ottawa. Later that evening, Morrison and Shirley Droughan were back at the Bennetts' home for dinner. They were a very social group.

After dinner that evening, Morrison excused himself and drove to the Hull jail where he picked up the prisoner that he had been sent to Ottawa to get. The prisoner was transported to the RCMP A Division Guard Room in Ottawa where he would be held until his flight to Winnipeg the following morning.[4] With these official duties completed, Morrison drove the rental car to the small village of Orleans, a few miles east of Ottawa, where he met Nikolai Ostrovskiy, who was waiting on the darkened street outside the Orleans Hotel. Ostrovskiy got in Morrison's car, and they drove across the main highway and stopped at a dead-end road near the Ottawa River. The isolated spot they found in the darkness suited them well. They would be able to see an approaching car for a considerable distance even though it was doubtful that anyone else would venture to this area at this time of night.

Ostrovskiy asked some perfunctory questions about Morrison's health and his family and then asked how long he was expected to remain in Winnipeg. Morrison informed him that it would be for some length of time. Ostrovskiy questioned whether Morrison had any new intelligence for him but was told that he did not. He told Ostrovskiy that he did not have an opportunity to discreetly ask anyone for information that he knew the KGB would be interested in.

Ostrovskiy then asked Morrison if he had heard anything new about "the man in Montreal." Morrison knew that he was talking about Yevgeni Brik. He responded by saying he had no new information. However, he posed a question of his own. Morrison asked whether the man had arrived safely back in Russia and if he would be returning to Canada. Significantly, and most surprisingly, Ostrovskiy confirmed that he had arrived back in Moscow but that he would not be returning.[5]

Ostrovskiy probed Morrison about Yevgeni's personal property at his apartment and photography studio in Verdun, and wanted to know what the RCMP was going to do with it. He pressed Morrison to find out about this and told him it was important that he obtain an answer to this question and pass it to him.

Ostrovskiy went on to question Morrison once again about RCMP Security Service surveillance radio frequencies and radio codes and informed him that it would be worth a great deal of money if he could obtain that information. And he asked Morrison if the Security Service had been able to penetrate the Soviet's telegram codes. Morrison told him that he had no knowledge of anything concerning such matters. And finally, Ostrovskiy asked Morrison if he had any knowledge, or if he could get information, about RCMP Security Service agents who may have been sent to Moscow as teachers, trade representatives, or in some other capacity.

In an effort to make communicating with the KGB more secure and out of the watchful eyes of the RCMP, Ostrovskiy provided details of a LLB that the KGB had arranged for Morrison's purpose. He was instructed to post a letter to Herrn Gustav Kush, FregerStrasse, 5 Leipzig, Germany,[6] and provide details of future trips he would be taking to Ottawa from Winnipeg. This would allow the KGB to prepare properly for each future meeting. Prior to this, Morrison had been mailing letters to Ostrovskiy's Goulburn Street, Ottawa, home.

Ostrovskiy also introduced the possibility of there being future clandestine meetings in Winnipeg. It was agreed that Ostrovskiy would write to Morrison to make arrangements for a Winnipeg meeting if it was deemed necessary. Morrison told him that the best place in Winnipeg for them to meet would be between the Parliament Building and the Assiniboine River. This area was wide open and would provide them with a good vantage point to watch if anyone was approaching.

Ostrovskiy also suggested that Morrison explore the possibility of travel to Mexico City where he could meet one of Ostrovskiy's superiors. The Soviets clearly wanted to get Morrison out of the country and away from the watchful eyes of the RCMP Security Service. The Soviets wanted to control the environment around their clandestine meetings with Morrison. They knew they could do this better in a neutral country. Morrison was given an envelope containing $1,500 in small denomination bills for information he previously provided. Once again, he signed a receipt in a false name. However, Morrison told Ostrovskiy that he could not travel to Mexico. Ostrovskiy also suggested that they could meet in Paris. With nothing settled, they parted company.

Morrison returned to Union Station in downtown Ottawa where he purchased one money order in the amount of $500. One of his long outstanding debts was about to be paid.

The following morning, Morrison flew back to Winnipeg with the prisoner he had been sent to retrieve. It was the first of many trips back to Ottawa to meet with the KGB. All of them were unknown to, and unauthorized by, his superior officers at the RCMP in Winnipeg.

Chapter Twenty-Three

All Appears Lost

In December 1953, during his incarceration and interrogation inside Luby-anka, Yevgeni was directed by Korznikov to write a letter to Mr. George Ta-ruska, who lived at 5385 Bannantyne Avenue, Verdun, Quebec. This was the same apartment building where Yevgeni lived and where his photographic studio, Portraits by Soboloff, was co-located. Taruska, an honorable man who had no knowledge whatsoever of Yevgeni's true identity or the fact he was a Soviet KGB Illegal, was Yevgeni's landlord. He resided on the apartment building's top floor, two levels directly above Yevgeni.

Korznikov instructed Yevgeni on what to include in the letter. However, he wanted the letter written in Yevgeni's own words. Korznikov wanted to allay any fears that Taruska may have harbored about Yevgeni's long absence from the building as well as any anxiety he may have regarding rent payments that were past due. One of the KGB's objectives was to eventually remove and take possession of Yevgeni's photographic equipment. They wanted to ensure there was no incriminating information or photographs in the cam-eras connecting him with any of the KGB assignments that had been given to him. They also wanted to get his one-time pads and shortwave broadcast schedules that they knew Yevgeni had hidden inside his apartment. The KGB also wanted to get their hands on the SX-71 Hallicrafters shortwave radio that Yevgeni had purchased in Chicago. It was the radio that Yevgeni used to re-ceive the encrypted Russian Morse code messages that had been transmitted to him from The Centre in Moscow.

In his letter, dated December 11, Yevgeni falsely informed George Taruska that he was presently in Paris and that five weeks earlier, he had fallen in love with a beautiful woman named Jane. He told Taruska that he and Jane got married on November 20. He continued by stating they were on their honey-moon and staying with some of Jane's Parisian relatives. He further explained that they expected to remain in Paris until February 1956, at which time they would move permanently to California.

Yevgeni mentioned that Jane's father had a large photographic studio in Southern California and that Yevgeni would be working with him. Yevgeni asked Taruska to forward any letters received at his Bannantyne Avenue address in Verdun to the address of Jane's relatives at 30 bis rue de Tilsitt, Paris. This was in fact the address of ADA, the KGB LLB who technically came under Yevgeni's sphere of responsibility.

Yevgeni also expressed concerns to Taruska about the rent money for his apartment. He mentioned that a friend of his owed him $280 and that this friend promised to send this money to Taruska. He asked Taruska to acknowledge receipt of this money by sending a note to the Paris address he provided. He reminded Taruska that there was also an $80 deposit that he had paid at the time of the initial rental. Yevgeni asked him to apply that money to the January 1956 rent.

Lastly, Yevgeni instructed Taruska to remove everything from his closets and added the notation that he would personally return to Verdun and pick up his personal items or he would have someone pick everything up for him. In a final gesture, Yevgeni wished Taruska and his family a very Merry Christmas and a Happy New Year.

Nikolai Korznikov then focused his attention on other matters. Under intense interrogation, Yevgeni had compromised the details of the May 20 Montreal meeting with Sweeny and Mitchell at the Queen Elizabeth Hotel. Korznikov and the KGB officers in Directorate S wanted to get their hands on the British SIS communications system that Yevgeni had been told would be placed in a Moscow dead drop for him. During his interrogation, Yevgeni provided Korznikov with the precise locations, dates, and times where the British would be watching for him in the city. By placing these locations under surveillance the KGB hoped to learn who it was within the British SIS station that was responsible for monitoring Yevgeni in Moscow. They also hoped the British officer would lead them to the dead drop where the communications equipment was stashed. They launched a plan that was designed to lure the British into believing that Yevgeni was safe and at liberty to walk the streets of Moscow.

Putting their plan into action, the KGB released Yevgeni from Lubyanka on December 30, 1955, and allowed him to return to his wife, Antonina, and their apartment at 5 Kalisevsaya Street. He had not seen her, or his parents, since 1951. Yevgeni was saddened to see how much his parents had aged and that his father was in failing health.[1]

During the time that he was free, Yevgeni began to scheme about how he could escape the USSR and return to Canada. In spite of the elaborate plans that SIS officer Leslie Mitchell had made Yevgeni memorize during their meeting in Montreal, Yevgeni devised his own strategy. It was dangerous, reckless, and had the potential to end very badly for him. For it to work, he needed the active participation of his wife.

Antonina was a science teacher at a local high school. Yevgeni knew that she had access to materials that could be used to assist him to escape from the USSR. Antonia was very reluctant to become engaged in what she considered was a reckless and dangerous scheme. She feared it could cost him his life and possibly, the lives of others. Yevgeni was persistent. He urged her to help him. Yevgeni asked Antonina to remove a quantity of sulphuric acid and other chemicals from the school's science lab and bring them to their apartment in glass jars. He explained to her that with his knowledge and experience of mixing photographic chemicals he believed he could create a homemade bomb. He tried to convince Antonina that they could escape the USSR together by taking the homemade bomb to the local airport and hijack an aircraft. They would then demand to be taken to Western Europe where they would defect to local authorities.[2]

His plan never had a chance to succeed. It was doomed from the very start. Prior to Yevgeni's release from Lubyanka, Korznikov had gone to Antonina's apartment and compelled her to act as a source of information about Yevgeni and his intentions. He left her no choice and she knew it. Antonina met surreptitiously with Korznikov, away from her apartment, on at least two occasions during the relatively short time that Yevgeni was living back at home. She had no choice but to reveal Yevgeni's activities and details of their conversations. She was fearful of the KGB and knew she could lose her apartment if she did not cooperate with Korznikov. Feeling trapped, she betrayed Yevgeni's ill-conceived plan to try to hijack an aircraft and fly to Europe by using a homemade bomb.[3]

Fearful that Yevgeni might elude the KGB surveillance that monitored his every move while free from Lubyanka, successfully execute his plan, and escape to Western Europe, the KGB recognized they had no choice other than to have him arrested once again. On January 7, 1956, two Ministry of the Interior (MVD) officers arrested Yevgeni at his apartment and returned him to Lubyanka and back into the hands of the KGB. Once again, Yevgeni was placed into solitary confinement. He began to hear whispers from his keepers that his interrogation was going to be turned over to a rather brutish MVD colonel who would not treat him as humanely as Korznikov did. Although the whispers and rumors lingered for several days, the MVD officer never materialized. Yevgeni's interrogation was continued by Korznikov.

Yevgeni knew that all was lost. He knew he would never again have the opportunity to return to his wife and parents.[4] He would never again sleep in the family apartment. It caused him great pain to know that he would never see his sick father again. And of course, he knew he would never return to Canada. He felt despondent, helpless, and defeated. He had no choice now but to accept his fate. Yevgeni had no doubt that he would be executed. He was certain that he would die inside the confines of Lubyanka. He knew the history and horror of Lubyanka and the stories of the countless political prisoners who had been tortured and then executed within these same walls over many years. Resigned to his fate, Yevgeni began to confess many of the things he had previously held back.

Chapter Twenty-Four

Merry-Go-Round of Clandestine Meetings

Several months after his prisoner escort trip to Ottawa at the end of October 1955, James Morrison returned to Ottawa again at the end of March 1956. On this occasion, his youngest son accompanied him. This trip, similar to several others that would follow over the next twenty-two months, was taken without written approval by Morrison's superiors in the force. All members of the RCMP were required to submit an annual leave request if they wished to travel outside of their detachment duty district. Failure to submit and obtain permission for annual leave was considered an offense against the RCMP Act and its regulations, and could result in discipline. The offending officer would be considered absent without leave, or AWOL. Morrison and his son flew over a weekend from Winnipeg to Toronto, changed planes, and continued on to Ottawa where he rented a car.

During an interview on August 6, 2013, James Morrison's youngest son made a startling disclosure. He indicated that he has never shared this information with anyone previously. He confided that when he was a young boy, his father, astonishingly, had taken him to meetings with the Soviets on three separate occasions. He did not meet or have any contact with any of the KGB officers. Rather, his father would leave him alone in the car while he conversed in the Soviet's vehicle. It is highly probable that Morrison brought his youngest son along as cover. He would have known that, if he was under suspicion by the RCMP Security Service and was under surveillance, that the RCMP would surmise he was simply out running errands with his son and not on an intelligence run to meet the KGB. Under the circumstances, Morrison would have known from experience that the Watcher Service would drop him.[1]

Fifty-five years later, the younger Morrison son stated that details of those trips with his father are vague. However, he remembers one meeting under the bridge connecting Ottawa and Hull, Quebec. It may have been the Champlain Bridge, as James Morrison and Nikolai Ostrovskiy are known to have met there. A second meeting was in a wooded area along a dark stretch of Alta Vista Drive. He remembers his father driving down the road, making a U-turn, and pulling up behind the Soviet's car. He remained in the car while his father walked up and got into the vehicle ahead of him. And he remembers a third meeting that took place down by the walking bridge that spans the Rideau River. It is understandable that details of these meetings are somewhat imprecise as he was a young boy of seven or eight years of age at the time.[2]

Back in Manitoba, Morrison's life fell into an abyss of spiraling debt. To exacerbate his financial troubles, he had been demoted from the rank of corporal to that of constable when he was quietly kicked out of the Security Service. He was fortunate that he had not been dismissed from the RCMP altogether. The corresponding loss of salary deepened his problems. He needed the KGB's money now, more than ever. But Morrison no longer possessed the top secret security clearance or direct access to classified documents that was needed in order for him to obtain the kind of intelligence the KGB was seeking. He knew they wanted information about Security Service operations against them in Canada as well as the nature and extent of operations that the KGB believed the Security Service was running against them in Moscow. He knew that Ostrovskiy would pay handsomely for information about the Security Service radio frequencies, especially those of the Watcher Service. Morrison always hoped that he might learn some useful intelligence from his friends in the Security Service that he could sell to Ostrovskiy during those unauthorized trips back to Ottawa.

On June 24, 1956, three months after returning from Ottawa with his son, the Commanding Officer of D Division, Assistant Commissioner Samuel Bullard, made the decision to transfer Morrison and his family to the attractive, rural farming community of Manitou, Manitoba.[3] Situated in the extreme south end of the province, Manitou is twenty miles north of the Canada-US border and approximately one hundred miles southwest of Winnipeg. Manitoba shares its southern border with both North Dakota and Minnesota.

In spite of his demotion in rank, Morrison was given more responsibility at the detachment in Manitou than that which he enjoyed in Winnipeg. It is fair to say that his superiors would have been assessing his abilities while he worked in Winnipeg. Morrison had been away from active police work for almost six years during the time he was in Ottawa. His RCMP personnel file showed that he had previous police experience working in rural detachments in Saskatchewan following the war. Satisfied that he would be able to run an active police detachment, Bullard's transfer elevated him to the position of senior constable at the detachment. In effect, he became the detachment commander. He was in charge of a small number of subordinate officers who were responsible for general-duty police investigations in the town and the surrounding area. The move away from Winnipeg was an unintended gift for Morrison. It provided him with the autonomy he needed while removing him from the direct scrutiny of his senior officers in Winnipeg. Morrison recognized immediately that it was an opportunity to exploit. And he did precisely that.

Morrison flew to Ottawa or Montreal on at least seven occasions between March 28, 1956, and January 27, 1958, under his own name and at least once, and possibly more frequently, using an alias.[4] On each of these occasions he met with Ostrovskiy and received KGB funds to cover his traveling expenses. Ostrovskiy's questions were always the same. He consistently asked Morrison about what was new, when was he planning on traveling to Paris, and when did he contemplate being posted back to Ottawa. Morrison's responses were purposefully vague. He wanted to string out his relationship with the Soviets as long as he could in order to receive additional funds.

Morrison did not have authorized annual leave from his superiors to be absent from his duty district for the majority of these trips. Neither his superior officers in Winnipeg nor the RCMP in Ottawa had any knowledge that he was taking these trips. However, the KGB did.

At the end of September 1956, Morrison wrote a personal letter to Ostrovskiy that he mailed to the LLB in Leipzig, Germany. His correspondence was a signal requesting a personal meeting in Orleans, Ontario, on October 4. In a surprising departure from his previous trips back to Ontario, Morrison borrowed a car from a friend in Manitou, Manitoba, and, together with his wife, Gwynneth, arrived in Ottawa on October 3 in a brand new Studebaker. The Morrisons were houseguests of the Bennetts, where they stayed for five nights. As arranged through the LLB in Leipzig, Morrison and Ostrovskiy met once again at 8:00 p.m. in Orleans and did their usual dance of the same old questions and vague responses. However, on this occasion, Morrison informed Ostrovskiy that he required additional funds. As Ostrovskiy did not have extra funds with him, the two agreed to meet once again, three nights later on October 7, in Somerset Park next to the Soviet Embassy.

On October 6, the night prior to the hastily planned meeting in Somerset Park, Morrison and Bennett visited together over drinks in Bennett's home and engaged in conversation about Security Service issues and problems as well as gossip about the various personnel who worked in the branch. Morrison also complained about the treatment he received from the force, his loss of a security clearance and removal from the Security Service, and he questioned Bennett as to whether it would ever be possible for him to be posted back to Ottawa. He also directly asked Bennett how the man in Montreal was doing, a direct reference to Yevgeni Brik. Morrison knew that Ostrovskiy and the KGB wanted to know what the RCMP intentions were respecting

Yevgeni's photographic equipment and other items in his Verdun apartment and photo studio.

Morrison met Ostrovskiy in Somerset Park as planned. Because of the proximity of the Soviet Embassy, Ostrovskiy walked to their rendezvous. Morrison received another $300. It is inconceivable that he would not have shared details that he learned, from an unsuspecting Jim Bennett, the previous night at his home.

Morrison was concerned that his unauthorized trips to Ottawa, especially those where he used an alias, could place him in jeopardy if they were discovered by Guernsey or Sweeny. He was also aware that these trips could potentially place his friends, Shirley Droughan and Jim Bennett, in very embarrassing and difficult circumstances should it be discovered that they were fully aware of his presence and had in fact socialized with him. Morrison decided that he would hence forth fly from Winnipeg to Montreal, where his parents resided, rather than to Ottawa. He would rent a car and drive to Ottawa for his meetings with Ostrovskiy.

The following morning, Morrison and his wife departed Ottawa and drove the Studebaker to New York City. They booked into the Sheraton Park Hotel and, using KGB funds received from Ostrovskiy, purchased tickets for Game 5 of the World Series between Mickey Mantle and the New York Yankees and Jackie Robinson and the Brooklyn Dodgers. As they joined more than sixty-four thousand fans at Yankee Stadium in the Bronx, they witnessed baseball history being made when Yankee right-hand pitcher, Dan Larsen, pitched the first no-hitter in the history of the World Series. Mickey Mantle drove in a home run in the fourth inning, and the Yankees won the game 2–0. Jim and Gwynneth Morrison spent the next day touring New York City and then drove back to Manitou, Manitoba, via the United States.[5]

Three months later, on January 2, 1957, KGB Illegal Support Officer Nikolai Ostrovskiy's posting to Ottawa ended, and he left Canada permanently.[6] On his watch, he successfully ran a very difficult and conniving RCMP Watcher Service "walk-in" and turned him into an access agent who provided critical intelligence to the KGB in Ottawa and Moscow. Because of this, the KGB was able to lure back one of their highly trained Illegals who had shattered their trust and had become a double agent for the RCMP Security Service. KGB Illegal Support Officer Rem Sergeyevich Krasilnikov replaced Ostrovskiy. His relationship with Morrison was about to begin. It didn't take long for it to become adversarial.

Chapter Twenty-Five

British SIS in Moscow

The KGB in Moscow was intent on getting their hands on the British communications system that SIS officer Leslie Mitchell had told Yevgeni about during their Montreal meeting in the Queen Elizabeth Hotel. Mitchell had advised Yevgeni that once they established he was safe, the communications radio, along with the gun, maps, and other items he would require in an escape attempt, would be placed in a dead drop in Moscow. Mitchell pressed Yevgeni at that meeting to memorize the location of two different dead drops, rendezvous locations, recognition signals, the warning signals he was to use if he was under KGB control, and the radio frequencies of the SIS radio. Yevgeni had told Korznikov the location of the dead drops and the rendezvous sites during his interrogation. However, he did not compromise the radio frequencies.[1]

Korznikov set a plan in action. He drove Yevgeni to the general vicinity of the dead drop, but a safe distance away from it. Surprisingly, a female KGB operative accompanied them. The two got out of the car and walked, as if they were a couple, to the area of the dead drop. Korznikov knew from his interrogation of Yevgeni that the British did not know and had never seen his wife. It was a major blunder on Korznikov's part.[2]

On the street, closely monitoring the pedestrian traffic pass by, was a young British female SIS officer who was in Moscow on her first clandestine overseas posting. Daphne Park, serving in Moscow under diplomatic cover as a Second Secretary, had just recently been briefed on the case and was informed that she would be Yevgeni's controller in Moscow. She had never met Yevgeni and only had a photograph to assist her in identifying him. Likewise, Yevgeni had no idea who the SIS would have on the street watching for him, and subsequently, did not know who he should be looking for as he approached the rendezvous site.[3]

Ms. Park, who would go on to have a stellar career both in government and out, saw Yevgeni approach. But she immediately saw that something was quite wrong. The female accompanying Yevgeni was out of place. He had been specifically instructed to arrive at the rendezvous site alone, completely unaccompanied. Daphne Park also observed that he was flying the wrong recognition signal. In an instant, she made a determination that everything was wrong. Was Yevgeni signaling the SIS that he was under KGB control? She rightfully aborted the meeting. The KGB operation was unsuccessful. But it was a costly one as well for Daphne Park and the SIS station in Moscow. KGB surveillance had covered the rendezvous site and Yevgeni as well, as he and the female KGB operative walked down the street together. The KGB did not get the sophisticated British radio that they so badly wanted. But their surveillance did discover that Daphne Park was a clandestine SIS officer working in the British Embassy. The failure to get the radio was on Korznikov's shoulders. He had made the decision to place the female KGB operative on the street with Yevgeni. In spite of the KGB surveillance team that was in place, was she there as a control figure to keep Yevgeni in line?

In the *Mitrokhin Archive: The KGB in Europe and the West*, Christopher Andrew and Vasili Mitrokhin offer an alternative scenario. They state, "Brik was not allowed to meet any member of the SIS station in the Moscow embassy, probably for fear that he would blurt out what had happened to him, but was instructed to arrange a rendezvous which he did not keep. By keeping the rendezvous site under surveillance, the KGB was able to identify Daphne (later Baroness) Park, the member of the British embassy who turned up there, as an SIS officer."

This analysis, although understandable, is incorrect. Mitrokhin got this wrong. It is known that Yevgeni did in fact attempt, under Korznikov's control, to meet with Daphne Park. He did fly a signal informing the SIS that he was under KGB control, which Park recognized and aborted the meeting.[4]

Back in Lubyanka, Yevgeni began to confess everything. He held nothing back. At the same time, however, while alone in his cell at night and feeling desperate, he began to scheme. He fabricated a story and committed it to memory. When Korznikov continued the interrogation the following day, Yevgeni told him that when he met SIS officer Leslie Mitchell in Montreal, Mitchell had provided him with an alternative plan that could be used in an emergency. He told Korznikov that if the SIS was able to see that he was trying to initiate this plan, they would load the dead drop with the radio communications system. He informed Korznikov that, according to the plan, he was to appear alone on the fifth-floor balcony of a certain government building in downtown Moscow, on certain specified dates, at a specific time. If viewed by the British, it was their signal to load the dead drop.

Yevgeni was counting on the KGB's resolve to obtain the radio and was hopeful that this desire would allow him to briefly walk out onto the balcony. In reality, Yevgeni was so concerned about being shot in the back of the head that he fabricated this scenario in the hope that it would provide him an opportunity to commit suicide by leaping over the balcony to a certain death. Korznikov was not swayed by this fabrication, saw through the ruse, and never gave Yevgeni the opportunity to put his plan into action. He remained in Lubyanka.

Throughout all of this, Yevgeni did not know that the SIS promise to provide him with a British communications system was completely notional. They did not wish to risk compromising him if he fell under KGB suspicion. There never was a radio in a dead drop for him to acquire, nor was there ever a plan to place one there.[5]

On a pleasant, sunny morning in late May 1956, a young man showed up at the 5385 Bannantyne Avenue apartment of George Taruska in Verdun. He informed Taruska that he was a friend of David Soboloff, one of Taruska's tenants. He presented a letter to him and said that Soboloff had sent it to him, along with some other things, and requested that the letter be delivered to Taruska. This, of course, was the letter that Yevgeni wrote during his interrogation at Lubyanka, which was demanded by KGB officer Nikolai Korznikov.

George Taruska was surprised to learn that Soboloff had married and was spending time in Paris with his new wife. He was pleased to see that provisions were made about receiving payment for rent owing to him. Taruska noted that the young man who delivered the letter appeared to be East European. He wondered if he was perhaps an immigrant from Czechoslovakia. The young man further informed Taruska that he hired a local trucking firm to assist him in removing Soboloff's photographic equipment, furniture, and other personal items. Taruska directed the men to Soboloff's apartment two floors below, and opened the door of 5381 Bannantyne for them. He noted that this young East European–looking man inventoried each item as the truckers removed them from Soboloff's apartment. In short order the men were gone. All the photographic equipment, furniture, and personal effects were removed from the moving truck and taken to an empty storage room at the Fraser Nordheimer Building at 359 St. James Street West in Montreal. They were never seen again.

Chapter Twenty-Six

Morrison's World Unravels

With Nikolai Ostrovskiy's departure from Canada and Rem Krasilnikov's arrival at the Soviet Embassy in Ottawa in early January 1957, Morrison's chaotic life became more difficult. He was still drowning in debt and had been engaged in check kiting from at least June 1956, and perhaps earlier. His bank account contained only $10.57.[1]

Kiting is a form of check fraud in which money is drawn from one bank account, which has insufficient funds, and then deposited into a second bank. Money is then drawn from the second bank and deposited back in the first to cover the insufficient funds in that account. The check writer, who has insufficient or no funds, takes advantage of the time it takes for the banks to clear the check. Kiting is an act of fraud and is a criminal offense. Morrison was kiting in several communities in Manitoba, particularly in Manitou, Miami, Carman, Morden, and Somerset. He was also kiting in Ottawa on those occasions when he returned there to meet Ostrovskiy.

Within days of Krasilnikov's arrival in Canada, Morrison flew east on January 15 to discuss the repayment of one of his debts to Mr. Burden, and to meet with Ostrovskiy. Nikolai Ostrovskiy had not told Morrison that his posting was over and that he was returning to Moscow.

Morrison quickly determined that Krasilnikov was a quieter, more reserved individual than Ostrovskiy. At their first meeting together in the small village of Orleans, east of Ottawa, Krasilnikov posed the same form of intelligence questions as did Ostrovskiy. He was particularly interested in pinning down Morrison for a date when he would travel to Paris to meet with the KGB, away from the attention of Canadian authorities. But once again, Morrison stated that he could not travel to Paris at this time. Krasilnikov did not press Morrison for answers. This was an introductory meeting, and Krasilnikov wanted simply to get to know Morrison better, and if possible, get him to commit for Paris.

Five months later, in early May, the Canadian government received a diplomatic note at the Department of External Affairs from the Soviet Embassy in Ottawa. The Soviet Ministry of Foreign Affairs asked for Canadian government approval to include Nikolai Aksenov's name to be added to the list of approved diplomatic couriers who would travel to Canada on official diplomatic business.[2] A diplomatic request of this nature, between counties, was not uncommon and usually was accepted by the host country, so long as there were no adverse traces pertaining to the courier. This was a preferred method for Soviet and East European intelligence services to clandestinely get one of their intelligence officers into the country. In this particular case, there were no identifiable adverse traces on Aksenov, and he was given a visa to travel to Canada.

In mid-May, Morrison received a letter in Manitou, Manitoba, which had been posted in Western Europe. The writer asked him if he was ready to fly to Paris for a meeting. Morrison replied by sending a return note to the Leipzig, Germany, LLB in which he stated that he was still not able to fly to Paris. Within a short period of time he received a second letter, this time from Krasilnikov in Ottawa, establishing a meeting in Orleans on June 22.

Aksenov, in the company of Vitali Berdennikov, another identified Soviet diplomatic courier, arrived in Canada on June 19 from Washington where they had arrived three days earlier. Prior to Washington, the couriers had been in Mexico City from April 29 to June 16, a period of time that is well beyond the norm for a standard diplomatic courier visit. Highly suspicious, it was much more in keeping with a visit by KGB officers who had other more important matters to deal with than delivering diplomatic mail. The Soviet Embassy in Mexico City has had a long history of KGB intelligence activity.[3]

As requested by Krasilnikov, Morrison flew to Montreal, where he borrowed a car from his brother and drove to Orleans where he met Krasilnikov in front of the Orleans Hotel at 10:00 p.m. Nikolai Aksenov had accompanied Krasilnikov to the meeting. Morrison, who had only recently met Krasilnikov, was now meeting with yet another KGB officer who he did not know. It was now evident that Aksenov was not a diplomatic courier. Rather, he was a KGB officer who had been dispatched to Canada with the probable objective of assessing Morrison's ability to continue as a recruited Soviet agent.

Although Morrison did not know who Aksenov was, he sensed that he was an experienced officer and very likely senior to both Ostrovskiy and Krasilnikov. Aksenov was approximately thirty-five years of age, stood six feet tall, and had fair, wavy hair. Morrison had the impression that had he traveled to either Mexico City or Paris, it likely would have been Aksenov that he would have met. This was somewhat confirmed when Aksenov informed him that the KGB wanted Morrison to travel to Mexico City where they would have the opportunity to teach him how to communicate using secret writing inks and paper. Aksenov assured Morrison that his travel expenses would be taken care of.

Aksenov's English was poor and required translation assistance during the meeting from Krasilnikov. It is evident that Aksenov's assessment of Morrison, or at least his ability to continue to furnish sensitive intelligence, was limited at best. Aksenov recognized that Morrison's posting in Manitoba, over thirteen hundred miles from Ottawa, could not benefit the KGB in the manner it did when he was working in the Security Service in Ottawa. Morrison's intelligence about Yevgeni becoming a double agent and information he provided about the makeup of the Security Service along with assessments of some of its officers was well received at The Centre. But they needed him to get back to Ottawa in order to get the kind of intelligence that mattered to the KGB. Insofar as the meeting was concerned, it didn't end well. He did not receive any remuneration, which was always Morrison's main objective.

Morrison returned to Montreal from Winnipeg five weeks later accompanied by his wife, Gwynneth. That evening, leaving Gwynneth in the city, Morrison and his brother took the two-hour drive to Orleans. Once again, his brother waited in the beer parlor of the Orleans Hotel while Morrison met with Krasilnikov. Morrison's inability to provide sensitive intelligence changed the complexion of his relationship with Krasilnikov and the KGB. Krasilnikov became angry and demanded that Morrison begin to cooperate during these meetings. He told Morrison that there would no longer be regular meetings. Morrison was wasting their time, and each meeting placed them in jeopardy of being discovered by the RCMP Watcher Service. He was told that there would only be future meetings when Morrison signaled that he had actionable or important intelligence to impart. On those occasions, Morrison was instructed to write to the Consular Division at the Soviet Embassy and that Krasilnikov would receive his note. With the meeting over, Morrison was shocked and upset that not only did Krasilnikov not pay him he also did not provide his travel expenses for the trip.[4] This of course placed Morrison in deeper financial crisis.

Upon his return to Winnipeg, Morrison wrote a letter to the KGB in Moscow and sent it to the Leipzig LLB. He informed The Centre that he was angry and fed up, and he complained bitterly about Krasilnikov's attitude. Morrison told the KGB that he had made up his mind to terminate his relationship with them. However, several weeks later, he received a letter, postmarked in Western Europe, that assured him that the entire matter had been a misunderstanding. It was a mistake. The Centre urged Morrison to meet with Krasilnikov once again.

Having received the letter of reassurance from the KGB, Morrison reconsidered his earlier decision and decided he would continue to meet with Krasilnikov. He desperately needed KGB funds to help him out of his financial quagmire, which of course, was of his own making.

Morrison and Krasilnikov met once again, this time on October 18 in Buckingham, Quebec. As previously instructed, Morrison sent a letter to the Soviet Embassy in Ottawa seeking a tourist visa to travel to Russia. He used a three-day date substitution, which meant that he would meet Krasilnikov three days after the date that he had identified in the letter for which he needed the visa. In order to detract attention from himself if the letter was ever intercepted by the RCMP Security Service, he signed it using the fictitious name, P. Borofsky. Krasilnikov would know that any letter signed with that name was actually Morrison in Manitoba.[5]

Surprisingly, airline records obtained by the RCMP Security Service show that Morrison flew back to Montreal again from Winnipeg, three days later, on October 21. This was a pattern that had not been seen previously. This situation begs the question: Why had Morrison returned to Eastern Canada seventy-two hours after he had just been there? Were the airline records incorrect? Having just been in Ottawa, was it likely Morrison would have used his personal funds to pay to return to Ottawa again? Did the KGB finance this trip? If so, what motivated them to do so? Had Morrison been tasked by Krasilnikov during their meeting on October 18, to which he was responding during his trip back east on October 21? Was there another explanation for taking two trips so close to one another? It made neither practical nor financial sense to take these two trips separated by only three days. Unless, there was an ulterior motive?

During their interrogation of Morrison fourteen years later, RCMP Security Service sergeants Claxton and Warren attempted to get answers to these questions. Morrison's response was that he could not remember ever taking two back-to-back trips to meet Krasilnikov or anyone else. During the 1971 interrogation, Morrison agreed that he met with the Soviets on every trip he made to Ottawa with one exception, the trip he took with his son. Claxton and Warren questioned Morrison closely but could not get him to recall or reveal anything in relation to these two back-to-back trips. They later reported that they were left with the impression that Morrison was being straightforward and honest. However, the fact that Morrison could not, or would not, remember taking these two trips does not provide convincing evidence to the contrary.

Morrison's final two meetings with Krasilnikov proved to be his undoing. On December 7, the two men met once again at the Alexandra Hotel in Buckingham. Krasilnikov's attitude had changed as he presented himself in a friendlier manner than the last time they had met. He spoke at length on socialism and talked about fraternal international relationships. He asked Morrison if he agreed with socialist principles and was told that there was some appeal for what Krasilnikov was talking about. In spite of the fact that Morrison had been meeting with the Soviets since 1955, Krasilnikov asked Morrison if he was prepared to assist their cause. Morrison indicated that he would do anything that he could to help. When asked if there was anything specific that Krasilnikov wanted Morrison to attend to, he was advised that he needed information on a number of things. They were the same issues that Ostrovskiy had identified.

Krasilnikov stated that he wanted Morrison to obtain information on the RCMP Watcher Service radio frequencies, secret codes of the Security Service, the organization and makeup of the Security Service membership, information about Security Service agents operating inside the Soviet Union, and any information about Security Service operations against Soviets at their embassy in Ottawa or their consulates in Toronto and Montreal. Morrison explained how difficult it would be to obtain that kind of intelligence, but assured him that he would do whatever he could to get the information. Krasilnikov responded by saying that he would send him $1,000 to $3,000 for expenses in an effort to acquire this information.

While attending their previous meeting, Morrison observed what he would later describe as "an unsavoury looking individual, wearing glasses, sitting in a metallic green Ford or Chevrolet in the area of their meeting." He looked out of place, and Morrison made a mental note of this. Once again, at this December 7 meeting, Morrison saw this individual again and pointed the man out to Krasilnikov and asked him directly if he was from the embassy. Morrison did not receive a response from Krasilnikov. For the first time since he began his treasonous activities with the KGB, Morrison began to worry that perhaps he was under surveillance by the RCMP Watcher Service.

Prior to departing, Krasilnikov inquired about the potential for promotional opportunities for Morrison within the police structure and whether it was possible for Morrison to get posted back to Ottawa where it would be easier for the two to meet.

In spite of his concern that the RCMP Security Service was possibly aware of his meetings with Krasilnikov, Morrison agreed to a future meeting that would take place in January or February 1958. After the two departed, Morrison went to the hotel in Buckingham where his brother was waiting for him. As the two brothers drove back to Ottawa, Morrison came to the conclusion that he would preempt any action the RCMP Security Service might take against him by going on the offensive himself. His next action would prove to be the beginning of his undoing.

Chapter Twenty-Seven

Yevgeni Brik's Final Days

Yevgeni had not seen Korznikov for several days. His only interaction with people was when the guards brought him his meals as he sat silently in the solitary confinement cell in Lubyanka. The loneliness and long hours played on his mind, and he imagined all manner of scenarios where he would be summarily executed. The interrogation sessions with Korznikov had slowed recently, and he sensed that his time was close at hand. The guards would not answer his questions, leaving Yevgeni only himself to talk to.

In mid-morning on September 4, 1956, two guards arrived at his cell, opened the door, and told him he was being taken out of Lubyanka.[1] No explanation was given as to where they were headed. But Yevgeni did not need to ask. He knew that his time had come. His primary regret was that he was going to die alone without having the comfort of seeing and holding his mother or wife again. His father had died earlier in the year. He had not been told of his death, nor any details of his funeral.

Yevgeni was marched down the barren corridors within Lubyanka. Nobody spoke. Nobody else besides the guards were seen. With every step, Yevgeni expected he would be summarily executed with a single shot to the back of his head by one of the guards who walked behind. Suddenly, they emerged within an inner courtyard where a vehicle was waiting. There was no sign of Korznikov. Perhaps he awaited their arrival at some other point where the execution would take place.

Within a few short minutes, the KGB vehicle pulled up to another building, one that Yevgeni was unfamiliar with. He was led up a back stairway and suddenly found himself inside what appeared to be a courthouse. As he looked around the courtroom, he was shocked to see his wife and mother sitting in the court. The two women looked frightened as they sat silently on the bench. Nobody was allowed to speak.

From a room off to the side, men emerged in full military dress. Yevgeni was told that he was being placed on trial before a Military Collegium of the Supreme Court of the Union of Soviet Socialist Republics. The chairman of the military tribunal was a full colonel, and three other uniformed officers were also present. One acted as a court recorder while the others represented the State's case against Yevgeni. Noticeably absent was any legal representation for him.

Yevgeni saw, for the first time, that Korznikov was seated at the back of the room. He neither spoke to, nor acknowledged, Yevgeni. On the table in front of the court recorder sat the bottle of chemicals that Yevgeni had planned to use in an ill-conceived plan to hijack an aircraft out of the USSR.

After the opening formalities of the court were dispensed with, the chairman read the Final Accusation, a charge under Article 58 of the Criminal Code of the USSR, which amounted to the offense of treason. The Final Accusation described Yevgeni's activities in Canada, his work as a double agent, and his betrayal of the USSR.

The chairman called Yevgeni's wife, Antonina, to step forward as a witness for the State. In response to his questions, she confirmed that Yevgeni was living with her at their apartment during the first week of January 1956. She confirmed that she obtained and carried home, at Yevgeni's behest, a jar of sulphuric acid, which he planned to use to hijack an aircraft at the airport in Moscow. Following a few other questions, the chairman asked Yevgeni if he had anything he wished to add to the evidence, or if he wished to make a statement. He asked the chairman if he could have a few minutes of privacy with his wife and mother. The chairman responded by asking him if there was anything more substantial that Yevgeni might wish to address with the court. The inference was that Yevgeni should be appealing to the court for clemency.[2]

Yevgeni knew that the punishment for treason, the crime for which he was accused of, was execution by the State. He also knew that any clemency appeal he might address would have been denied. There was no doubt in his mind that the sentence was a forgone conclusion that had been worked out between KGB general Serov and the chairman of the court.

Yevgeni's request to have a few quiet moments with his wife and mother was denied. The chairman made his ruling; Yevgeni was led from the chamber. There was complete silence save for the soft crying of his mother and Antonina.

Chapter Twenty-Eight

The End of the Road

James Morrison believed that he might be in jeopardy. The peculiar-looking man that he saw in the green-colored Ford or Chevrolet while he was having a clandestine meeting with KGB officer Rem Krasilnikov could have been a member of the RCMP Watcher Service. Morrison decided to take control of the situation and confront the problem head on. However, it is obvious that he rushed to judgment and failed to analyze the situation thoroughly. Nor is it likely that he fully considered the consequences of his action plan.

Morrison's career in the RCMP and his life as a spy began to collapse on December 8, 1957, when he telephoned Charles Sweeny at 1:15 a.m. on Sunday morning. Sweeny, who was now a commissioned officer with the rank of inspector, was attending a private house party at the time. Morrison told him that he was calling from a pay telephone booth behind Union Station, that he was in Ottawa without an approved leave pass, and that he had important information to provide him. He told Sweeny that he wanted to see him right away as he would be returning to Montreal shortly. When asked what that information was, Morrison told him, cryptically, that he had been in contact with "the boys in the big house." This was a direct reference to the Soviet Embassy in Ottawa. Sweeny, his senses on high alert, questioned Morrison on who precisely he had been in contact with. He responded by stating it was "our old friend Nick." Sweeny knew instinctively that he was referring to KGB officer Nikolai Ostrovskiy.[1]

Sweeny knew all too well the reason why Morrison had been kicked out of the Security Service. Misappropriation of RCMP funds was a serious offense. In most cases, this type of behavior resulted in both criminal charges and loss of employment. Sweeny didn't trust Morrison, nor did he like him. He told him that he did not wish to see him at this hour. He advised Morrison to register at a local hotel and that they would get together in the morning.

So there would be no misunderstanding, he informed Morrison that this was not a request, it was a direct order. Morrison told him that he would register at the Château Laurier across from Union Station.

Sweeny's mistrust of Morrison caused him concern that perhaps Morrison wanted him to attend to a meeting right away so that Ostrovskiy would see him and be able to identify him in the future. He reasoned that if that was the case, Ostrovskiy would have learned that Sweeny would not be coming to meet Morrison until the morning and would likely have left the area. An hour later, Sweeny went to the Château Laurier and inquired as to Morrison's room. He was told that he had registered into room #569, but had just left the hotel on foot in order to get a coffee. The clerk further informed Sweeny that there was another man with Morrison and that they had arrived at the hotel in a 1958 Chevrolet. Sweeny decided he would check the local coffee shops near the hotel to see if he could find them. As it happened, he bumped into the two men shortly thereafter. The second man was James Morrison's brother. Sweeny and Morrison went up to Morrison's hotel room while his brother was asked to wait in the hotel lobby.

In spite of the very late hour, Sweeny telephoned RCMP inspector Leslie Higgitt and briefly described where he was and who he was with. He advised Higgitt that it was very important for him to immediately join them at the Château Laurier. While waiting for him to arrive, Morrison described his initial meeting with the KGB in Ottawa. Higgitt arrived within half an hour, and Sweeny asked Morrison to repeat the entire story to him. Neither Sweeny nor Higgitt believed Morrison's story but directed him to put everything he had just told them in writing. Sweeny pulled out a drawer from a desk in the room and handed Morrison several pages of Château Laurier letterhead and instructed him to write all the details out for him. He told him that he wanted his formal written report by noon on December 9. He was ordered not to communicate with anyone and that he was to remain in the Château Laurier.

After Higgitt and Sweeny left Morrison's hotel room, they met privately and agreed on a course to proceed on. They decided that disciplinary action could wait as it was secondary to determining what, if any, damage had been done by Morrison's contact with the Soviets.

Several hours later, Sweeny met with Special Constable Harry Hurd of the Watcher Service. Hurd provided him with a copy of the Watcher Service "Beaver Book," which contained the photographs, biographical information, addresses, vehicle descriptions, and licence numbers that were identified with all of their targets. This highly classified book was the Watcher Service's bible that they used on a daily basis in the performance of their duties. Sweeny described the KGB officer who had met Morrison the previous night along with the licence number A65337 or A56337, which the Soviet was driving. Morrison had also said that the car was a blue and white two-tone 1953 or

1954 Chevrolet. Hurd, without hesitation, was able to inform Sweeny that this was the vehicle normally driven by Rem Krasilnikov.

On December 9, Sweeny picked Morrison up at the Château Laurier just after noon and drove him to Ottawa's Uplands Airport where he was to take the Trans-Canada Airlines flight back to Winnipeg. Prior to boarding the aircraft, Morrison handed Sweeny the handwritten report that he wrote on the Château Laurier letterhead. Sweeny showed Morrison the Beaver Book and asked him to point out the KGB officer he had met on December 7. Morrison looked at the photographs and immediately identified the photograph of Krasilnikov.

Before Morrison left to board the plane, Sweeny laid out a list of orders that he was to follow explicitly. He was ordered not to deviate from any of them. Morrison was advised to return directly to the RCMP detachment in Manitou, Manitoba. Under no circumstances was he to tell anybody about his trip to Ottawa. He was to wait until he received further instructions from Sweeny or Higgitt as to his future conduct. He was specifically ordered to have no further contact with any representative of the Soviet Embassy unless authorized and supervised directly by Sweeny himself. Morrison was told to gather the various letters and cards he had received from the Soviets and retain them in his possession until such time as he could turn them over to Sweeny or Higgitt. He was forbidden to destroy them. And he was to take immediate steps to obtain the Christmas parcel that reportedly was sent by Krasilnikov. This was the parcel that Krasilnikov said would contain up to $3,000. Morrison was told to leave the parcel unopened. Sweeny wished to examine and open the parcel personally.

On the day of Morrison's departure from Ottawa, Sweeny prepared an official report for his senior officer, Terry Guernsey. He strongly suggested that Morrison was holding back critical information and that he had very likely been in contact with the KGB for a considerably longer period than what he admitted to. Sweeny wanted to ensure that they got the full story of Morrison's treachery. He therefore recommended that the RCMP not take any immediate disciplinary action against Morrison at this point that might cause him to stop talking. Sweeny suggested that they do nothing until after Morrison received the Christmas package from Krasilnikov containing the promised money. He advised Guernsey that the RCMP should conduct a thorough investigation of Morrison's finances for the previous three years. He stated that Morrison's father and Mrs. Mabel Vidian-Jones, his mother-in-law, should be interviewed in an effort to determine whether they provided Morrison with the money to discharge his debts as he claimed they had. He stated that their statements would have to be corroborated with financial records.

Sweeny further recommended that Morrison would have to be thoroughly interrogated, particularly by an officer from the Security Service's Counter

Intelligence Branch. Sweeny suggested that the Security Service might wish to consider allowing Morrison to keep his next rendezvous with Krasilnikov, which was tentatively scheduled for some time in mid-January 1958. Sweeny suggested that it might offer them an opportunity to introduce some disinformation to the Soviets. And finally, he suggested that the Commanding Officer D Division, as Manitoba was known within the RCMP, not be consulted at this stage of their investigation.[2]

On January 27, 1958, Morrison arrived at Uplands Airport and took a taxi to the Lord Elgin Hotel. He had been advised by Sweeny that he should fly to Ottawa and prepare to meet with Krasilnikov in accordance with their planned meeting for the following night. Once at the hotel, he contacted Inspector Higgitt, who told him to lay low for the balance of the day and to take a taxi to RCMP Headquarters late the next afternoon.

The following afternoon, Morrison made his way over to RCMP Headquarters and then left in the early evening for his meeting with Krasilnikov at the hotel in Buckingham, Quebec. Higgitt, Sergeant Henry Tadeson, and Corporal Harry Donner in Tadeson's private vehicle accompanied Morrison. They would make themselves scarce well prior to the meeting. The Watcher Service was also covering Morrison's rendezvous with Krasilnikov in an effort to determine if Krasilnikov was alone or accompanied by someone else from the KGB Residency. Uncharacteristically, Krasilnikov did not show up. Nor did he turn up at the designated backup meeting the following night. Krasilnikov's failure to appear either evening had never happened before. Was something wrong? Had he been warned off ahead of time by Morrison? Or by someone else? Did the Soviets see the Watcher Service? Sweeny and Higgitt had to consider whether Morrison had lied about this meeting.

In accordance with their original plan, Morrison was ordered to appear at RCMP Headquarters in the early morning of January 30. Deeply distrustful of all that he had initially told them, Sweeny, joined by Higgitt, took Morrison to a private room where they began a systematic interrogation of him. Throughout the morning, Morrison stuck to his original story but made a number of contradictions that was not lost on the interrogators. By the afternoon, Morrison had completely changed his story and was now deploying a new tactic. He claimed that the entire affair was an invention. He never met the Soviets. He told them that it was all a lie. He naively tried to convince Sweeny and Higgitt that he made up the story with the hope that he would be transferred back to Ottawa and into the Security Service once again. He was counting on them believing his story and that his contact with the KGB would be seen as an invaluable operational opportunity to deploy against the Soviets.

To bolster this new story, Morrison stated that the letter that he reportedly received from Krasilnikov summoning him to Ottawa for this latest rendezvous was a fabrication. This was the same letter he had turned over to Higgitt. Morrison told them that he had actually written the letter himself, using his left hand rather than his right. Seizing the initiative, Sweeny handed him a piece of paper and pen and instructed Morrison to recreate the letter. The words were dictated to him rather than allowing him to see the manner and style of how the original letter was written. Morrison's attempt wasn't even close.[3]

Morrison continued to claim that the $500 he used to pay off his debt was a loan he received from his father. Unknown to Morrison as he was making this claim, RCMP sergeant Andrews had just completed an interview with Morrison's father in Montreal. He stated categorically that he had not given or loaned his son $500.

Morrison's responses to questions during the afternoon continued to be contradictions of earlier statements he had made. One such contradiction revolved around the Gustav Kush KGB LLB in Germany. Morrison changed his original story and lied once again, stating that he made up the German name and overseas address. Unfortunately for Morrison, an allied intelligence agency had already confirmed its existence. At the end of the day, Morrison was placed under arrest and taken to the single men's quarters inside RCMP Headquarters where he was confined, under RCMP guard, in one of the rooms.

When the interrogation resumed the following morning, Morrison stated that he wished to unburden himself and tell Sweeny and Higgitt the complete, truthful story. He spent most of the morning discussing his abysmal financial situation and the extensive, illegal kiting he was engaged in to keep the creditors at arm's length. Most, but not all, of the kiting was undertaken against banks in Manitoba. He eventually found himself in a position where the kiting could no longer cover the checks drawn against a bank in Ottawa. With each check that he wrote, the accrued amount of debt spiraled upward until he got to the point where he ended up with two checks and a total debt of $5,950. It was an enormous amount of debt for 1958. For Morrison, it represented almost three years' salary. It was evident that Morrison was attempting to focus the interrogation on his financial situation as opposed to the treachery he was engaged in with the KGB. Sweeny and Higgitt allowed Morrison to continue with his story.

Sweeny and Higgitt took a brief break in the interrogation during the afternoon of January 31 and paraded Morrison before Subinspector Louis R. Parent in what is referred to in the RCMP as an Orderly Room, a throwback from the British army. It is a quasi-judicial hearing where members of the RCMP are paraded before a senior officer, usually an adjutant. Those appearing in the Orderly Room were Mounties who were charged with a breach of RCMP Rules and Regulations. In Morrison's case, he was charged with several counts of being absent without leave from his duty district at the RCMP Detachment in Manitou, Manitoba. As adjutant in the Orderly Room, Subinspector Parent remanded Morrison in custody until February 7 in order that his interrogation could continue.[4] Following the brief hearing, the officers retreated back to the interview room where the interrogation continued. As the afternoon grew later, it was quite clear to Sweeny and Higgitt that Morrison had lied about his involvement with the Soviets. It was now quite evident that he had volunteered his services as opposed to the KGB approaching him.

The questioning of Morrison was put on hold for the weekend. This gave Sweeny and Higgitt an opportunity to review his statements and to prepare for the continuation of the interrogation on Monday morning. It also gave Morrison an additional two full days in confinement to think about his predicament and consider how much the RCMP really knew about his activities with the Soviets.

On Monday, February 3, when the interrogation resumed, Morrison changed his story once again and admitted to his interrogators that it was he who initiated contact with the KGB and not the other way around. He informed Sweeny and Higgitt that he approached KGB officer Nikolai Ostrovskiy at the Grand Hotel in early July 1955. He tried to minimize his treachery by claiming that he simply provided worthless information to Ostrovskiy and steadfastly denied having compromised anything of value. Under intensive questioning, Morrison admitted that he provided Ostrovskiy with the names of RCMP assistant commissioner Clifford Harvison, Superintendent Ken Hall, and inspectors Norm Jones, Terrance Guernsey, and himself, Charles Sweeny. Ultimately, Sweeny and Higgitt were convinced that Morrison was still holding back important information that he simply was not prepared to expose.

After another night of confinement, and knowing that Sweeny and Higgitt were not about to stop the interrogation, Morrison's resolve broke on the morning of February 4. He confessed that he had betrayed the Security Service's most important counterintelligence case for money. He admitted that he provided Ostrovskiy with all the information he knew about the "man from Montreal," which was sufficient for Ostrovskiy to identify Yevgeni Brik as being a double agent. He told his interrogators he was paid $3,000 for this information. Morrison also admitted having compromised the identities of the RCMP Security Service members of the Watcher Service and the cars they operated. In fact, he told everything he knew about the Security Service and its operations to the KGB. He stated that he received an additional $500 for that information. He admitted that in addition to Ostrovskiy, he also met clandestinely with KGB officers Rem Sergeyevich Krasilnikov and Nikolai Aksenov. Morrison provided details of, and the locations of, the various clandestine meetings he had with them.[5]

The following day, Morrison provided a complete statement of his espionage activities on behalf of the KGB that, ironically, was recorded by his old friend, Shirley Droughan, in the company of Sweeny and Higgitt.

On February 6, RCMP commissioner Leonard H. Nicholson, Superintendent Hall, and inspectors Sweeny and Higgitt met to discuss what course of action the RCMP would take with respect to Morrison. He had admitted to espionage and to compromising what was considered to be the most important counterespionage operation in Canada since the outbreak of the Cold War. The Canadian and British governments were in agreement that the fate of a KGB double agent, if caught by the Soviets, was death by execution. There was little doubt that Yevgeni had died at some point after he was last seen by British SIS officer Daphne Park near the rendezvous site in Moscow.

James Morrison was escorted back to Winnipeg by RCMP Security Service sergeant Andrews in a police aircraft. Morrison was sent back to Manitou Detachment, while Andrews remained in Winnipeg where he briefed the Officer Commanding D Division and Superintendent Spalding, officer in charge of the RCMP Criminal Investigation Branch in Winnipeg. Sergeant Andrews discussed all of Morrison's fraudulent check activities in Manitoba and Ottawa. He was not authorized to discuss any aspect of his espionage activities on behalf of the KGB. This was clearly a decision that had been made in Commissioner Nicholson's office during the meeting that was held there on February 6. Critics may argue that this was the beginning of an RCMP coverup to protect its image at all costs.

On March 3, 1958, an executive decision was made at D Division Headquarters to transfer Morrison from Manitou Detachment back to an administrative position in Winnipeg. Nine weeks later, on May 12, having been formally charged with false pretenses under section 304(1)(9) of the Criminal Code of Canada, Morrison was convicted of his crimes. He was given a two-year suspended sentence and ordered to make full restitution to the banks involved.[6]

Two days later, the Officer Commanding D Division, working under the authority of the commissioner of the RCMP, charged Morrison with an offense under section 252 of the RCMP Rules, Regulations, and Orders of 1945. The section, which was still in effect in 1958, read, "Other ranks convicted of an indictable offence, or otherwise bringing discredit on the Force, or whose conduct has been so reprehensible as to render them unworthy of continuing in the Service, may be dismissed forthwith from the Force by the Commissioner."[7]

James Douglas Finley Morrison was dismissed from the force on May 12, 1958. He never faced criminal or Official Secret Act charges for his treachery. The Canadian public never learned of his betrayal. Morrison was the first member of the RCMP to commit treason and to send another person to what was known to be an execution. Because he was never charged for these Official Secrets Act offenses, the RCMP's reputation was kept intact. That illusion would be shattered in the years ahead.[8]

Chapter Twenty-Nine

Exposed by the Media

Twenty-four years after he was fired by the RCMP in 1958 for misappropriating government funds, the last person in the world that James Morrison was thinking about was Yevgeni Brik. However, three significant back-to-back events changed the landscape for Morrison in ways he would never have imagined.

Celebrated Canadian author and journalist John Sawatsky was about to expose what Morrison and the RCMP had hoped was buried forever. Sawatsky, a Michener Award winner in 1976, was investigating national security matters for a second book about the RCMP Security Service. His first, in 1980, *Men in the Shadows: The RCMP Security Service*, was one of the first books to publish details about the inner workings of the Security Service. His next book, *For Services Rendered: Leslie James Bennett and the RCMP Security Service*, was a sensation and received broad media and public attention when it was published in 1982. It was this latter book that illuminated the public's consciousness and awareness of a Soviet KGB Illegal who had become a double agent working for Canada who was in turn betrayed by an RCMP Security Service officer.[1]

Sawatsky's book was not focused on this particular case. Rather, he concentrated on the life and career of Leslie James Bennett and the internal controversy as to whether Bennett was a KGB mole working at the heart of Canada's counterintelligence branch. As earlier stated, Bennett was fully exonerated by the Canadian government. He was a completely innocent man. This fact was confirmed in Parliament on March 31, 1993, when, in response to a question by Member of Parliament Edna Anderson from the riding of Simcoe Centre, the Honourable Doug Lewis, Solicitor General of Canada, provided the following statement. Addressing the Speaker of the House of Commons, he stated, "Mr. Speaker, I want to assure Mr. Bennett and the

House, that the Government of Canada believes that Mr. Bennett was never a KGB mole. I was struck by his request that we make a categorical denial or statement to that effect and I am pleased to have this opportunity today to put that on the record."[2]

Nevertheless, Sawatsky was the first to identify and document the story of Yevgeni Brik and James Morrison. He did not publicly identify either individual in his book. Perhaps he did not know their actual names. However, he did expose their codenames as being GIDEON and LONG KNIFE, respectively. He also told the Canadian public that the RCMP codename for the case itself was KEYSTONE. These files, created by Terry Guernsey in 1953, had languished in the Security Service's top secret archival vaults for years.

Certain important details of the KEYSTONE case, which Sawatsky described in his book, contained a number of significant errors. Anyone within the Security Service who had access to these classified case files could readily see the mistakes that had been made. But this should neither be surprising nor a point of criticism, as Sawatsky, of course, did not have access to the top secret KEYSTONE operational case file. Nor did he have any contact or connection with Yevgeni Brik, who had disappeared in 1956. Regardless of the inaccuracies, Sawatsky's book blew the lid off one of the most important and closely guarded counterintelligence operations during the early stages of the Cold War.

Sawatsky's revelations caused heated debate in Canada at the time. The vaunted RCMP received a great deal of public and official government criticism. The question, of course, was why hadn't the RCMP charged Morrison with espionage offenses under the Official Secrets Act, as opposed to minor summary conviction offenses under the Criminal Code? National television news outlets, radio talk shows, newspapers, pundits, and others were all over the story. Numerous academics and consultants of all kinds, most claiming to be national security experts, provided their opinions to a national audience through the Canadian media. Various mistakes that appeared in Sawatsky's book were repeated by other authors and journalists and became circular reporting. There was shock, bewilderment, and disbelief from Canadians right across the country. They simply could not believe that a member of the RCMP would willfully commit treason. It was unheard of. The revelation resulted in diminishing respect and a corresponding loss of reputation that the Mounted Police had carefully forged since it was created in 1873. The RCMP was a Canadian national symbol. The RCMP Musical Ride was recognized and revered around the world. This kind of bad publicity for the force was unheard of.

Following closely on the heels of Sawatsky's book, a Canadian Broadcasting Corporation (CBC) television production of its popular news magazine series, the *Fifth Estate*, took the KEYSTONE story to a new level. Producers had found Morrison and, unbelievably, convinced him to appear on the weekly series. Morrison's appearance on the *Fifth Estate* on November 9, 1982, was a calamity that cost him dearly. He sat under heavy lights wearing a pathetic-looking disguise before seasoned journalist, Eric Malling. Morrison's wig consisted of a thick mop of dark, unmanageable hair and his fake mustache hung lopsided on his face. He was a pitiful sight and no match for the highly professional journalist.

Malling informed the national television audience that the *Fifth Estate* agreed not to identify Morrison. However, addressing him directly, Malling suggested that it was just a matter of time before he was publicly recognized and identified. Malling suggested, "Why don't you forget about the disguise and just admit who you are, explain your position?" Morrison's response was an abrupt, "No way."

Later in the interview, Malling asked Morrison to describe the significance of what he told the Soviets about GIDEON. He asked him how important the RCMP double-agent case was for Canada. Morrison responded that he didn't actually know how important the operation was because he wasn't involved in the actual handling of the case. Not to be deterred, Malling rebutted, "But you knew about him, and you told the Soviets this guy was playing both sides." Morrison incriminated himself by responding, "That's right . . . yes."

Continuing, Malling posed the question, "Do you ever think about what happened to GIDEON?" Morrison's telling response was, "Well, when you engage in espionage you have to expect whatever the consequences are. I have thought about it, yes."

Malling countered with, "Do you think there was any doubt he was killed?" Morrison responded, "I wouldn't know, but that would appear to me to be their standard policy." Morrison went on to say that he received approximately $3,500 from the Soviets and that money was sufficient to cover his immediate debts. He went on to say that the RCMP engaged in a coverup when they kicked him out of the force as they wished to preserve the honor of the RCMP.

One of the most damaging exchanges between Malling and Morrison occurred when Malling stated, "You took one of the most sensitive operations Canadian security had ever run, an opportunity to find out about Soviet intelligence. It probably resulted in a man being killed. You did it for $3,500 paid to you by the Soviets and you don't consider yourself a traitor?" Morrison provided a very weak response by simply saying, "I wouldn't apply that word, no."[3]

Four days following the broadcast of the *Fifth Estate*, *Winnipeg Free Press* reporter, the late Mike Ward, interviewed Morrison over the telephone. During that November 13 conversation, Morrison once again admitted to being

LONG KNIFE. He spoke at some length about his belief that the RCMP would not charge him with espionage offenses under the Official Secrets Act because they did not have sufficient evidence to do so. He also intimated that the government of Canada would be "opening a can of worms" if they did so. He practically boasted that he had additional information about RCMP operations that he knew the government would not want to be made public. Ward had no such agreement with Morrison to keep his identity secret. He publicly identified Morrison in the articles that he wrote.[4]

The *Fifth Estate* television broadcast, Sawatsky's book, and Ward's news articles combined to create a perfect storm for Morrison. The Canadian public wanted answers as to why the RCMP never charged him under Official Secrets Act legislation when he was fired in 1958. They wanted to know if he would now be charged after having incriminated himself on national television.

The Canadian public was not alone in asking these questions. Six days after journalist Mike Ward identified Morrison by name in a *Winnipeg Free Press* exposé, Morrison's name was raised in the Parliament of Canada during Question Period in the House of Commons. The Honourable Allan Lawrence, a Progressive Conservative Member of Parliament for the riding of Durham-Northumberland, rose and addressed the Speaker of the House, the Honourable Madame Jeanne Sauvé. He stated:

Madame Speaker, my question is directed to the Minister of Justice. LONG KNIFE, the codename for the RCMP Security Service corporal who allegedly received $3,500 from the Soviet KGB for betraying a double agent in Montreal, has now been identified in the *Winnipeg Free Press* as an ex-RCMP corporal by the name of James Morrison. Well over a week ago, even though the government has been aware of these facts for five years, the Solicitor General referred the question of whether or not there would be a prosecution to the Minister of Justice. Surely the Minister of Justice has made up his mind. Will there be a prosecution, will there not be a prosecution and, if he has not made up his mind, why not? When will we hear whether or not there will be a prosecution?[5]

Prime Minister Pierre Elliott Trudeau's Minister of Justice in the Liberal Cabinet was the Honourable Mark MacGuigan, who represented the Ontario riding of Windsor-Walkerville. He responded by saying, "Madame Speaker, since receiving the request from the Solicitor General, I have directed that an inquiry be made. I do not know when the results will come to me for a decision, but I can assure the Honourable Member that when the recommendation comes forward, I will act on it very quickly."[6]

The RCMP, meanwhile, was conducting the investigation that the Minister of Justice had referred to in his response to Parliament. The threshold they had to meet was whether sufficient evidence existed in order to lay Official Secrets Act charges against Morrison. Ontario Provincial Court judge Mr. Charles Scullion issued search warrants that had been prepared for the court by the RCMP. Warrants were executed against journalists John Sawatsky, Mike Ward, the newsrooms of the *Winnipeg Free Press* and the *Fifth Estate*, and the Toronto offices of Doubleday Canada Ltd., who was Sawatsky's publisher.

In the months that followed, the question whether Morrison was going to be charged with espionage offenses came up in Parliament a number of times. On January 24, 1983, the Minister of Justice informed Parliament, "I have to admit that I have not yet received an opinion from the Department."[7]

On March 4, the Honourable Mr. Lawrence brought up the matter once again. His frustration at not receiving a definitive response was evident. He stated, "I do not know how much more bluntly, simply, or directly, I can put it to the Minister? Will James Morrison be charged or not?"[8]

Three months later, on June 3, 1983, RCMP superintendent Rodney T. Stamler "swore an Information and complaint in the Supreme Court of Ontario (Criminal Division), alleging that James Douglas Finley Morrison, between the first day of April 1955 and the 31st day of January, 1958, at or near the City of Ottawa and elsewhere in the Province of Ontario and Quebec and elsewhere in Canada committed offences contrary to the provisions of the Official Secrets Act and of the Criminal Code, such Information and complaint having come before the Provincial Court (Criminal Division) of the Judicial District of Ottawa-Carleton."[9]

Four days later, on June 7, RCMP inspector Douglas H. Egan met with Morrison who, at the time, was living at 1792 Sloane Avenue, Prince Rupert, British Columbia. Morrison was informed of the charges against him and was asked if he wished to provide a written statement. Morrison declined. He did sign a document that had been prepared in advance that outlined the precise offenses he was accused of. The document also informed him that anything he said may be given as evidence at trial and that he had the right to engage and instruct legal counsel without delay. In addition to not wanting to furnish a written statement, Morrison advised Egan that he did not wish to retain counsel. The following day, June 8, 1983, Morrison met with Egan once again and was placed under arrest. Twenty-five years after clandestinely meeting KGB officers Ostrovskiy, Krasilnikov, and Aksenov, and, having engaged in espionage for financial gain, Morrison was now going to have to face justice and the Canadian judicial system.[10]

Canada's Official Secrets Act was adopted from the United Kingdom in 1889. It was amended in 1990 and remained the country's primary legislation in matters dealing with national security investigations and prosecutions until the Security of Information Act following the al-Qaeda terrorist attacks on September 11, 2001, replaced it. Although amendments had been made to this legislation over the years, it was the instrument used by the government throughout World War I and World War II, the Korean conflict, and the Cold War. It could not keep up with changing technology or methods that spies used to conduct espionage. The government of Canada only prosecuted twenty-two cases under the Official Secrets Act, and most of them were directly related to the Igor Gouzenko revelations in 1945. Another celebrated case was the 1989 Stephen Joseph Ratkai prosecution in St. John's, Newfoundland. This combined Canadian and American operation against the Soviets resulted in Ratkai being convicted of espionage and sentenced to nine years in prison.

James Morrison, who wisely changed his mind and retained legal counsel, challenged the charges against him in court. His lawyers strenuously argued that they were a violation of the Canadian Charter of Rights and Freedoms and should be quashed as they denied Morrison the right to be tried within a reasonable amount of time. A Preliminary Hearing was held in January 1984 in the Ontario Provincial Court (Criminal Division) to ascertain whether there was sufficient evidence to proceed with the charges. At the commencement of the hearing, His Honour Judge Beauline issued a publication ban with respect to the hearing. The Preliminary Hearing concluded with Judge Beauline ruling that there would be a stay of proceedings against Morrison. Judge Beauline further ruled that the federal government had violated Morrison's Charter of Rights and Freedoms by waiting more than twenty-five years to bring charges against him.

Federal Justice minister Mark MacGuigan questioned Judge Beauline's decision to issue a stay of proceedings against Morrison and denied that the federal government had violated his Charter of Rights and Freedoms. He advised that the federal government would examine its legal options to appeal these Provincial Court decisions.

On June 22, 1984, Mr. Justice J. Holland of the Supreme Court of Ontario quashed an earlier Provincial Court (Criminal Division) decision that had granted a stay of proceedings to Morrison on the charges in the Information. He also dismissed an Application to the Supreme Court of Ontario under the Charter of Rights and Freedoms, section 24(1), for a stay of proceedings on the charges in the Information. This set the stage for Morrison's criminal trial, which began on January 20, 1986, in the Provincial Court House in Ottawa. Mr. Justice Coulter Osborne presided. Crown Prosecutor Mr. Doug Rutherford represented the Government of Canada. Defense Counsel Mr. John Nelligan represented James Morrison. Morrison had entered a not-guilty plea at the commencement of his trial. Four days later, on January 24, Morrison stopped the proceedings, changed his plea to guilty, and admitted that he betrayed Yevgeni Brik to KGB officer Nikolai Ostrovskiy. The Crown dropped two of the charges. In discussing the penalty that awaited Morrison, defense lawyer John Nelligan explained to the court that Morrison had paid his debt to society and that the matter should be forgotten. Mr. Justice Osborne set the sentencing date to May 26, 1986. On that occasion, he sentenced Morrison to serve eighteen months in prison.

Morrison always claimed that his wife had no knowledge of his dealings with the KGB or that he had received payment and expenses from them. I believe this to be true. He was a con man, a liar, a thief, and a philanderer. There was never any evidence to suggest that Gwynneth knew of her husband's espionage. After he was charged and received national notoriety, there is little doubt that this caused his wife great shock and pain. She certainly knew about his philandering, but there is no doubt that she was completely unaware of his activities on behalf of the KGB. Nevertheless, a stoic and dignified Gwynneth Morrison traveled to Ottawa with her husband and attended his January 1986 trial, while she stayed at the home of their youngest son. Gwynneth quietly supported him in public and stood by his side. How she felt internally can only be a matter of conjecture. One would surmise that she was grateful that her long-suffering father, Lieutenant Commander Gerrard Laurie Vidian Jones, the father who would not attend his daughter's wedding to Morrison, was not present at his son-in-law's espionage trial. His intuition and displeasure with James Morrison in 1941 and his deep unhappiness about his daughter's choice for a husband caused him years of pain. Gwynneth's father was spared this hurt and pain as he had died thirty-one years earlier in Ottawa on February 24, 1955. Shortly after his death, Gwynneth's mother, Maylar, moved back to England where she died some years later.

Chapter Thirty

An Astounding Revelation

The CSIS was born from the rib of the RCMP, Security Service. There had long been a heated debate as to whether a country's security intelligence responsibility should be a part of, or divorced from, that same country's national police force. Fierce lobbying within Canada called for the separation of the Security Service and the creation of an independent security intelligence organization after media exposés of RCMP wrongdoing, particularly, but not exclusively, in the Province of Quebec.

These exposés caused Canadian prime minister Pierre Elliott Trudeau and his Liberal government to establish, on July 6, 1977, what was known as the Royal Commission of Inquiry into Certain Activities of the RCMP. The commission quickly became known simply as the McDonald Commission, so named after Justice David C. McDonald. He was charged with the responsibility of investigating a number of alleged illegal activities, perpetrated by both the RCMP Security Service and the RCMP's Criminal Investigations Branch (CIB), which surfaced in the late 1970s. Justice McDonald subsequently issued three reports to the federal government. The first, which had the title Security and Information, was issued in November 1979. The second, Freedom and Security under the Law, was issued in January 1981. And the third report, Certain RCMP Activities and the Question of Government Knowledge, was issued in May 1981. There were a number of findings and recommendations identified by Justice McDonald. Chief among them was the recommendation to separate the Security Service from the RCMP and create an independent security intelligence organization with civilian review mechanisms.

Prime Minister Trudeau accepted this recommendation and directed that the Solicitor General's Department in Ottawa create a Transition Group that would study Justice McDonald's recommendation and establish a legal framework for the new agency. On July 16, 1984, the CSIS was born. Its initial Director, Thomas D'Arcy "Ted" Finn, was a former assistant secretary to the Federal Cabinet for Security and Intelligence in the Privy Council Office.

With the dissolution of the RCMP Security Service, a new headquarters was immediately required to house the staff and branches of the newly established CSIS. The membership of the new Service moved from RCMP Headquarters on Alta Vista Drive to the East Memorial Building, 284 Wellington Street, Ottawa, directly across the street from the Supreme Court of Canada. The CSIS Regional Office in Ottawa was located at 400 Cooper Street in the center of the city. Regional and District Offices were established across Canada.

The transition from a police environment and mentality to a civilian spy agency evolved over the initial years of its existence. The Service moved into a brand new headquarters in Ottawa in 1995. It was a purpose-built, state-of-the-art, billion-dollar complex that was completed under budget and ahead of schedule. It quickly became the envy of the federal government and equally so with foreign intelligence services that visited the facility.

Late in the afternoon of April 11, 1992, the internal telephone rang on the desk of CSIS senior investigator Donald G. Mahar. His office was located in the Counter Intelligence Branch at CSIS National Headquarters in the East Memorial Building. This was his second posting to headquarters. He had previously been a desk head in the Ottawa Regional office where he worked target areas and recruitment operations with the Service's legendary recruiter, the late Frank Pratt. A twenty-three-year veteran of the RCMP, RCMP Security Service, and now CSIS, Mahar was the Service's Foreign Agent Recruitment Coordinator. The recruitment of Canadian government–mandated targets, including foreign intelligence officers, foreign diplomatic staff, and locally engaged staff was a priority for CSIS. It allowed the Service to gather and inform the Canadian government about hostile intelligence operations and intentions against Canada. It was a position that Mahar aspired to since the creation of CSIS in 1984. During the past sixteen years, he worked in Counter Intelligence, primarily against Soviet and East European as well as Asian targets. In 1987 he worked in Asia on a temporary assignment.

Following RCMP training in 1969 to 1970, in Regina, Saskatchewan, Mahar was posted to Saskatoon where he was employed on general police duties. Two years later he was transferred to the small Saskatchewan farming community of Colonsay. He married Carol Anne Westran on September 11, 1971, a registered nurse from his hometown who had traveled to Saskatchewan so they could be together. In 1974, their son Scott was born in Saskatoon. A little over six years after he graduated from the RCMP training academy, he received the posting he had been working for from the very beginning of his career.

A telex arrived at the small, rural RCMP Detachment in Colonsay, inform-ing him that he had been accepted into the Security Service and was being posted into the prestigious B Ops Branch in Ottawa. He knew immediately that he was about to be deployed at the heart of the RCMP's Soviet Counter Intelligence Branch.

Formerly from London, Ontario, where he attended Oakridge Secondary School and Fanshawe College, Mahar is a graduate of Carleton University with a bachelor of arts degree in political science and law. His core subjects included Soviet and East European Studies.

It was near the end of the workday when Mahar answered the telephone on his desk. The caller was John Cummings. As deputy director general, Operations, or DDG (Ops), Cummings was Mahar's immediate supervisor. Without explanation, he simply asked Mahar to walk the short distance down the hall to his office.

Cummings was a very experienced and respected counterintelligence of-ficer. Most officers who were subordinate to him recognized that they were indeed fortunate to have Cummings as their supervisor and mentor. He demanded nothing less than total professionalism from his officers. He was known for demanding the same of himself. Mahar had known and worked with Cummings for a number of years, considered him a friend and mentor, and respected him tremendously.

At forty-nine years of age, Cummings was trim, silver-haired, and always impeccably dressed in a navy blue business suit, starched white shirt with cufflinks, and highly polished shoes.

Born in Cape Breton, Nova Scotia, Cummings grew up in southern Ontario. He joined the RCMP in 1962 and had various jobs in the early part of his career, including being a member of Prime Minister Lester B. Pearson's Protection Detail. Athletic and with a passion for baseball, Cummings quickly earned a reputation for being very good at his job. He became a member of the Security Service, B Ops Branch in the Ottawa Regional Office in 1964, was transferred to the Montreal Regional Office in 1971, and transitioned to CSIS in 1984 back in Ottawa. While working at CSIS Headquarters, Cummings held the coveted position of head of Recruitment Operations. He rounded out his career by spending two years as the director general of the CSIS Physical Surveillance Unit (PSU), four years as DDG (Ops) of Counter Intelligence, and a year as director general of Internal Security. The substantive portion of his career was spent in counterintelligence. He ran Counter Intelligence at headquarters in 1990 while the director general of the branch, Geoffrey O'Brian, attended a year at the Royal College of Defence Studies in the United Kingdom.[1]

Cummings and Mahar crossed into O'Brian's office and took a seat. O'Brian always did his best to make his guests feel relaxed. It was obvious to

Mahar when he entered the office that a matter of some urgency was about to be introduced. It was also evident that Cummings and O'Brian had discussed the subject before Mahar had been summoned.

As director general of Counter Intelligence, Geoffrey O'Brian sat at the pinnacle of the country's efforts to counter and defeat hostile intelligence service operations against Canada. Everything went through him. O'Brian was not a career intelligence officer, nor had he been a member of the RCMP. His background was in law.

O'Brian was born in Toronto, Ontario. He obtained his undergraduate degree in 1969 at Trent University, a small liberal arts university in Peterborough, Ontario. He followed this with a bachelor of law degree from the University of Toronto and was subsequently called to the Bar in 1975, where he practiced law in Toronto for two years.

O'Brian moved to the world of politics in 1978 and obtained a position in the office of the Minister of Finance on Parliament Hill in Ottawa. He spent five years working on Parliament Hill culminating with a position in the office of Canadian prime minister Pierre Elliott Trudeau.

O'Brian's transition into the world of security intelligence began in September 1981 when he became a member of the Security Intelligence Transition (SIT) Group that had been established following the publication of the second and third reports of the McDonald Commission and the government's acceptance of separating the police and security intelligence functions. He spent nearly three years with the SIT Group. Importantly, they established the framework of the Service, crafted the CSIS Act, and maneuvered it through the various committee stages in Parliament. When the CSIS Act was passed in June 1984, O'Brian was offered a position in the new Service. In 1990, he was selected to attend the prestigious Royal College of Defence Studies in the United Kingdom. While in the United Kingdom, he was informed by CSIS director Reid Morden that he would be assuming the position of director general, Counter Intelligence back in Ottawa when his course ended in December 1990.[2]

Although somewhat eccentric at times, O'Brian possessed a keen intellect, a wonderful sense of humor, and would often find unorthodox but brilliant solutions to problems. He maintained good relationships with his staff and allied Service representatives from around the world. He was supported by, and received operational advice from, the highly experienced Cummings and the other officers who worked for him. Geoffrey O'Brian was always prepared to listen to the counsel of others and then would make up his own mind.

O'Brian handed Mahar an urgent message that had been received at CSIS Headquarters late that afternoon. It had come from the SIS in London. The top-secret message contained extraordinary intelligence, if it was in fact true.

Mahar's first thought was that this was a practical joke. On reflection, he wondered if this was something more sinister on the part of the newly formed Russian Foreign Intelligence Service Sluzhba Vneshney Razvedki (SVR), which had replaced the KGB's First Chief Directorate (Foreign Intelligence) in December 1991. Was it simply one of the SVR's "operational games" that they were so good at? But what possible motive could they have for resurfacing this operation after so many decades? The three men had difficulty believing the information contained in the telex could be true.

The British telex advised that on January 27, 1992, an elderly man had walked into the British Embassy in Vilnius, Lithuania, and asked to speak with one of the diplomats. The receptionist informed him that nobody was presently at the embassy. She suggested he return after lunch, at which time someone would hopefully see him. The old man returned and sat down in the reception area. A short while later, a gentleman emerged and introduced himself as the deputy ambassador. He asked the older man what his nationality was and what it was he wanted. The older man asked the deputy ambassador if they could speak confidentially. They moved to a small room off the reception area and spoke softly.

The older man stated that he wanted to get in touch with the Secret Intelligence Service (MI6). He stated that it would be good for Britain, but more significantly, it would be good for Canada. The deputy ambassador was compassionate and assured the older gentleman that he was prepared to listen. The older gentleman removed two small pieces of photographic film from his pocket. Each had been wrapped in tin foil. He stated that the two photographic films contained coded messages. He further advised the deputy ambassador that the key to breaking the code was a poem from Sinclair Lewis's book, *Babbitt*. The older man then took the time to write out the passage.

The old man took great care to inform the deputy ambassador that if the Russian Intelligence Services found out about the details contained in the coded message, and the fact that he confided this information to the British, that he would be arrested and executed. The two men discussed future meeting arrangements and agreed it would be safer to meet again in Vilnius rather than in Moscow. The old man agreed to return to the embassy again on April 11.

O'Brian, Cummings, and Mahar discussed the situation and were incredulous about what they read in the British message. Cummings and Mahar were both well aware of the KEYSTONE case of the 1950s. In fact, when Mahar arrived in B Ops. Counter Intelligence in 1976, former RCMP inspector, the late Bill Walker, had given Mahar permission to study all the RCMP Security Service operational case files directed against the Soviet and East European intelligence services from the 1950s and 1960s. Mahar recognized the opportunity and privilege that had been given to him by Walker and devoured the case files, one after the other. Operation KEYSTONE was clearly the most important one during the early stages of the Cold War and was the most intriguing and fascinating to read. It was widely believed within the RCMP Security Service and SIS in the United Kingdom that Yevgeni Brik had undoubtedly been executed by the KGB when he failed to return to Canada in 1955 or 1956. The question that now had to be satisfied was whether this old man, who turned up at the British Embassy on January 27, was in fact Yevgeni Brik, or whether this entire affair was a canard.

In spite of the lateness of the day, Director General O'Brian asked Mahar to go down into the basement vault that contained the archival records of the RCMP Security Service and to search for the 1950s KEYSTONE file. O'Brian had arranged to have a records management official to assist with this task. The objective was to scour all the volumes that made up the KEYSTONE file and come up with three questions that only the true, real-life Yevgeni Brik would be able to answer correctly.

The vault contained the history of security intelligence in Canada going back to the defection of Igor Gouzenko in 1945. Artifacts and spy paraphernalia from many cases sat on the shelves beside the boxes of files. Mahar read through the KEYSTONE volumes, Guernsey's diary, and Sweeny's notebooks. He emerged from the vault at 3:00 a.m. and was surprised to see both O'Brian and Cummings still in the office. A message containing the three questions was hastily sent to London and subsequently forwarded to the British Embassy in Vilnius to be put to the old man when he arrived at the embassy for his April 11 meeting.

The coded message that the old man had given to the deputy ambassador on January 27 on the photographic films contained instructions for meeting him in Moscow. The message was intended for both the RCMP and MI6. It stated that he would be at the Mayakovskiy subway station at 12:00 noon every first and third Tuesday each month. He would be standing at the downstairs platform wearing sunglasses and holding a red bag with a red strap over his left shoulder. He also included a brief parole to be exchanged. He signed his coded message with the words: Gene / Dave 53 5. This was an obvious signal identifying his real name, Yevgeni (Eugene), and the identity he adopted in Canada of David Soboloff. The 53 5 represented the years that he worked for the Canadians, being that of 1953 to 1955.

As arranged, the old man arrived at the British Embassy in Vilnius on April 11. He had a brief meeting with diplomats in a private office. He advised them that this was the first opportunity he had to speak with either the Canadians or British in over thirty years. One of the diplomats asked him why he required three months between meetings at the embassy in Vilnius. He said that he believed it would take up to ten days for SIS to get the photographic negatives. Then time would be required to decipher the coded message and for SIS senior executives to decide what course of action they would follow. Additional time would be required to consult with the RCMP Security Service in Canada. In the old man's analysis, he believed that ten weeks between meetings would be sufficient time to get an answer.

The three questions that CSIS had transmitted to SIS in London were asked. The old man answered them flawlessly. Nobody else could have done so. It was now evident that Yevgeni Brik had not been executed as believed and that he was now rising from the ashes thirty-seven years later. Following further discussions, Yevgeni was asked to return to the embassy the following day.

Having been informed that Yevgeni answered the questions correctly, Geoff O'Brian briefed CSIS senior executive officers and informed them that Yevgeni Brik was indeed alive and desirous of returning to Canada. The appropriate officials at the Department of External Affairs and Immigration Canada were also contacted and briefed.

CSIS requested a meeting of the Interdepartmental Defector Committee to advise the committee members of the situation with Brik and to determine whether he met all the requirements to be accepted into Canada as a defector. The membership of the committee included External Affairs, CSIS, RCMP, Department of National Defence, and Immigration. John Cummings was the CSIS representative and had the lead with respect to this meeting. It was his responsibility to convince the committee members that Yevgeni met all the requirements and that the committee should approve the CSIS request. It had already been decided by External Affairs that they would not be taking the lead to get Yevgeni out of Russia through diplomatic channels and back to Canada. The British had also advised CSIS that they would not take the lead in exfiltrating Yevgeni from Russia but that they would assist CSIS in doing so. The committee agreed that Yevgeni Brik met the requirements of a defector and would do whatever was legally necessary to help him escape.

Yevgeni returned to the embassy the following day and was informed of the decision by the Canadians. He removed another piece of tin foil from his pocket that contained two photographic negatives along with two black-and-white passport-sized photographs that he had taken of himself. He was given a sum of money and was told that it was from the Canadians. This cash was to be used for travel costs, the purchase of clothes, and bribes if necessary, to anyone necessary during his escape. He was told to return to his home in Aleksandrov, northeast of Moscow, and wait until the day of his escape. It was agreed that day would be June 19, 1992.

Chapter Thirty-One

The Devil Is in the Details

Preparations to mount an exfiltration operation overseas had to begin immediately considering the day of extraction was set as June 19, just sixty-nine days away. A great deal of operational and administrative planning had to commence immediately. It would require the skill and time of several within CSIS and other Canadian government departments to ensure a successful outcome. Chief among the tasks that had to be completed judiciously was the requirement to inform the solicitor general of Canada, the Honourable Doug Lewis in Prime Minister Brian Mulroney's cabinet, of the situation. His authority and approval to move forward with the operation was critical.

An Aide Memoire describing the situation was prepared for the minister along with a case brief describing events of the 1950s, who Brik was and details of Brik's betrayal at the hands of an RCMP officer. The Aide Memoire was hand delivered to the minister by a senior CSIS executive officer. It in turn made its way to the prime minister's office. After being briefed on the astonishing turn of events and the fact that Yevgeni Brik was alive and desirous of escaping Russia and returning to Canada, Prime Minister Brian Mulroney wrote his endorsement on the face of the Aide Memoire. He stated, "Every consideration will be given to this man who was betrayed by the cowardice of an RCMP officer."

With these astonishing words, the planning of the operation to extract Yevgeni Brik from Russia began. It was to be accomplished with the assistance of the British.

Geoffrey O'Brian informed Mahar that the Canadian planning and execution of the extraction would be his responsibility to draft and that he would support it when all their requirements had been met. Mahar had CSIS Facilities Management personnel install an additional safe in his office and had all the KEYSTONE and related operational case files moved from the vault in the archives to the new safe in his office. He spent days deliberating over these files searching for details that would help in the planning of the operation. Mahar knew that a legend, a fictitious cover story, would have to be created for Yevgeni Brik as well as an operational plan that would complement this legend.

With a legend, documentation to support it would be essential. In stepped a thoroughly professional and experienced officer who immediately took responsibility for these matters and set to work.

Modest, patriotic, and completely reliable, Robbie McLeod was brought up in a rural setting on a poultry farm in northern New Brunswick. Besides his poultry business, McLeod's father was also engaged in commercial salmon fishing, logging, construction, and working with cranes and other heavy equipment. McLeod's strong work ethic and commitment to the task at hand was forged by the example and influence that he learned from his father. He became a bit of a jack of all trades as he was growing up during his teenage years.

McLeod attended Wilfrid Laurier University, a midsized university in Waterloo, Ontario, located an hour west of Toronto. The university is named after Canada's first francophone prime minister, Sir Henri-Charles Wilfred Laurier, who was Canada's seventh prime minister. McLeod obtained a bachelor of art's degree with a major in political science.

Robbie McLeod joined the RCMP in September 1972 and, similar to other recruits at the time, trained at RCMP Depot in Regina. Upon graduation, he was seconded to the RCMP Centennial Review. The Review, which celebrated one hundred years of RCMP history in Canada, visited communities across the country where the members performed various demonstrations before huge audiences. He was subsequently posted to Newfoundland where he was engaged in general-duty policing in three different detachments over the next few years.

McLeod became a member of the Security Service in Toronto in 1976 and had a number of postings in Kitchener, RCMP Security Service Headquarters in Ottawa, and back to Toronto B Ops Counter Intelligence on the day that CSIS was created on July 16, 1984. McLeod transitioned to CSIS on that day and was subsequently transferred to the CSIS Calgary District office two years later where he became responsible for counterterrorism investigations.

As a senior investigator, McLeod was posted back to CSIS Headquarters in Ottawa in 1989, where he worked in the very sensitive area dealing with human source operations in conjunction with the Counter Intelligence branch.[1] He was considered by most to be the perfect person for this delicate position. It required discretion, knowledge, tact, and common sense. These are some of the attributes that best describe McLeod.

Mahar and John Cummings worked closely as they evaluated various scenarios and discussed the pros and cons of one potential plan after another. Every contingency had to be planned for. They had to think about potential issues and problems of getting Brik from Aleksandrov to Moscow and then from Moscow to Vilnius, Lithuania. What if he had an unexpected emergency at the last minute in Aleksandrov? What would happen to the plan if the train was late getting into Moscow and the connecting train to East Europe had already departed? Yevgeni was no longer a young man. Would he have the strength of character, stamina, and courage to overcome any potential problems with Russian or East European immigration and customs officials or uncompromising border guards?

As Mahar fine-tuned the details of Brik's legend and the various aspects of the operational plan, McLeod was taking care of other vitally important details, slowly and methodically. He searched for and collected the kind of personal items that any Canadian traveler would expect to have on his person. These were items that Brik would have with him at the time of his escape. He found an old, used leather wallet and filled it with photographs and Canadian, Swedish, and Lithuanian currency. Credit cards, driver's licence, and an odd assortment of receipts were all stuffed into the wallet next to a couple of lottery tickets and some Canadian postage stamps. Brik had chosen to use the name Eugene Thompson for his cover identity. He wanted to use the Anglicized version of his first name. He chose the surname Thompson because it was a name he was familiar with from a British foreign radio broadcast that he listened to on his shortwave radio in Aleksandrov.

For Brik's safety and security, all government documentation that Brik would carry during this operation was genuine and legally obtained from the respective department or agency that had the authority to issue these documents. Yevgeni Brik's documents, credit cards, and driver's licence all reflected the name Eugene Thompson, the chosen name of his false persona.

Mahar arranged for the proposed operational plan to be sent by secure communications to the Canadian High Commission in London, England. Situated in the prestigious Grosvenor Square acreage across the park from the US Embassy, the office of the CSIS Security Liaison Officer (SLO) was situated in the secure portion of the High Commission. Only authorized Canadian diplomatic staff and vetted visitors were permitted access to the area. The secure message containing the proposed plan was received by this office and secured.

The following day, Mahar flew to London, met with the CSIS SLO, and retrieved the plan. Within the hour the two CSIS officers were in a cab headed to Century House, the twenty-two-floor, drab-looking headquarters of the SIS, or more colloquially known as MI6. They met with their British counterparts, and Mahar presented the plan and discussed the legend and documentation that Brik would be using. The British offered suggestions on how the plan might be improved and built upon to suit everyone's needs. When the discussions were completed, and all were satisfied, Mahar returned to Ottawa and briefed Geoffrey O'Brian and John Cummings on his meeting with SIS.

The exfiltration date was still a few weeks away, but there was still much to do. The false documentation for Yevgeni Brik was still being prepared and other complementary items collected. Arrangements for Mahar to be issued with an official Government of Canada red diplomatic passport were being made. To support Brik's legend, it was necessary to acquire a suitcase and fill it with the necessary clothing and trappings of an older Canadian gentleman who was traveling internationally.

This represented a much larger problem than we had bargained for. What size clothing should be purchased? What size shoes would he require? From the Canadian perspective, he had not been seen for over thirty-seven years. Due to a complicating factor, we could not get in touch with the SIS officers who saw Brik in the British Embassy in Vilnius. The correct size of clothing became an issue. The legend called for North American clothing, not East European.

Mahar searched the 1950s files for any references to Brik's height. According to those yellowed pages on file, his height ranged from five feet, one inch, to five feet, seven inches. How much did he currently weigh? What size pants would he need? Unable to come to a reasonable conclusion about clothing size, Mrs. Carol Anne Mahar, the wife of CSIS officer Don Mahar, suggested that clothing be purchased for a man who approximated the size of her late father, F. Howard Westran. A registered nurse by profession and the mother of an eighteen-year-old son, she improved this aspect of the operation by adding a woman's touch to what would be needed to properly outfit Brik as a Canadian. Over the next couple of days, several hours were spent shopping for a suitcase, all manner of clothes, socks, shirts, underclothing, toiletries, hankies, and other items a senior citizen might carry in his suitcase.

Mrs. Mahar came up with a brilliant idea on how to handle the issue about clothing size. She took the suit pants and turned the legs inside out, removed the thread from the cuffs and replaced it with Velcro strips. The pants had an elasticized, adjustable waistband. All Brik would have to do would be to remove his East European clothing, pull on the pants, and adjust the leg length using the Velcro strips and add the belt that had extra hole punches in it to assure a proper fit. Everything inside the suitcase was of North American purchase. Mrs. Mahar took all the clothing and put them through the wash several times to remove the touch, smell, and appearance that all the clothing was brand new. All the clothing items and toiletries were packed into the suitcase. Luggage tags, in the name of Eugene Thompson, were put away separately until such time as they were to be given to Brik overseas in a safe house. Like the wallet that had been assembled for him, letters and other personal items were placed inside the suitcase.

In mid-June, Mahar returned to London to meet with SIS officials once again to finalize plans and to provide a personal briefing to Mr. Gaetan Lavertu, the Deputy High Commissioner at the Canadian High Commission. Mr. Lavertu was, as expected, highly professional, asked relevant questions, and offered the assistance of his office if required. The following day, Mr. Mahar flew to Stockholm, Sweden, where CSIS officer Mr. Gordon Gramlick joined him. Together, they provided a briefing to Canadian ambassador Michael Phillips. As was the case with Deputy High Commissioner Lavertu, Ambassador Phillips was totally professional, generous with his time, and likewise offered any assistance that might be required of him.[2]

All that remained was for Mahar to return to Ottawa, take possession of the suitcase and cover documentation, and return to Europe in time to execute the escape plan on June 19.

Everyone was cognizant that, in the days ahead, when Mahar and Gramlick would meet their British counterparts they would do so with the knowledge that, during an operation of this magnitude, anything could happen. The devil is always in the details.

Chapter Thirty-Two

Into the Breach

Approximately ten days before the official launch of the exfiltration operation, Geoffrey O'Brian called Don Mahar down to his office in the Counter Intelligence Branch. Once again, John Cummings was sitting with him discussing the upcoming operation.

When Mahar arrived at the office, O'Brian confirmed some additional details with him in respect to the operational plan and then indicated that he was worried. He was concerned about Brik's state of mind. He wondered whether Brik might be getting anxious about the pending date of his escape, and he worried that Brik might take some precipitous action that could compromise him and the operation itself. With this in mind, O'Brian said that he would feel much more comfortable if Mahar would return to Scandinavia as soon as could be arranged in the event Brik tried to make an escape effort on his own. O'Brian stated that Mahar and Gramlick should meet again in Stockholm and wait there for the June 19 operation to begin. If Brik took action on his own, then the two CSIS officers would be in theater and, hopefully, be in a position to assist Brik.

In Aleksandrov, Brik continued to take the train back and forth to Moscow, partly to bolster his confidence that he could do so without interference from authorities and also to shop for items he might need during his escape. Brik would wander around the massive GUM department store on Red Square across from the Kremlin searching for items he might need at the time of his escape. At the end of the day, he would take the return train to Aleksandrov.

In order to test Russian and other East European border controls again, on June 2 he took the train all the way back to Vilnius, Lithuania. This of course was completely outside the parameters of the operational plan, and he knew it. He was "free styling" and could easily have derailed the operation before it even started. Nevertheless, while in Vilnius, Brik heard radio reports that

Russian president Boris Yeltsin decreed that it was urgently necessary to tighten border control points and alert customs officers to prevent foreign intelligence services from infiltrating agents into Russia from the Baltic States and Kazakhstan. Geoffrey O'Brian's earlier concerns were legitimate. Problems were beginning to materialize inside Russia. Were similar problems beginning to manifest themselves with Brik? Was he losing his nerve? With this worrisome news in hand, Brik nervously took the long train ride back to Aleksandrov and made certain that everything was in order for his escape.

On June 19, as scheduled and according to the operational plan, CSIS officer Don Mahar left Stockholm and flew to Kastrup International Airport, situated on the island of Amager, eight kilometers south of Copenhagen, Denmark. The previous day, the British SIS officers had taken up their positions. CSIS officer Gramlick had left Stockholm two days earlier and had flown into Vilnius International Airport. From this starting position, the exfiltration operation to get Yevgeni Brik out of Russia and back to Canada began.

Specific details about exfiltration operations are, by their very nature, highly sensitive and must remain classified. Methods of operation in successful cases may be used again in subsequent cases in the same country or in other parts of the world. Lessons learned from unsuccessful operations must be thoroughly analyzed and, where possible, changes must be introduced so these mistakes are never repeated. Such mistakes could cost the liberty, or worse, the life of the individual who is being helped to escape. Most importantly, nothing must ever be said that could possibly compromise human sources that may have played a role in effecting the escape of someone else.

And what about Yevgeni Brik himself? What was he thinking just before and after the operation began? How would he cope throughout the day? He was placing his fate into the hands of complete strangers. Did he ever wonder if his trust was misguided? At the moment of truth, would most people wonder the same thing?

Brik knew, of course, that he was not protected by diplomatic immunity if something dreadful went wrong during the operation and the participants were arrested. Because of the Geneva Convention, the Canadian and British intelligence officers, each with diplomatic passports, would be released and most likely declared persona non grata from Russia or whatever other country they were in if everyone was caught in the act. Not Brik. He would have no such protection.

Throughout the escape, he remained calm, assisted in part by a mild sedative that he consumed. It helped that he followed instructions and directions that were given to him. His moment of intense and emotional relief came after everyone was safe inside the secure area of Copenhagen's Kastrup International Airport. They made it. The operation was a success and remained secure. But he was not back in Canada yet.

With a flurry of handshakes, smiles, and a few photographs, the Canadian and British officers split up and went their separate ways. They would not meet as a team again. Everyone was immensely satisfied with the success of the mission. Everyone had parked their egos at the door for the good of the operation and, of course, for the good of Yevgeni Brik. Good intelligence, thorough planning, the ability to remain flexible, a dash of lady luck, and solid documentation assured a successful outcome.

Don Mahar and Yevgeni Brik found a quiet place to sit and unwind as they waited for a connecting flight to Stockholm. It had not been necessary to go through immigration or customs controls in Copenhagen as Mahar and Brik did not leave the secure area of the airport.

Following a brief wait in Copenhagen, their plane landed at Stockholm's Arlanda International Airport in the Sigtuna Municipality of Sweden, thirty-seven kilometers north of Stockholm. Swedish authorities, who previously had been briefed by Mahar, met them at the door of the aircraft and escorted them through the airport. Mahar went through the normal immigration and customs formalities while Swedish authorities, fully aware of Brik's cover name and documentation, escorted him behind the lines and down to a waiting car. When Mahar was clear of the Swedish controls, he joined the others and was driven into central Stockholm where a couple of large and comfortable suites were waiting for them at the Sheraton Hotel. The Swedish authorities were professional, helpful, and highly efficient.

CSIS officer Gordon Gramlick arrived at the Sheraton Hotel a couple of hours later and joined Mahar and Brik, who had settled into their suites. Gramlick produced a fine bottle of champagne, and the three men toasted the success of the mission as well as good health and a long life in Canada for Brik. Tired but jubilant, the men agreed that a good meal was in order. Exhausted from events of the day, they chose to order room service. Brik led the way, selecting sufficient food for himself that would have been more than adequate for all three. The following morning, prior to checking out, Mahar noticed that Brik had completely emptied the room bar fridge of all its liquor bottles and in-room snacks. As he was completely sober, it was evident that he stashed all the items in his suitcase for a future celebration.

The SAS flight from Stockholm to Heathrow International Airport north of London was uneventful. Brik was still using the Eugene Thompson documentation and experienced no difficulties whatsoever with immigration or customs officials. The Canadian Airlines 747 flight to Toronto was comfortable. Arrangements had been made to place Mahar and Brik in the upper deck of the aircraft. They were the only passengers in the section.

A few hours into the flight, Brik expressed an interest to the flight attendant that he would like to see the flight deck of the huge 747. Twenty minutes later, the flight attendant went forward and secured permission for Mahar and Brik to visit the captain and first officer. Brik was in total awe as he surveyed the flight deck. He was incredulous that there were only two pilots in the cabin. When he flew from Rio de Janiero to Paris in 1955 in the Super Constellation, there were two pilots, a navigator, and a radio operator on the flight deck. Brik was a little alarmed to see that both pilots sat in their chairs with their arms folded. When asked who was flying the plane, the pilot calmly responded that all the work was being done by the aircraft's onboard computers. Brik just shook his head and smiled.

During the trans-Atlantic crossing, Brik posed many questions about books and writers, musicians, and others in the arts that he enjoyed while he was living in Canada almost four decades previously. He loved reading the works of philosophers Friedrich Nietzsche and Bertrand Russell. Brik also studied Sigmund Freud, George Bernard Shaw, and Jean-Paul Sarte. He appeared amazed and somewhat shocked that the books of these famous writers were not staples in everyone's home library.

Even though Mahar and Brik were the only two passengers on the upper deck of the aircraft, there was very little discussion with respect to what had happened to him following his return to Moscow in 1955. Mahar knew that he would be spending months debriefing Brik in what would be a chronological, structured investigation of those lost thirty-seven years. He did not wish to burden Brik at this point as he knew his emotions during the past two days were highly charged.

As the Canadian Airlines 747 approached Lester B. Pearson International Airport in Toronto, Mahar knew that Canadian immigration officials had been prepped for their arrival. Mahar took possession of all the false documentation in the name of Eugene Thompson and stowed it away in his double-locked attaché case. At the same time, he removed an envelope that contained the preauthorized Minister's Permit. It contained Brik's photograph and was made out in his true name, date of birth, and country of origin. The permit, formally called A Permit to Come into or Remain in Canada, IMM 1263, was authorized in Ottawa on June 2, 1992, prior to Mahar's departure for Sweden to initiate the operation. The permit contained no other personal information about Brik or any details about his background. That information was contained in classified records in Ottawa that CSIS had shared with immigration officials after the operation had been approved at the senior government level.

The front-line immigration officer inside the arrivals hall at Lester B. Pearson International Airport reviewed Brik's IMM 1263 and Mahar's diplomatic passport and quietly directed them to immigration's secondary screening process area. There, another officer reviewed the IMM 1263 and stamped his permit accepting him into Canada. It was June 20, 1992. Brik was back in

Canada after a thirty-seven-year absence. The exfiltration operation and the journey back to Canada went off without a hitch. A promise made to him by Charles Sweeny on behalf of the Canadian Security Agency/RCMP Security Service to look after his interests was fulfilled. A promise made and a promise honored. It was an important moment in the life of one of Canada's most important and sensitive operations during the early stages of the Cold War.

The two fatigued men, intelligence officers from two different parts of the world, walked out of immigration and headed for their next departure gate for the final leg of their journey.

Mentally and physically exhausted from two days of subterfuge and travel, Mahar and Brik walked into the Ottawa International Airport arrivals lounge and were warmly greeted by CSIS officer Robbie McLeod, who had made temporary accommodation arrangements for Brik at a local hotel. A very nice surprise was having the CSIS Counter Intelligence deputy director general (Ops) Mr. John Cummings and his very classy wife, Susan, greet and welcome Brik to Canada. Susan Cummings presented him with a lovely bouquet of flowers, and then the entourage departed for downtown Ottawa.

The first couple of days in Ottawa were quiet ones for Brik. He needed the rest. There was no intention of commencing the lengthy debriefing of him until after he had ample time to recuperate and to become familiar with his surroundings.

During those early days, Carol Anne Mahar took Brik around the community and showed him how to shop in Canadian grocery stores, how to take a bus and pay for his fare, and how to use street-side pay telephones. Being seventy-one years of age, Brik needed help finding things he would need in the local pharmacy. Being a registered nurse, Carol Anne Mahar helped him find various items in the pharmacy and impressed upon him how helpful, trustworthy, and discreet pharmacists are. The two spent time together visiting small shops, corner stores, and how to adjust to the neighborhood he was living in. His accommodations were temporary. It was intended that he would likely remain in the upscale apartment that McLeod had rented for him until such time as Mahar's debriefing was completed. The time period would allow McLeod to get to know and understand what sort of long-term accommodations would be suitable for Brik and where he might wish to reside. Neither McLeod nor anyone else with knowledge of this case within CSIS recognized in the early days how much of a challenge this was going to present Robbie McLeod personally, or the Service in general.

A number of days after he had settled in to his new apartment and was feeling comfortable about his neighborhood, Mahar decided it was time to commence a comprehensive debriefing. Brik was introduced to Geoffrey O'Brian at CSIS National Headquarters in the East Memorial Building on Wellington

Street. O'Brian invited Brik and Mahar into his office for coffee and a courtesy visit with Brik. They were joined shortly thereafter by John Cummings. O'Brian welcomed Brik to Canada on behalf of the Service and asked about his well-being. Brik spoke briefly about his life the past few years and expressed his appreciation for what CSIS had done to help get him to Canada.

In the weeks and months that followed, Brik told a harrowing story about what had happened to him after the KGB failed to manipulate a meeting between him and SIS officer Daphne Park on the streets in Moscow.

Chapter Thirty-Three

The Lost Years

Yevgeni Brik's operational debriefing began in earnest a week after he arrived in Ottawa. These daily sessions were always conducted by Don Mahar. As their meetings progressed, Robbie McLeod would occasionally take charge of Brik for a day and take him off to view another apartment or deal with some other facet of his personal requirements. Health coverage, medical and dental examinations, and financial requirements were all matters that had to be attended to. McLeod was thorough and handled each of these important matters professionally and efficiently.

There was no expectation that Brik possessed time-sensitive intelligence of value to CSIS, the government of Canada, or to any of Canada's allies. The decades had past, and so too had many of the principals who were involved in this case.

But from a historical perspective, Brik filled in the huge gaps of knowledge that were created after his departure from Canada and his eventual arrival back in Russia.

He described to Mahar what it was like being taken by the KGB to face trial for treason. Standing before the Military Collegium in Moscow on September 4, 1955, Brik felt weak as he held onto the railing in front of him. He stood on trembling legs and felt that he might collapse. Brik knew what was coming. He waited for the military judge, a colonel in full uniform and adorned with campaign medals, to order his execution. He wished that his mother and wife were not in the courtroom to hear those awful words. He could scarcely process the colonel's command, to him and the officers present, that he was sentenced to a period of incarceration for fifteen years. Those surprising, unexpected words bounced off the paneled walls of the court and seemed to linger in the air forever. On either side of him, KGB minders were placing leg irons and handcuffs on Brik and pushing him toward the side room situated to the left of the judge.

Brik was confused and disoriented as he rode in the back of the prisoner truck as it returned to Lubyanka. Reality had not yet sunk in. He believed that the State was going to execute him. He knew that the penalty for treason was death. Yet here he was bouncing around in the back of a truck driving through the streets of Moscow. Was it all a frightful dream? Was it a trick? Would he be shot in the head when he least expected it, after he returned to Lubyanka?

Brik explained to Mahar that his new normal was sitting alone again in his solitary confinement cell in Lubyanka. His only activity came about when Nikolai Korznikov showed up with photographs for him to view. However, this only happened occasionally. Korznikov would show Brik a selection of images in an attempt to identify RCMP Security Service officers Terry Guernsey and Charles Sweeny and SIS officer Leslie Mitchell. The task was confusing to Brik as he only knew these men under the pseudonyms by which he was introduced to them. During earlier debriefings, Korznikov pointed out to Brik that he had been duped by Guernsey and Sweeny into thinking that he was working for the CSA. There was no such organization.

All the photographs that Korznikov produced for Brik's perusal appeared to be ordinary black-and-white passport photographs. There were no images of men in RCMP uniform, nor were there any photographs that appeared to have been taken surreptitiously by KGB officers out on the streets in Ottawa.

But most of the time, Brik sat in his cell and read. Guards would come by and provide him with a list of available books, and he would read until Korznikov made his next appearance. This boring routine continued for six months. What, if anything, was going on within the KGB about his case was never mentioned by Korznikov. Brik could not shake the notion that he still might be quietly taken aside and be summarily executed. He wondered if that was the reason he was being kept in Lubyanka rather than transferred to a prison as stipulated by the court. During his debriefing, Brik informed Mahar that he was never treated harshly by Korznikov or any of the guards while at Lubyanka.

One of the most frequently asked questions by those CSIS officers who knew that Brik had been exfiltrated from Russia and brought back to Canada was why he had not been executed for treason. It was a legitimate question. The KGB has a long history of eliminating its own officers and citizens who betrayed their country and cooperated with their adversaries throughout the decades. These executions have not stopped. One only needs to look at the Russian body count in more contemporary times. At least a dozen Russians who had been cooperating with the CIA and FBI were arrested, interrogated, and executed in the mid-1980s due to the respective betrayals by CIA officer Aldrich Ames and FBI officer Robert Hanssen. Nobody has documented this better than Sandra Grimes and the late Jeanne Vertefeuille, both former CIA officers, in their ground-breaking book *Circle of Treason: A CIA Account of Traitor Aldrich Ames and the Men He Betrayed.*[1]

Historians estimate that between eight and ten million people died as a result of decrees from Soviet dictator Josef Stalin and his KGB head, Lavrenti Pavlovich Beria. Following Stalin's death on March 5, 1953, scores of KGB officers who had been loyal to him were arrested and executed or, alternatively, sent to Soviet labor camps in the Gulag Archipelago. Beria himself was arrested on June 26, 1953, interrogated, tried, and executed on December 23, 1953.[2]

Yevgeni Brik believed that his life may have been spared due to the fear that certain KGB officers lived under because of who they backed within the intelligence service, or due to operational failures that they were directly linked to. Brik arrived back in Moscow two years after the death of Stalin, and the memory of the purges and killings were still very fresh at Lubyanka. Aleksandr Semyonovich Panyushkin, head of the KGB's First Chief Directorate (Foreign Intelligence), and others knew that he had betrayed the KGB and had been cooperating with the RCMP Security Service. It reflected badly on those working at The Centre. Although Brik did not have any personal knowledge of other KGB failures overseas, senior officers at The Centre were fully aware that the Directorate S, Illegals Department had suffered additional operational failures in other countries throughout the world.

Brik offered another possible explanation as to why he was not executed. The KGB in Ottawa maintained a dialogue with James Morrison, such as it was, and may have felt it advantageous to keep Brik alive in order to vet Morrison's statements with him.

Following the death of Stalin, hundreds of thousands of prisoners were released from the Gulag. The Soviet Criminal Code changed, and many who had been convicted under Section 58 of the Code for political crimes against the State, such as Brik, were incarcerated rather than executed. Nevertheless, the forced labor camps continued to flourish for many more years.

Brik advised Mahar that, as far as his memory could recall, he was removed from Lubyanka in approximately April 1957. Without any advanced warning, a KGB guard entered his cell and ordered him to collect his personal belongings. Guards escorted him to a truck and placed him into a cage that had been built into the back of the vehicle. Brik told Mahar that Korznikov was nowhere to be seen. Brik was certain that he was being taken to some remote location where he would be executed. It was very late at night or possibly early in the morning. Brik couldn't tell which. He rode in complete darkness and silence. There was no other person in the cage. He was afraid and hoped that he wouldn't be hanged. He knew that a firing squad would be quick. Brik was sorrowful that he was not given an opportunity to say farewell to either his wife or mother. He didn't want to die alone in the dark.[3]

Confused and disoriented, Brik was removed from the truck and walked to a railway carriage that was sitting on a spur, just off the main line. The carriage, a former passenger car, had been remodeled and converted to a prisoner carrier. Ten separate cells had been constructed in the carriage, with each cell fitted with four bunks. All the carriage windows were covered with steel bars. Brik was placed alone in a cell. The other cells were mostly empty, but Brik could see that there were prisoners further down the carriage. Armed guards entered the car and ordered complete silence. Within a half hour, Brik felt a strong jolt and the carriage rock as other cars were added. Shortly thereafter, the train began slowly to pull away.[4]

Brik informed Mahar that he didn't know it at the time, but he and the other prisoners were being transported to the ancient city of Vladimir, 180 kilometers northeast of Moscow. Situated on the Klyazma River, it is the home of the infamous Prison #2, of the Ministry of Internal Affairs. It is more commonly known as Vladimirskaya Tsentral or Vladimir Central Prison.

Brik was processed and given the opportunity to receive prison garb or the option of wearing his own clothing. He chose the latter. He was taken to the prison hospital and placed alone in a two-person cell separated from the other prisoners. The prison authorities knew nothing about his intelligence activities in Canada or the fact that he had become a double agent who had betrayed his country and the KGB specifically. Prison officials only knew that he had been convicted under Article 58 of the Soviet Criminal Code. Brik was not ill. Following instructions from the KGB, he was placed in the hospital block so that he could be watched closely while being isolated from the other prisoners.

Brik described the hospital block as being a three-level structure with twenty-five two-person cells on each level. The cells were separate from the actual infirmary itself. There was a small exercise yard where Brik would spend his time alone, never with other prisoners, while a guard watched over him. Lights remained on all night.

His daily routine changed very little during the years he spent in solitary confinement in the hospital block. Each morning at 0600 hours, a guard would stop outside his door and slip a plate of food through the opening. It was not always nutritious and seldom warm. He, along with other prisoners in the prison, seemed perpetually hungry. He was given a cup and sufficient tea to last throughout the day. Because he was in the hospital block, he also received a cup of milk each day.

There was a pail in the corner of his cell, and Brik would be given the opportunity each morning to take it to the toilet area to wash it out. After breakfast, prison staff would enter the cells in the general population and lock the bed up against the wall. However, the beds in the hospital block remained down where the prisoners could relax. There was a single chair that was permanently affixed to the floor. Brik told Mahar that he remained in his cell for most of the day and had little, or no, conversations with anyone. If he needed to use the toilet, he would have to ask a guard to release him from his cell. The guard would then escort him to the toilet area. After lunch, Brik would be taken to the exercise yard for an hour.

Brik confided to Mahar that he and the other prisoners had liberal use of the prison's library books. He would be provided with a list of holdings from which he could request four or five books. He stated that he read most of the books in the library, and some titles several times.

Once a month, Brik's mother would take the train from Moscow to Vladimir so that she could have a thirty-minute visit with her son. All prisoners were permitted to receive a small package of food or clothing. Brik's mother would do her best to bring him warm socks, blankets, and other clothing or food that was not available at the prison.

His wife, Antonina Lazareva, visited him in the early days of his incarceration, but her monthly visits dropped off and then ended all together. Brik learned that she met someone else, fell in love, and divorced him. He understood and accepted this. They had been apart for many years. She only saw him sparingly during his two years of KGB training in Moscow. He then left for Canada where he spent an additional four years separated from her. And now, he was in prison for an additional fifteen years.

Brik's only other visitors in the hospital block were KGB officers from Moscow who brought photographs for him to view. They were still attempting to identify Guernsey, Sweeny, and Mitchell. These visits were few and far between and offered nothing in terms of human comfort for him as he sat in isolation. Korznikov was never among the KGB visitors. Brik told Mahar that he never identified any of the photographs he was shown.[5]

After spending several months in solitary confinement, the prison guards interrupted his daily routine by placing another prisoner in his cell. Brik stated that it was both pleasing and awkward at the same time. He had become somewhat used to having his own private space and wasn't certain how he would accept this stranger. On the other hand, he had nobody to interact with on a daily basis and he missed having conversations with another human being.

Brik did not confide his background to this new cell mate. He did not know if he had just arrived at Vladimir Central Prison or whether he had been transferred to the hospital block from elsewhere in the prison. Brik would eventually come to know that his new cell mate was Grigori Moiseyevich Maironovsky.

A Soviet biochemist by education, Maironovsky became a member of the Bolshevik Party in 1920. He eventually worked at the Bach Institute of Biochemistry in Moscow and became head of the KGB's Laboratory No. 1 in 1938. His classified work for the KGB was focused on establishing and managing the KGB's secret poison program that would be used, when directed by higher authority, against enemies of the Soviet Union. It included experimentation with various poisons and injecting them into political prisoners who were awaiting execution by the State. Maironovsky's work was not restricted to the laboratory. It is reported that he personally participated in a number of assassinations of individuals who authorities considered to be anti Soviet. The late Soviet spymaster, Pavel Sudoplatov, who himself was incarcerated at Vladimir Central Prison, documented in his book *Special Tasks: The Memoirs of an Unwanted Witness, A Soviet Spymaster* that Maironovsky was directly involved in a number of assassinations. According to Sudoplatov, he had personal knowledge of assassinations that Maironovsky had conducted in 1946 and 1947. They were often conducted in the context of Maironovsky administering a needle during a routine medical checkup. In his book, Sudoplatov mentions the deaths of A. Shumsky, a Ukrainian nationalist, Archbishop Romzha of the Uniate Church in Western Ukraine, a Polish engineer named Samet, and Isaiah Oggins, a citizen of the United States.[6]

Sudoplatov speculated that Maironovsky injected a vial of poison into Swedish diplomat Raoul Wallenberg inside a highly classified unit called the *spetsialnie laboratornaya kamera* and that his body was later cremated as a result of a direct order issued by Viktor Semyonovich Abakumov, Soviet Minister of Security. Sudoplatov's theory has never been proven and has been discredited by others.

Chapter Thirty-Four

Strange Bedfellows

As the weeks and the debriefing of Yevgeni Brik progressed at CSIS headquarters, it was evident that he was unhappy in regard to his personal life, and this manifested itself in the operational debriefings as well. Brik's problems of a personal nature fell to Robbie McLeod to address. Brik was annoyed that he had not been awarded Canadian citizenship when he entered Canada or that he did not receive a Canadian passport shortly after he was settled. He was dissatisfied with his Landed Immigrant status, which he obtained when he entered Canada in Toronto on June 20, 1992. Nor was he content with the Canadian travel document that McLeod labored behind the scenes to get for him. Brik was beginning to exhibit some of the less savory aspects of his personality that were so evident in his relationship with RCMP officers Terry Guernsey and Charles Sweeny in the 1950s. These problems intensified when Brik made it clear that he did not like the attractive, partially furnished apartment complex that McLeod secured for him on Albert Street in Ottawa. Brik knew that it was not intended to be his permanent residence. McLeod had rented it on a month-to-month basis. It was to serve as his residence during the period of his debriefing by Mahar, as well his address while he was being resettled in Canada. McLeod was already seeking other suitable accommodations for him.

It was also around this same time when Brik dropped a bombshell during a debriefing with Mahar. He had previously mentioned having a girlfriend in Aleksandrov with whom he had been dating for twenty years. He briefly dropped her name to Mahar during their trans-Atlantic flight to Toronto, but stated clearly and unequivocally that they were simply friends. He stated that they each had their own apartment, lived separate lives, and simply dated.[1]

These facts changed dramatically when, during a debriefing with Mahar, he made the announcement that he was in fact married and that he wished to sponsor his wife to Canada and that he expected CSIS to help him make this happen. He explained that his wife, Galina Aleksandrovna Berezhnaya, knew nothing of his plans to leave Russia. He stated that he married her days before he left Aleksandrov for the exfiltration operation. He indicated that the reason he married her was so she could legally inherit all of his assets. Now that he had his feet planted in Canada, he wanted to bring her to Ottawa. Mahar learned from McLeod that he, too, had been told that Brik denied being married and only changed his story after he was reasonably settled in Ottawa.

As the operational debriefings resumed, Brik continued to speak to Mahar about his incarceration in the solitary confinement cells in the hospital block inside Vladimir Central Prison. His long isolation had initially been broken when prison authorities assigned Grigori Moiseyevich Maironovsky to share his cell. This partnership endured for several weeks. However, Maironovsky was removed from the cell and Brik was back living on his own again. In time, other prisoners would join him for various periods and then, they, too, would be rotated out. Considering Brik's career as a KGB Illegal, some of his cell mates made for very strange bedfellows.

Leonid Aleksandrovich Eitingon, also known as Naum Isakovich Eitingon, shared Brik's cell for a little over two months. Eitingon, a long-serving member of Soviet intelligence, was responsible for many kidnappings and assassinations. He was given responsibility of running the KGB Illegals program in the 1930s. One of his most successful operations was his management of the Manhattan Project at Los Alamos, New Mexico, and Berkeley, California. There were as many as forty KGB agents involved in the Manhattan Project that Eitingon was responsible for among the scientific community. The agents consisted of Russian Jews who had left Russia prior to the Russian Revolution.[2]

Two years after Brik and Eitingon shared a cell, prison authorities placed Brik and Pavel Anatolivich Sudoplatov together in the hospital block. As deputy director of Foreign Intelligence, Sudoplatov was an important and influential figure in Soviet intelligence.[3]

Josef Stalin had called on Sudoplatov and instructed him to organize the assassination of Leon Trotsky who, at the time, was living in exile at Coyoacan, just outside Mexico City. Trotsky vigorously opposed Stalin and authored numerous anti-Soviet and anti-Stalinist letters, editorials, and speeches, all of which infuriated the Soviet dictator. Sudoplatov oversaw and directed the planning of the assassination operation and selected Eitingon to lead it. Eitingon established two separate and independent operational teams, each with the aim of murdering Trotsky. Ramon Mercader del Rio, a Spanish communist, was a member of one of the teams. He established a romantic relationship with Sylvia Ageloff, a Trotskyist who had volunteered to work at Trotsky's home. The operation was set for August 20, 1940. Mercader gained access to Trotsky's home on that date through the assistance of Ageloff. She arranged for Mercader to have a private meeting with Trotsky in his personal study. It provided Mercader the opportunity to attack Trotsky with an ice axe, striking him over the head and severely injuring him. Trotsky survived the attack but died the following day in the hospital. Mercader was immediately apprehended by Trotsky's bodyguards, but Eitingon, who was waiting in a car outside Trotsky's home, escaped.[4]

Brik informed Mahar that he was moved from the hospital block and transferred to the five-person cells in the general population in early March 1960. He remembers the timeframe because it was two months before captured American U-2 pilot Francis Gary Powers arrived at the prison. Powers's U-2 aircraft had been shot down on May 1, 1960, twenty miles southeast of Sverdlovsk. The international incident caught President Dwight D. Eisenhower in an embarrassing web of deceit. He initially tried to convince the world that the U-2 was a weather plane that had accidently penetrated Soviet airspace. Having ensnared Eisenhower in a trap, Soviet president Nikita Khrushchev exposed Eisenhower's lies when he informed the Supreme Soviet that not only did they have parts of the U-2 wreckage, they also had Powers in custody. The remains of the U-2 were exhibited in Gorky Square where curious citizens rushed to see it. A show trial was held in Moscow with Powers's wife and parents in attendance. Expecting to be executed, Powers received a sentence of ten years and was sent to Vladimir Central Prison where he was incarcerated. He would spend seventeen months in captivity.

Francis Gary Powers was exchanged for Soviet KGB Illegal Colonel Vilyam Fisher, also known as Rudolph Abel, on February 10, 1962, at the Glienicke Bridge in Berlin. An American student who was being held in East Berlin was also swapped as part of this negotiation. He was released to American representatives at Checkpoint Charlie.[5]

While living in the five-person cells, Brik was given the job of cleaning out the toilets in the mornings. Occasionally, he would see Powers as he walked in the corridor as he headed out into the exercise yard. They never had a conversation or even exchanged words. The prisoners knew that Powers was among them. Brik told Mahar that the guards could not keep that kind of information to themselves. From the very beginning, Powers shared a cell with Zigurd Kruminsh, a Latvian political prisoner.

Brik advised Mahar that there were several other prisoners of note who were in the same prison block or who shared space in the five-person cells with him. One such person was Maksim Steinberg. Like Brik, he was a KGB Illegals Resident who functioned as a Swiss businessman in the 1930s. Steinberg and his wife refused to heed a recall to Moscow during the purges and remained in Switzerland. They later returned to Moscow following the death of Stalin, believing that amnesty protected them. This was not the case. Maksim Steinberg was sentenced to fifteen years and his wife to ten years.[6]

During his years at Vladimir Central Prison Brik's mother continuously advocated for better conditions for him. At one point, Brik was removed from his cell and taken to a private room where he was met by Colonel Shevchenko, the head of the Vladimir District KGB. Shevchenko admonished Brik and told him that his mother was constantly bothering and irritating Nikolai Korznikov in Moscow about Brik's conditions. She wanted prison authorities to provide him with warm clothes, extra food, and blankets. Brik told Mahar that it was true that Korznikov had kept in touch with his mother over the years and did what he could to assist her. Shevchenko instructed Brik to do what he could to influence his mother to stop bothering Korznikov. Sometime later, during a thirty-minute meeting with Brik, his mother told him that Korznikov had spoken to her and confided that Shevchenko was lazy and didn't want to work. He told her to ignore Shevchenko.

Brik remained in the five-person cells until January 1964. His mother, always agitating for her son, was responsible for what happened to him next.

Chapter Thirty-Five

Temnikovskiy Department of Camps

During a break in the debriefing protocol with CSIS officer Don Mahar, Yevgeni Brik spent additional time with CSIS officer Robbie McLeod. One of Brik's sincerest wishes was to obtain an Ontario driver's licence and to purchase a new vehicle, a GMC Tracker. McLeod had very good relations with key individuals within the provincial and federal government departments. He was quite prepared to speak with his contacts in the Ontario Department of Motor Vehicles. But before he could do so, Brik struck out on his own and tried, in his normal fashion, to ram a square peg into a round hole. When things didn't go the way he wanted, whether it be at the Department of Motor Vehicles or any other place, he would get obnoxious, rude, and try to intimidate people to get what he wanted. It didn't work in this case. He was told that his application was rejected due to poor vision. Shocked and upset, Brik took the news badly. This subject became an ongoing issue and matter of complaint while working with McLeod.[1]

On another occasion, Brik disappeared after McLeod had arranged for him to get a Canadian travel document. He had not given McLeod, or anyone else, any indication that he was going away. He was under no obligation to do so. Nevertheless, it was disconcerting that he disappeared.

It was later established that Brik had taken a bus to Montreal and then crossed the Canada/US border as a passenger on an Amtrak train. Within hours he was in New York City. He visited the old Flatbush neighborhood of Brooklyn where he and his parents lived in the late 1920s and early 1930s, and found his childhood home at 1119 Foster Avenue. He walked the streets and found the play yards and his old elementary school. This is where it had all started for him. During the next several days, Brik visited different neighborhoods and toured the Empire State Building, the Chrysler Building, NBC Studios, and Times Square. He returned to Ottawa the same way that he left.

Although Robbie McLeod and others were worried about his sudden disappearance, it was understood that he needed this break and found comfort in the nostalgia of visiting his childhood home.[2]

In his leisure time in Ottawa, which he had a lot of, Brik would wander the Bank Street, Elgin Street, or Byward Market areas of the city searching for used books and other bargains. He would occasionally telephone Mahar from a street phone and excitedly inform him of the price of bananas that day or describe a book that he purchased that he originally read in the 1950s. His mood would change from day to day, and one never quite knew which Yevgeni Brik was going to show up. Some days he was easy to get along with. Alternatively, he would quite literally be an uncompromising, nasty individual.

Brik was never satisfied with the very nice, comfortable accommodations that McLeod found for him. He would complain bitterly about his apartment, McLeod would find another, and he would complain again. On one occasion, Brik went out and purchased sheets of plywood and then nailed them to the walls and across door openings as he closed off a portion of a very nice apartment because he felt it was too large for him.

Brik decided on his own that he wished to move into a certain high-rise building on Rideau Street. McLeod did his best to discourage his choice as the building had a bad reputation and was notorious for being a problem spot. It also had a troubled reputation for attracting undesirables. Brik would not be deterred. Against his better judgment, McLeod rented Brik a one-bedroom apartment on the eighth floor of the building. The two went out shopping to local stores to furnish it. In time, Brik added a number of bookshelves that he built himself inside the apartment. He would travel by city bus to lumber supply stores, have the wood precut, and then ride the bus back to his apartment carrying a few pieces of wood on each trip. He subsequently moved to a two-bedroom apartment in the same building on the eleventh floor.

When the operational debriefings resumed with Don Mahar, Brik spoke of his mother's intervention with prison authorities in Vladimir. She was tenacious in advocating for better conditions for her son. In spite of Colonel Shevchenko, she continued to petition Soviet officials in Moscow and Vladimir during the eight years that he was imprisoned. Brik was surprised to hear that because of his mother's advocacy she was instrumental in having officials convene a special tribunal to discuss his case. Her objective was to get her son out of prison and transferred to a labor camp where he would serve out the remainder of his sentence in conditions where he would have more liberty and be outdoors. She hoped his life would be easier in the camps than it currently was being caged up in a small cell with four other men. She was aware that many prisoners had been abused inside the confines of Vladimir Central Prison. But Brik assured his mother, a point he reinforced during his debriefings, that he was never physically mistreated.[3]

In January 1964, the tribunal ruled in his favor and Brik was released from Vladimir and placed on a train for the long journey on the Kazanskaya Railway System to the Mordovian Autonomous Soviet Socialist Republic. The railway line ran from Moscow to Saransk, Mordovia. His destination was the Temnikovskiy Department of Camps, which was a collection of nineteen labor camps. It was part of the Gulag, which was constructed on the orders of Josef Stalin. The Soviet's referred to them as work correction camps. The headquarters for the Temnikovskiy Department of Camps was located in a small village named Yavos, which was situated close to Camp #12. The nineteen labor camps were stretched out over the twenty-five-kilometer main railway line.

Between Gorky and Saransk, there is a railway stop at a village called Potma where convicts are removed from the trains and transported to a distribution camp. The prisoners are divided into groups dependent upon which section of the Soviet Criminal Code they were convicted of. The prisoners do not serve their time at the distribution camp. As Brik was convicted under Article 58 of the Code, he was sent to one of the camps designated for Article 58 offenders. The train ran between Potma and Temnikovka twice per day. One run facilitated transportation for local residents of the villages, camp workers, and Soviet Ministry of Internal Affairs (MVD) officials. The second run was for the transportation of prisoners to the various camps.

Much has been written about the horrors and deaths in the Gulag over the years. Millions died, entire families wiped out. In 1953, following the death of Stalin, the Soviet government declared a general amnesty to all common prisoners who were incarcerated in the labor camps. The camps emptied as the surviving prisoners were released. However, the general amnesty did not apply to political prisoners who were convicted under Article 58 of the Soviet Criminal Code. These convicts were enemies of the State.

By 1958, the camps were filled to capacity once again, primarily with political prisoners. It is believed there were approximately fourteen million political prisoners in the camps across the USSR. In an effort to alleviate this problem, Working Committees of the Supreme Soviet began hearings at the various camps in an effort to release political prisoners back into Soviet society. Tens of thousands were released under the authority of these committees.

Brik was sent to Camp #7 directly from the distribution center. It is situated near the village of Sosnovka, which is simply a railway station stop. He spent three years in Camp #7, between 1963 and 1966. Cooks, carpenters, electricians, and MVD officials who worked at Camp #7 lived in Sosnovka. Conditions were basic for both prisoners and the workers.

Brik had only basic knowledge of the makeup of the Temnikovskiy Department of Camps and no knowledge at all of some of them. There were two camps that were strictly for women offenders. Camp #2 was one of these, but Brik did not know the other. The main infirmary for the Temnikovskiy Department of Camps was located in Camp #3. There were separate infirmaries for men and women. Only the most seriously ill or injured prisoners were admitted to these infirmaries. All the other camps had smaller medical facilities that were used for those suffering minor injuries or illness.

All foreign prisoners were held in Camp #5. It was generally known among the prisoners that conditions in this camp were better than others. The prisoners were common criminals from foreign countries who had been convicted of drug offenses and other similar crimes. No political prisoners were held in this camp.

One of the most difficult and abusive camps was Camp #10, which contained repeat criminal offenders. Brik stated that stories about what happened in this camp were particularly brutal and frightening.

A second camp for political prisoners was Camp #12, near the village of Yavos. In 1966, many of the prisoners from Camp #7 were transferred to Camp #12. Brik was one of them. He remained in Camp #12 until 1970.

Camp #19 was a third camp for political prisoners. It, however, functioned as a clearinghouse as prisoners from Camps #7 and #12 were sent here approximately six months prior to their release date from custody. Brik was transferred here in February 1970. The camp was located near the village of Temnikovka.

All the camps were administered by the Soviet Ministry of the Interior (MVD). There were guard towers surrounding each camp with heavily armed MVD officers standing watch. None of the MVD officers who worked inside the camps carried weapons. Armed MVD officers with dogs patroled the outer perimeter on a twenty-four-hour basis.

Brik informed Mahar that when he arrived at the Temnikovskiy Department of Camps it was generally believed there were approximately 2,500 political prisoners in Camp #7. Most were from Russia or the Baltics who had fought with the Germans against Russia during World War II. They all were Article 58 offenders who had been convicted of everything from anti-Soviet behavior to treason.

Brik was housed in a barracks-like facility. There were forty bunk beds in one long room. There were only two doors in the building, one at each end. The aisle space down the length of the room was narrow, measuring one and a half meters in width. The building was of wood construction, and there was a common bathroom with showers in the middle of the building. Outside the building was a wooden security wall, topped with barbed wire, which stood five meters high. Beyond it was a no-man's-land or neutral zone, ten meters wide, which was covered with a layer of fine sand that was raked regularly by

MVD officers. A prisoner's footprints would be readily observed if anyone should attempt an escape. Beyond the neutral zone was a second, outer fence constructed of barbed wire.

The concept of escape may have often been in the minds of prisoners. However, in reality, there had only been three successful attempts during the period of time that Brik was in Camp #7. In each case, the prisoner was arrested shortly after he cleared the outer, barbed wire fence. During one of the escapes, the prisoner was spotted by the guards who opened fire on him. He lost an arm and very nearly his life. All three prisoners had an additional three years added to their sentences.

Each night two unarmed MVD officers walked through the barracks room every two to three hours. The prisoners were awakened daily at 0600 hours and had their bathroom break and cleaned up their sleeping area. They would go to the dining hall for breakfast, which normally consisted of cereal. By 0730 hours the prisoners would form up outside of their barracks. There were approximately two hundred prisoners who lined up outside Brik's building. An MVD official would take roll call by calling out each prisoner's family name. The prisoner would respond with his given name, then his patronymic name, and finally his year of birth. When this was completed, the prisoners, under the watchful eyes of the MVD officers in the towers and those on the ground, would be marched out the gate and off to a work area in another part of the camp.

The political prisoners of Camp #7 spent eight hours per day in the wood-working building. They were fed lunch in a designated eating area where they were working. At 1700 hours, they were lined up once again, at which point MVD officers searched each prisoner for screwdrivers, nails, chisels, or anything else that could potentially be used as a weapon. If caught with such an item, the prisoner would be harshly dealt with.

The prisoners would then be marched back through the gates and to their individual barracks where they were dismissed. They were free to mix with each other or lie on their bunks. Following dinner, the prisoners played chess, engaged in soccer, wrote letters, or read books that they got from their camp library. One night per week, movies were projected against a white bedsheet that was hung on a wall in the barracks. Due to the isolation of the camp, the boredom, and loneliness, the movies played an important role in the morale for the prisoners, the MVD, and camp workers. It was common for the prisoners and the others to swap movies. Although this was strictly against regulations, the reality was that the movie swaps provided some variety from the dreary existence for all who resided and worked in the region. Camp #7 had a decent library and reading room that could accommodate forty prisoners at a time. Brik was a frequent visitor to the library. Guards and prison workers often supplemented the library with books they obtained elsewhere.[4]

In describing personal circumstances, Brik spoke to Mahar about daily living in Camp #7. Personal clothing was strictly prohibited. All prisoners wore standard prison garb. The prisoners' heads had to be shaved and kept that way. They were given very little money. Each prisoner could receive one five-kilogram parcel of food from relatives every six months. The monthly visits that Brik had with his mother while he was in Vladimir Central Prison was reduced to one visit per year.

Brik stated that the guards were not abusive to the ordinary prisoners in the camp. The vast majority of prisoners caused no trouble while incarcerated. They burned off their frustrations and angry emotions on the soccer field or when playing volleyball. However, when there was violence, it was brutal and fell along ethnic lines where long-standing feuds would be settled. In this context, murders within the camp were not uncommon, nor was suicide. Brik was aware of several prisoners who had taken their own life in Camp #7.

Brik confided that during his many years at the Temnikovskiy Department of Camps the KGB never visited him. His final meetings with them had been while he was still a prisoner in Vladimir Central Prison. He never saw KGB officer Nikolai Korznikov again. He heard that Korznikov lost his stature within the KGB, was demoted, and was exiled to a less important Republican KGB office away from Moscow. Brik heard from others that Korznikov, having been demoted and marginalized, had fallen into alcoholism. Brik privately wondered if Korznikov had become the convenient scapegoat for the problems and failures within Directorate S and paid the price.

In February 1970, Brik was advised to gather his few belongings and prepare to be transferred to Camp #19. He had been an inmate in camps #7 and #12 for seven years. Let there be no doubt, Brik was a survivor.

A few years back, he was aware that there were prisoners who were being pardoned of their crimes and released from the camps. For the most part, these were prisoners who had family members who had emigrated from the USSR to Germany. The Soviet and German governments were discussing and negotiating protocols for family reunification. Brik knew one of the Russian prisoners who everyone anticipated would be released and sent to Germany in order to reunite with his family. Brik confided to Mahar that he wanted to write a letter to Canadian authorities to inform them that he was alive and in the Gulag. But he didn't know who the Russian should approach in Canada. He wanted them to know that they had a traitor within their ranks. But he knew that the prisoner would be thoroughly searched before he would be released from the labor camp. He knew nothing about RCMP Security Service officer James Morrison, but he did know that he himself had been arrested, detained, and incarcerated because someone from Canada had betrayed him. If the traitor wasn't Canadian, then perhaps it might have been someone in British intelligence, perhaps even disgraced former SIS officer Kim Philby himself. In the end, Brik knew there was too much risk to the Russian who would be leaving for Germany, and too much risk for himself. He abandoned the letter idea.

Brik had become well acquainted with two respected Soviet writers who were prisoners in Camp #12 while he was there. Nikolai Erdman and Mikhail Volpin were successful writers and filmmakers.[5] They wrote about tyranny in the USSR and smuggled their work out to France where they were published. Brik was fond of the musical play they wrote called *Hello Moscow*. He struggled with the idea of confiding his story to the writers and asking them to contact authorities in Canada. However, he didn't have the courage to do so. They eventually left the camp not knowing anything about Brik's story.

With his imagination working overtime, Brik once again began to plot the hijacking of an aircraft from inside the USSR to Western Europe. His previous ill-conceived hijacking plan in 1955 never materialized after his wife informed KGB officer Korznikov. That plan was used against him at his trial. However, while in camp, Brik heard news that the countries of the United Nations had enacted harsh penalties for anyone hijacking aircraft and flying them to UN country destinations. He gave up on his latest hijacking fantasy and fell into depression.

Throughout the years in the Temnikovskiy Department of Camps, Brik never confided his true story to any of the prisoners. When anyone asked of his background, he simply stated that he had been in the United States working as a translator at the United Nations. He had the knowledge of New York and a solid backing of English to make this a believable story. Years earlier, he had been warned not to divulge any information about his background or activities in Canada. He believed the KGB had informers within the prison and labor camp population and he did not wish to get in trouble with them again. He knew he would face retribution from the KGB if they learned that he disobeyed them.[6]

Chapter Thirty-Six

Time Served

It was a gorgeous summer day as the sun drenched the prisoners and workers at Camp #19, along with the inhabitants of the nearby village of Temnikovka. It was August 19, 1970, precisely fifteen years to the day that Yevgeni Brik had arrived back in Moscow from Ottawa in 1955. So much had happened to him after he descended the stairs from the aircraft and was driven to KGB headquarters at Lubyanka by KGB officer Nikolai Korznikov.

A few days earlier, Brik was summoned to the Camp #19 administration office and asked where he intended to travel to when discharged from the camp. MVD officials had to purchase a train ticket to his destination. These same officials had already prepared an internal passport that he would have to carry on his person at all times. It would be given to him on discharge. The second page of his internal passport was stamped to show that he was a convict and that he had been imprisoned at Vladimir Central Prison and the Temnikovskiy Department of Camps.

He received no instructions from Soviet officials dictating where he would be required to live. But after years living in the prison system, he knew there were rules that he had to adhere to. As a convicted prisoner, he was forbidden to reside in any of the capital cities of the Soviet Republics. Although he privately wished to go to Moscow, Brik told the MVD officials that he wanted to live in Aleksandrov.

Twenty-two years later, while sitting in CSIS officer Don Mahar's office, Brik confided that he was fearful of being released from the camp and walking through the gates. He had heard stories of prisoners getting their hopes up on the day of their release only to have them dashed when MVD officers took them instead to the trains and sent them to the labor camps at Tyanya along the Lena River in Siberia. The stories were punctuated with anecdotes of prisoners who went to Tyanya that were never released from there. The MVD added to the prisoner's fears by stating that the MVD officers who were sent to work in the camps at Tyanya never left there either.

Brik told Mahar that on the day of his release from the Temnikovskiy Department of Camps he was taken to the administration office and given his internal passport and what few personal belongings were his. Some of the clothes he received back were the very clothes that he wore fifteen years earlier when he was arrested at KGB headquarters. Brik was taken back to the Distribution Camp at Potma and was given a form that would allow him to obtain a train ticket to Aleksandrov. Brik was also given a food package that provided him with sufficient herring, bread, and cheese for three days. He also received three thousand rubles that he saved while in the camps. He had received eighty rubles a month while a camp inmate and paid back forty rubles a month for his food and housing. Not only did he lose his liberty for years but also he had to pay for it. Each prisoner was permitted to spend seven rubles per month, which left them savings of thirty-three rubles each month.[1]

Brik took the travel voucher he had just received, walked to the train station, and exchanged it for a one-way ticket to Aleksandrov. He sat quietly and kept to himself as he rode the slow train back to Moscow. He had received permission to stay overnight in Moscow, and then he would be required to continue the train trip to Aleksandrov the following day. He had not seen Moscow in fifteen years. So many things had changed; so many things remained the same. He felt self-conscious in his old 1950s clothing. But he shouldn't have worried as people were too busy to notice. The traffic and the abundance of cars took him by surprise.

Brik told Mahar that he also felt intimidated and paranoid. He believed everyone was watching his every move. He tried to determine if he was under KGB surveillance and could not trust anyone for fear they were KGB informers. He was elated to be a free man again but questioned whether he was really free.

Brik sought directions and then walked to the closest militia station. Once again, defying rules and regulations that prohibited convicted prisoners to reside in Moscow, he attempted to register himself as a resident of his mother's Moscow apartment. Naturally, the militia asked him to produce his internal passport and readily saw that he was a convicted person who had served fifteen years in prison and the labor camps.

Brik once again boarded a train and traveled north of Moscow to a small village approximately forty kilometers from Pereslavi where his aunt resided. His aunt went immediately to the local militia office and registered Brik as being a resident of her home. He remained with her for a few days, moved on to Pereslavi for a few more, and then completed his trip to Aleksandrov where he began to look for a place where he could live permanently.

While Brik found temporary, short-term housing, his aunt contacted a friend in Aleksandrov and asked for her assistance in finding something permanent for Brik. This friend and her divorced daughter, Galina Aleksandrovna Berezhnaya, searched in vain for an entire month on Brik's behalf but found nothing. Berezhnaya become rather ill and required medical assistance. Brik was grateful for the work she and her mother had done on his behalf. He showed his gratitude by accompanying her to Moscow where he assisted her to get admitted to the hospital. He had not had female company in fifteen years and had become attracted to Berezhnaya during the month she was searching for an apartment for him. She was admitted to a ward with four other ladies on the fifth floor of the hospital. Brik asked her to go to the window in her room and stand where he could see her from the street below. Brik, who had found employment in Aleksandrov as a photographer, would leave work every day at six o'clock in the evening, take the train to Moscow, and go to the hospital and stand on the street at nine o'clock. She was always standing in the window waiting for him. Defying regulations again, he would then go to his mother's apartment and spend the night with her. He would get up at four o'clock in the morning, go to the Moscow train station, and take the three-hour train trip back to Aleksandrov and go to work. He did this every day for an entire month. On the one day a week when he had a day off, he would spend the full day with Berezhnaya in the hospital where they would visit and talk.

Brik and Berezhnaya dated regularly throughout 1971. The following year, they announced that they would live in a common-law relationship. However, they both chose to keep their respective apartments, choosing to live off and on together three or four times per week. They did not marry, nor did they register with local authorities that they were living in this type of arrangement. In 1970, the head of the local MVD had authorized Brik to reside in Aleksandrov. However, he warned that if he ever married, authorities in Moscow would not register the marriage, nor would they ever allow Brik to reside in Moscow. Brik and Berezhnaya lived with this type of arrangement for the next twenty years.

Brik worked as a professional photographer in a local photographic studio from the time he settled in Aleksandrov until he left the small company in 1974. He alleged that the people he worked with were drinking on the job, did substandard work, and were skimming money from the cash receipts. He quit from the studio and obtained employment at the Aleksandrov railway station. His new responsibilities were not very onerous. He was employed as a security guard where he watched over the railway's grain storage areas. It was exactly the kind of job he was looking for. He worked twenty-four-hour shifts, then had three days off until his next shift started again. Although it was completely against railway regulations, he slept throughout the night without any fear of retribution because his supervisors slept as well. Brik was issued a World War I revolver that he wore during all of his shifts. Brik told Mahar that the irony of him being a convicted prisoner carrying a loaded weapon was not lost on him. He believed that the Moscow KGB never knew of this.

Drinking on the job was commonplace among the security guards at night. However, Brik had not had any alcohol since he was in Paris in 1955. Several of the guards he was working with would allow people into the grain compound to steal grain and sunflower seeds. The guards would receive bottles of vodka in return. Having spent fifteen years in prison and the labor camps, Brik was not about to jeopardize his liberty only to be incarcerated again. He kept this job until 1978.

Having three days off after his shift provided Brik with plenty of time to spend with Berezhnaya and to take the train to Moscow to visit with his aging mother. It also was sufficient time for him to establish his own photography business in order to supplement his income.

He continued to work at the railway but received a transfer from the security guard position to that of a railway dispatcher. Four years later, Brik retired on pension. It was short-lived. In order to augment his pension, he was employed once again at the railway station, this time working outside in the train yards. The following year he found work in the baggage department. It was all heavy, manual work, but he was earning a good wage.

Brik went into full retirement from the railroad in 1985. He was sixty-four years of age. In addition to his pension, he had earned a lifetime railway pass that would prove, in time, to be more valuable than the pension he received. He continued to operate his photographic studio and kept busy doing school graduations and other similar photographic jobs. He had acquired good equipment and had built a complete developing lab in his apartment, similar to the one he had at Portraits by Soboloff in Verdun, Quebec.

Brik's mother had moved from Moscow and was living at Brik's apartment where he was taking care of her. She was eighty-eight years of age and in poor health. During the next two years, he would feed her daily, and Galina Berezhnaya would go to Brik's apartment and bathe her three times per week. His mother, Natalia Stepanovna Brik, the attractive teacher from Novorossiysk, the only person who devoted years to look after his personal comforts, the mother who loved him, died in 1987. She was ninety years of age.

Brik confided to Mahar that he had only one contact with the KGB from the time of his release from the Temnikovskiy Department of Camps in August 1970 until his mother passed away in 1987. And that was a contact he initiated himself following his first retirement in 1982. Brik told Mahar that he ran into a problem while preparing the submission of pension documents. In order to be eligible for his full pension, he had to account for the years he was in training to become a KGB Illegal as well as the years he spent in Canada. Brik took the train to Moscow and walked to Lubyanka where he sought advice from the duty officer at the KGB reception room. He had not been to Lubyanka since he was transported to Vladimir Central Prison. He admitted to Mahar that he felt very strange walking into the den of the KGB. The last time he was there he expected to be executed. He subsequently received a certificate that stated that he had been working at Plant #347, which was described as a Soviet government facility. There was no information provided related to the name of the plant or what it produced. Brik submitted the certificate with the other required forms and began to receive his full pension. His pension benefits rose quickly over the years, particularly during perestroika. In 1990, Brik was receiving a very respectable 1,500 rubles a month as a pensioner who was also a war veteran. He had been wounded twice during the Great Patriotic War and had been awarded the Red Star First Degree and also the Red Star Second Degree.[2]

The KGB frequently visited the Aleksandrov train station while Brik worked there, but those visits had nothing to do with him or his activities of the past.

Events in Eastern Europe, and inside Russia itself during the late 1980s through to 1991, had a profound effect on Brik, as they did of course with Russians of all walks of life. It was then that Brik recognized the true value of his train pass.

Chapter Thirty-Seven

Perestroika, Glasnost, and the Soviet Railway System

During his years of imprisonment, Yevgeni Brik wanted to reach out to Canadian intelligence. But in spite of this, he instinctively knew that there was virtually no chance that he would ever see Canada again. Or, for that matter, any other country outside the Soviet Union.

When perestroika started, Brik believed that it was simply the beginning of a boisterous campaign that would lead nowhere. He had lived through the governments of Stalin, Khrushchev, Brezhnev, and others and believed that perestroika would die a horrible death like all the other ill-conceived plans they put forward. But things were changing.

In 1988, Soviet president Mikhail Gorbachev's expansion of glasnost declared that the press was free to report and ask questions on everything. No subject was taboo or off limits for open discussion in the media. It started slowly and took several months to take hold. But as Brik explained to Mahar, the Soviet press became more independent and, in his words, democratic.

He was also fascinated to see that many Russians were obtaining exit visas that allowed them to travel abroad temporarily, especially to the United States. He understood that convicted political prisoners, such as himself, those considered enemies of the people, would never be granted an exit visa from the Soviet Union.

The collapse of the Berlin Wall on May 9, 1989, was a watershed moment for Brik. It illustrated to him that people would no longer remain subjugated by communist authorities. This was never so evident than the reunification of East and West Germany. The public repudiation and outright challenge of communism was shocking to him. What did it all mean? What did it portend?

Brik was very skeptical in the spring of 1990 when Lithuania proclaimed its independence from the USSR and the Hitler/Stalin pact was denounced in Moscow. He did not believe that the Lithuanian experiment would succeed.

Nevertheless, he reasoned that if it did, perhaps he could become a Lithuanian citizen because his father was born in Libawa, Lithuania. He rationalized that with independence, the Soviet military would be pulled back to the USSR, which would give him the opportunity to travel to Vilnius and seek out the Canadian Embassy. He saw this as being the first real chance of escaping the USSR. However, to his disappointment, he began to discount this scheme when he read newspaper accounts of travelers having to clear both Soviet and Polish checkpoints. He spent many nights conjuring up different ideas and methods of how he could obtain a Soviet exit passport and take the train to Vilnius. He considered using some gold coins that he received from his father's estate. Brik had hidden them but wondered if he could use them now as a bribe in order to get the documents he required. In the end, he did nothing. He was fearful of being discovered and sent back to prison.

In August 1991, following the putsch in Moscow, Lithuania and Latvia demanded the removal of the KGB from their respective territories and that they be returned to Moscow. Brik informed Mahar that it was a very significant event for him personally because it was the presence of the KGB in these countries that caused him great concern with regard to potential escape scenarios. Several articles appeared in local newspapers that documented the sacking of KGB headquarters in Vilnius with citizens, and even members of the Lithuanian parliament, stealing KGB files. Events such as these emboldened Brik to reconsider escape scenarios through either Lithuania or Latvia.

In the wake of these developments, Brik approached Galina Berezhnaya and asked her if she would consider moving with him to Lithuania. She turned him down flat, indicating she could not leave her adult son. She was concerned about his ability to look after himself. Her previous husband had serious alcohol issues, and she did not want to see her son end up the same way. It was then that Brik decided that he would formulate escape plans on his own.[1]

At the end of August 1991, Brik took the train to Moscow from Aleksandrov and went in search of one of the several Information Bureaus in the city. Finding one, he approached a female attendant and, without identifying himself, asked her for the address of the British Embassy. He paid her a small fee and received the information he was looking for. He then asked her for the address of the Canadian Embassy. She returned with the address and the telephone numbers as well. He left the Information Bureau feeling good. He had accomplished something that might assist him in his escape. He knew that a year earlier, such information would have been considered secret. He had no doubt that the attendant, at that time, would have contacted the KGB.

Brik left the Information Bureau and began walking in search of the Canadian Embassy. He intended to ask for an appointment with a French Canadian diplomat, a First Secretary, who he had seen being interviewed on a Moscow television network. The diplomat had appeared in the interview alongside a second Canadian diplomat, a Second Secretary, who had a Ukrainian-sounding name. Brik confided he would not speak to the Ukrainian Canadian because, as he told Don Mahar during the debriefing, he would not be able to trust him.

As he approached the Canadian Embassy, Brik saw that there was a militia officer standing next to a long line of visitors to the embassy who were waiting to get in. He suspected they were all Soviet citizens seeking visas for Canada or to get documents notarized. He confided to Mahar that he walked past the embassy, eyes straight ahead, and never once even glanced in the direction of the militia officer. He did not wish to bring any attention to himself whatsoever. Brik made his way to the railway station and returned to Aleksandrov.

Brik returned to the Canadian Embassy the following week. Once again, he saw there was a long line of people waiting to gain access to the embassy. His strategy was that he would approach someone in the line and begin a general conversation. He noticed that everyone in line was holding papers of some description. He wondered if they were letters of invitation to Canada from family members, other Canadian citizens, or perhaps private companies or universities. He approached a gentleman and began asking him what exactly he needed to get into the embassy. The man responded, too loudly, that he didn't know but that Brik should ask the militia captain standing by the embassy door, just a few feet away. Brik wanted to turn and run. However, the captain, who had heard the exchange, inquired about what it was that Brik wanted. Brik told him that he had an elderly relative in Canada who wrote to him every few months. He explained that he had not heard from this relative for quite a long time and he wanted to seek the assistance of the embassy to determine his relative's fate. The militia officer barked at him and told him to go to the International Red Cross. Brik turned and left and never returned to the Canadian Embassy in Moscow again.[2]

Back in Aleksandrov, Brik worked on a different strategy. He visited the library on a regular basis and read all the newspapers and magazines he could find to become better acquainted with what was going on in the Baltics, East Europe, and Scandinavia. He devoured the newspapers of Vilnius in an effort to determine if Canada had opened an embassy in Lithuania. He then decided to use his rail pass and take a trip to Riga, Latvia, to test whether he could leave Russia without being stopped and returned to Aleksandrov. He felt he would be able to get a good sense of what was going on in the region by visiting Riga. To his surprise and delight, Brik was able to exit Russia and travel without difficulty to Riga. Once there, he was astounded by the presence of anti-Russian elements everywhere he looked. Everything Russian was being denounced. At one point, he asked some people for directions. Finding out that he was Russian, he was sent a long way in the opposite direction. He stayed in Riga overnight and returned to Aleksandrov the following day.

In early September 1991, Brik rode the train back to Moscow. On this occasion, he visited the Lithuanian Embassy. Noting that there were no militia officers stopping visitors from entering the embassy, Brik stepped in and spoke to a woman at the reception desk. He informed her that he would like to speak to one of the diplomats about obtaining information concerning the possibility of immigrating to Lithuania. He was directed to a side room where he found two diplomats working at their desks. He inquired about general conditions in Lithuania and whether many countries had formally recognized their independence. If so, had any of these countries established embassies in Vilnius? Receiving a positive response, he asked whether the United States, the United Kingdom, Germany, or Canada had opened diplomatic premises. The ladies responded by confirming that all those countries were now represented in Vilnius. When asked for the addresses of each of these embassies, Brik was told that, as these developments were all new, they did not have that information yet. But they were certain that these countries had opened temporary embassies in major hotels in Vilnius. Brik thanked the ladies for their assistance and indicated that he would return the following month, by which time he hoped they would be able to provide the addresses of the embassies in Vilnius. One of the diplomats advised that she would do her best to accommodate him. When Brik stepped outside, he noted that there were still no militia guards present. There was, however, a Polish guard by the gate who was not paying close attention to those arriving at the embassy.

Testing his ability to travel outside of Russia a second time, Brik once again took the train from Aleksandrov to Moscow and from Moscow to Riga, Latvia. He had no difficulties whatsoever crossing out of Russia. He chose not to stay overnight in Riga on this occasion. As he had arrived two hours before the shops were open, he washed and shaved in a filthy bathroom in the train station. Brik walked the streets until the shops opened up and found a small café where he had breakfast.

The train trip from Moscow to Riga took fourteen hours. It was important for Brik to take another journey of this nature because he had read in the newspapers that Lithuania and Latvia had instituted customs and immigration controls at their respective borders. However, Brik saw no evidence of this when he crossed the international borders. No papers were checked. There were no officials present. There were no controls of any kind. He returned home and did nothing that would signal that he wished to immigrate to Lithuania or Latvia.

On December 25, 1991, Mikhail Gorbachev became the first president in the history of the USSR to resign. He declared the office of the presidency of

the USSR extinct and handed rule over to the new president, Boris Yeltsin.
The following day, the Supreme Soviet dissolved the existing Union of Soviet
Socialist Republics ratifying Soviet declaration No. 142-H. It acknowledged
the independence of the Soviet Republics and created the Commonwealth of
Independent States (CIS). Over the next several months, all the individual
republics signed the Alma-Ata Protocol, which formally established the CIS
and gave finality to the dissolution of the USSR. It ceased to exist. Only the
Baltic States and Georgia failed to sign the agreement at the time.[3]

Brik continued to speak to Mahar about his train travel to the Baltic States
to test immigration and custom controls at the Russian border. Following the
dissolution of the USSR, Brik was concerned that new controls may have
been established. He decided he would take the night train once again to
Latvia. It was January 11, 1992, sixteen days following the collapse of the
USSR. Brik arrived in Moscow and walked to the Latvian Embassy. However, he found that it was being guarded by militia guards. He had hoped to
obtain the addresses of the British and Canadian embassies in Riga.

Brik had stayed in Moscow for the day, then, as planned, took the night
train to Riga. He was relieved to see there was still no problem for him to
exit Russia. Fourteen hours later, when he arrived in Riga, Brik went to the
Information Bureau that was situated right next to the railway station. When
asked about the address of the British and Canadian embassies, the attendant
refused to provide him with any information. He was told that if he wanted
to obtain the addresses of foreign missions he had to go to the Latvian Ministry of Foreign Affairs. When Brik asked her where that was, she wouldn't
provide him the address until he paid her a bribe. After a difficult search,
he located the Ministry and spoke with an official who handed him a slip of
paper with the address and telephone number of the British Embassy. It was
located inside the Hotel Rigas.

After a brief call to the British Embassy, Brik secured a last-minute appointment with the ambassador, who was about to leave for the airport. While
setting up the quick meeting, Brik informed the administrative assistant that
his name was Gene Thompson, he was not Latvian, and he could not remain
in Riga very long. When he arrived at the embassy, he saw that there were
three Latvian men standing in the entranceway. One was standing in the doorway, a second was standing behind a desk, and the third man appeared to be a
visitor. Brik walked right past them, and the man behind the desk challenged
him and asked where he thought he was going. Brik responded that he had
an appointment with the ambassador. He was told that he couldn't simply
walk upstairs. He had to sign for a pass. He was instructed to make an internal embassy call and confirm that he actually had an appointment. Although
frightened, he made the call and spoke with the same administrative assistant

he had called earlier. When she advised him to complete the paperwork for a pass, Brik confided that he was not really Gene Thompson and he didn't wish to sign for a pass. He asked her to come to the lobby and he would explain.

Moments later, the British ambassador appeared in the lobby and walked over toward the three Latvian men. Brik got his attention and asked if he could speak to the ambassador privately and confidentially. Brik informed the diplomat that he was Russian but considered himself a de facto Canadian. He told him that he wished to speak with MI6, the Secret Intelligence Service, but that his real intention was to connect with the RCMP.

The ambassador informed Brik that he was on his way to the airport to greet some visitors. He told him that he would go upstairs and speak with his administrative assistant and have her find the address and contact information for the Canadian Embassy. Brik asked the ambassador to give his word that he would keep their conversation confidential. He repeated that he wanted to speak to someone from MI6 or from the RCMP. The ambassador gave his assurance that their conversation would remain confidential. As he was leaving, he asked Brik to telephone his assistant two hours later, at which time she would have the information he required. When he called her as arranged, he was given the address details for the Canadian Embassy in Riga. However, he was informed that the embassy was only open two days per week. She stated that the Canadian diplomat who staffed the Canadian Embassy on those days traveled to Riga from Stockholm. She offered to contact the Latvian Ministry of Foreign Affairs and request information about which days the Canadian Embassy is open. Brik thanked her for her offer but requested that she drop the matter. He did not wish to have her make any further inquiries, as he had another idea. He returned to the train station, and fourteen hours later he was back in Moscow.[4]

Chapter Thirty-Eight

Vilnius, Lithuania

Yevgeni Brik informed Don Mahar that he changed his strategy in January 1992. He decided his next trip would be to Vilnius, Lithuania. In preparation for his last trip to Riga, Latvia, Brik had created a cypher message that he intended to hand over to the British ambassador. However, he judged at the time that conditions were such that he would not risk giving it to him. He simply did not have sufficient time to explain the situation before the ambassador left for the airport. He decided he would take it with him to Vilnius, and if the situation allowed he would attempt to pass it to whomever he might meet at the Canadian or British embassies. The cyphered message contained future meeting arrangements in Moscow on the first and third Tuesday of each month at the Mayakovski subway station, at noon, on the downstairs platform. He indicated that he would be wearing sunglasses and would have a red bag with a red strap over his left shoulder. Brik also included a short parole. The person meeting Brik would ask the time. Brik would respond that his watch had stopped. The other person would tell him to wind it. Brik would respond that it was broken.

Although it sounds awkward and contrived, the parole was a necessary element of the meeting arrangements. If one or the other did not know the correct parole, it would signal that he was not meeting the correct person. He would move on.

Brik signed the message with the words: Gene / Dave 53 5. The signature he used would allow the intelligence personnel reading the decrypted message to properly identify him. Gene represented his true name in English: Eugene or Gene. Dave represented his KGB cover legend in Canada, David Soboloff. And 53 5 represented the years, 1953 to 1955, that were the years he cooperated with the RCMP Security Service/(aka CSA). His encrypted message warned the prospective readers that the secrecy of the information was very important.[1]

To encrypt and decrypt the message, Brik used Sinclair Lewis's classic 1922 novel *Babbitt*. Using *Babbitt*, Brik encrypted the written message from plain text to a series of numbers. He photographed the sheet with the numbers on it and produced a photographic negative. It was a practice he had done countless times in Canada when receiving KGB coded messages from The Centre in Moscow. Brik took the photographic negative, made a copy for himself, and wrapped the negative in tinfoil.

It was Brik's intention to provide the encrypted message to Canadian or British representatives in Vilnius. He would then travel back to Riga or possibly Tallinn, Estonia, where he would provide the key to Canadian or British diplomats. In each case, he would ask that the encrypted message and the key be sent to the RCMP and SIS in Ottawa and London, respectively. It was at this time that Brik learned that the government in Tallinn announced that they would be enforcing strict border controls due to organized crime syndicates operating in the country. The government was trying to gain control of the problem. Brik had to change his plans with respect to Estonia.

After a number of previous trial runs into the Baltics, Brik left Aleksandrov on January 26, 1992, for Moscow and Vilnius. It turned out to be one of the most important journeys that he had undertaken with respect to future escape plans. As was the pattern in previous trips, Brik did not encounter any difficulty leaving Russia. Nor were there any immigration requirements when he arrived in Vilnius. He had to wait an hour for the Information Bureau to open. It was located next to the train station. After it opened, Brik obtained the address for the British Embassy and walked to its location.

When he arrived at ten o'clock in the morning, he saw that there were no militia officers on duty outside the embassy reviewing documents. However, Brik saw that there was one just inside the doorway of the embassy. When asked where he was going, Brik simply told him that he wished to speak to the woman at the reception desk. He walked straight toward the reception area without being questioned further.

Brik lied to the receptionist, advising her that he was a Lithuanian and that he would like to speak to one of the diplomats. She advised him that all the diplomats were out at the moment and requested that he return after lunch. Brik accepted this and walked away. As requested, he returned after the lunch hour and was directed by the receptionist to be seated. There was a man seated at a desk behind the receptionist who paid little, if any, attention to him. Brik could hear voices from an adjoining area. After a considerable wait, the receptionist disappeared into the adjacent room and presumably told them that Brik was still waiting to see someone.

A gentleman appeared and identified himself as the deputy ambassador and asked Brik what he wanted. He asked if Brik was Russian. Brik responded in a similar manner as he had in Latvia. He stated that he was born in Russia but considered himself to be a de facto Canadian. Brik informed him that he wanted to speak to him confidentially, so the two men entered another office and closed the door. Before they began to talk, Brik asked if the diplomat was certain there were no bugs or listening devices in the room. They began to speak in hushed tones, which gave Brik confidence that he was being taken seriously.

Brik told him that he wished to get in touch with MI6 and with the RCMP in Canada. He related that it would be good for both countries. When Brik saw that the diplomat did not stand up and walk out, he decided to trust him. He produced the two photographic films that were wrapped in tinfoil and showed the deputy ambassador the contents, informing him that they were encrypted messages. The British official placed the photographic negatives and the tinfoil into an envelope and assured Brik that he would send them off to London. Brik told him that the encrypted messages would be of no value to MI6 without having the key necessary to decrypt them. He confided that the key was a poem that was contained in Sinclair Lewis's book, *Babbitt*. Brik recited the poem and then wrote it out. The deputy ambassador was reassuring and told Brik that everything would be all right.

Brik informed the British diplomat that the coded messages described future meeting arrangements in Moscow. However, over the period of time that he was waiting to return to the embassy, he had come to the conclusion that it would be both easier and safer for him to meet with British or Canadian intelligence officials in Vilnius rather than Moscow. He was asked when he thought he would be able to return to Vilnius. Brik suggested April, and the two men agreed on April 11. Brik thanked the British diplomat and departed the embassy. He took the next train back to Moscow and another to Aleksandrov.

Brik kept a very low profile after he returned to Aleksandrov and made certain that he did nothing over the next few months that would draw attention to himself. He obtained his Moscow-Vilnius train tickets for the April 11 meeting in Vilnius at the train station in Moscow. He did not wish to advertise in Aleksandrov that he was going back to Lithuania. He had worked at the train station for seven years and knew everybody there. His long-standing girlfriend, Galina Berezhnaya, was also employed at the train station. Brik could use his train pass to go to Moscow without others taking much notice. Going back to Vilnius again so soon after his last trip would certainly have people talking. He wanted to avoid that at all costs.[2]

Brik returned to the British Embassy in Vilnius on April 11, 1992. He was asked if he would stay the night and return to Aleksandrov the following day. Everyone was satisfied that an exfiltration operation by the Canadians and the British would go ahead as planned. The date of that operation was set for June 19, two months down the road. The details of how it was accomplished must remain classified.

Epilogue

Following the successful exfiltration of Yevgeni Vladimirovich Brik in June 1992, he lived in Ottawa, Ontario, for nineteen years. At one point he moved to a new apartment, one that CSIS officer Robbie McLeod tried very hard to dissuade him of but Brik insisted. In the greatest of ironies, it was just a short walk from the Russian Embassy on Charlotte Street.

Brik declined an offer from CSIS to formally change his name and be resettled in another city or small community in Canada. He could have been relocated to any province of his choosing. He was looked after financially and could have lived a comfortable, quiet existence in total anonymity. But he wanted no part of that. He lived under his true name, had a public telephone, and a home computer. He did not try to hide. There was general shock and disbelief when the media learned a few years after his return to Canada that he was never executed by the KGB as originally believed, that he was in fact alive, and that he had been exfiltrated back to Canada where he was resettled. Various news agencies, journalists, and other pundits made claims that he was living in Canada under an assumed identity. These claims, like so many others, were simply not true.

Brik was angry when he read a report about his life in which an author claimed he arrived in Halifax in the fall of 1952, using false documentation, identifying him as an American citizen. In fact, Brik arrived in Halifax on November 4, 1951, a full year prior to what had been said about him. He arrived using a false Canadian passport, not American. That same report stated that he boarded a train for Montreal the following day and later obtained the David Soboloff Canadian passport that had been taped to the bottom of the toilet tank at the train station. None of this happened.

The actual truth was that he met Leonid Dmitrievich Abramov, his KGB Illegal Support Officer, in Montreal at the Botanical Gardens on November 14, 1951. In a small café away from the park, the two men exchanged documents. It was at this time that Brik received the David Soboloff identity papers. But there was no Canadian passport among them. Brik did not receive one until he was living in Toronto where an elderly dentist signed his passport application as his guarantor.

During those almost two decades in Ottawa, Yevgeni Brik was angry, cantankerous, and calculating. CSIS officer Robbie McLeod, the man who took care of his resettlement in Canada, characterized Brik as being an evil, mean-spirited little man. Many would agree with that assessment. Having spent fifteen years in Vladimir Central Prison and the Temnikovskiy Department of Camps could have played a significant part in making him this way.

However, CSIS officer Don Mahar, while conducting research in the archival files at CSIS headquarters prior to the exfiltration, saw plenty of evidence to convince him that Brik was a very difficult man. This was evident in the penned entries in the classified, personal diaries of RCMP Security Service officers Terry Guernsey and Charles Sweeny. The Operation KEYSTONE case file is rife with examples of his abhorrent behavior. The KGB too had great difficulty with his demeanor and lack of discretion. He disobeyed KGB officer Sergey Sergeyevich Sergeev and went home and blurted out to his wife and parents that he was now a KGB officer who would be working overseas. And of course, he compromised his position with the KGB when he informed his lover, Larissa Cunningham, about his true identity. And then he compromised himself and his double-agent role when he advised the news editor at the *Montreal Gazette* that he was both a Soviet Illegal and an RCMP double agent working against the Soviets.

Galina Berezhnaya immigrated to Ottawa and lived with Brik at 190 Lees Avenue, a downtown apartment building. Galina was a pleasant woman who was liked by the small circle of friends and acquaintances she had. With very limited English, her circle of friends was small. These same friends were not enamored with Brik and found him to be rude, unfriendly, and unpleasant to be around.

In his later years, Brik's life became even more difficult due to a medical diagnosis of dementia. It became necessary to have him committed to the hospital. Yevgeni Vladimirovich Brik died on May 25, 2011. He was eighty-nine years of age. His remains were cremated, and his wife returned his ashes to Aleksandrov. Unfortunately, friends of Galina Berezhnaya in Ottawa learned that she too died shortly after returning to Russia.

There is no evidence on record to substantiate that disgraced RCMP corporal James Douglas Finley Morrison ever served a day in prison following his conviction in an Ottawa court in 1986. Rather, it is believed he was sent to an Ottawa halfway house where he served two-thirds of his sentence and was then released. His oldest son used to visit him at the halfway house in Ottawa. Almost thirty-one years had elapsed from the time of his traitorous activities until his conviction in court. When he was released from the halfway house, he and his long-suffering wife, Gwynneth, returned to Western Canada where they resided in White Rock, British Columbia, for a period of time. They also lived in Stuart and Squamish, British Columbia.

Gwynneth Morrison stayed by her husband's side throughout the years of his indebtedness and philandering. The young British lady who had attended finishing school and was expected to marry a young naval officer died in 1991 in Edmonton, Alberta. Her parents were disappointed in her selection of a husband. They both knew she never reached her potential in life.

James Morrison settled in Victoria, British Columbia, after Gwynneth died. He spent his last years living in the basement apartment of a lovely home on Beach Street in the Oak Bay area. He was a regular at a local pub where he would have drinks with a few friends. He would arrive at the pub in his Jaguar accompanied by a friend's sheepdog. Haggis would enter the pub with him and go and sleep behind the bar until it was time to go home. Morrison's colleagues at the bar were concerned when he and Haggis never showed up for several days. They went to check on him and found him on the floor in his basement apartment. He was taken to Royal Jubilee Hospital on Bay Street in Victoria where he remained for about ten days.

Morrison's only surviving but estranged son flew to Victoria when he learned of the situation. There was no love lost between the two men. The son indicated during an interview for this book that he did not want to go Victoria to see his father. He knew his father lived his life as a con man and was always broke but tried to convince people otherwise. His father dishonored his mother over the years by having many mistresses. He showed little affection toward either of his two sons and acted as if he didn't care for them.[1]

James Douglas Finley Morrison died on April 2, 2001. He was cremated and his ashes scattered in an unmarked, common ossuary at First Memorial Funeral Service on Falaise Drive in Victoria. There is nothing to indicate or to memorialize his final resting place. The ossuary is located below a gravel walking path and rests below a concrete slab. If you did not know the location of the ossuary you would simply walk over it and continue along the path. The ossuary contains the remains of approximately four hundred people, several of whom were homeless street people. There was nobody at Morrison's burial other than his youngest son. There was no service, no music, no prayers, and no eulogy.[2]

Terrance (Terry) Munson Guernsey retired from the RCMP with the rank of superintendent. He was a man way ahead of his time and was considered by many to have been the "father" of the RCMP Security Service. He was recalled from retirement in 1984 to testify as a witness at the trial of James Morrison. Sadly, Terry Guernsey died a tragic death in an apartment fire in Toronto on May 13, 1992. His death came five weeks before the exfiltration operation to get Yevgeni Brik out of Russia. Although he hadn't seen Brik since 1955, he had been discreetly told that he was alive in Russia and that an operation was being undertaken to bring him back to Canada.

John Charles Sweeny retired from the RCMP on April 16, 1973, with the rank of assistant commissioner. He had an exceptionally successful career and worked in Alberta, Ontario, Quebec, Newfoundland, and at headquarters in Ottawa. He died on April 8, 1986, and is buried at Pinecrest Cemetery in Ottawa.

The two British SIS officers from the 1950s, Leslie Herbert Mitchell and Daphne Park, are both deceased. Park had a very successful career in SIS with postings in the USSR in 1954, Belgian Congo in 1959, Zambia in 1964, and Hanoi in 1969. She was invested into the Order of the British Empire (OBE) in 1960 and Companion of the Order of St. Michael and St. George (CMG) in 1971. Park was appointed Controller Western Hemisphere in 1975. No other female SIS officer had ever received a promotion to that level. She retired from the SIS in 1979 and was elected principal of Somerville College, Oxford. In 1990, she was appointed a Life Peer in the British House of Lords and became Baroness Park of Monmouth. She died March 24, 2010.

Retired RCMP officer Sandy McCallum, one of the few principals from this story who is still living, is a full-time resident in a retirement home in southern Ontario. He has exceptional recall for the 1950s and 1960s and provided detailed information about events of the time. His room at the residence is adorned with his RCMP photograph, various awards that he received, and his medals. Sandy is trim, stands straight as a pillar, and is fond of wearing an RCMP vest in the residence. He is a proud Canadian and has served the country with distinction.

Nothing is known about former KGB officers Abramov, Bourdine, Ostrovskiy, Krasilnikov, Aksenov, Korznikov, Sergeev, or others. Two separate initiatives were taken in 2015 and 2016 to seek informed comment and archival records from the current Russian SVR, at the Russian Embassy in Ottawa, and via the official SVR website, without success. Vladimir Central Prison remains an active prison to this time. The Temnikovskiy Department of Camps have been discontinued. However, one of the original buildings remains a prison.

Espionage remains a key foreign policy initiative for the Russian Federation which is, for the most part but not exclusively, exercised by the SVR. The practice of using SVR Illegals will continue throughout the world and in

North America specifically. Although the specter of espionage and the spy tradecraft has evolved with advancements in technology, the continued use of Illegals who penetrate sensitive government departments, the military, the high-tech industry, and research and development companies will continue. It remains a tremendous challenge to counter these initiatives at a time when resources are heavily allocated to the protection of the Canadian people, our institutions, and way of life. Our first priority must always be public safety. Nevertheless, we must not drop our guard against the threat posed to Canada by hostile intelligence services from many identified target countries.

The men and women of the CSIS, as well as those who were members of the former RCMP, are owed a debt of gratitude by the Canadian government and, especially, the Canadian people. We all should be very proud of them.

Notes

CHAPTER THREE

1. Author Interview with Yevgeni Vladimirovich Brik.
2. Declassified Top Secret Document obtained from the Canadian Security Intelligence Service (CSIS) through Canadian Access to Information and Privacy legislation.
3. Ibid.
4. Author interview with Brik.
5. Ibid.

CHAPTER FOUR

1. Author interview with Brik.
2. Ibid.
3. Ibid.

CHAPTER FIVE

1. Vladimir Kuzichkin and Frederick Forsyth, *Inside the KGB: My Life in Soviet Espionage*, 83, and author interview with Brik.
2. The term *dead drop*, which is a concealment location used to hide money, instructions, film, or anything else used in the world of espionage, is used interchangeably with the term *dead letter box* or DLB.
3. Author interview with Brik.
4. Ibid.
5. Ibid.
6. Ibid.

7. Ibid. The original plan was for Brik to sail to New York from Paris. For reasons never explained, Brik sailed from Marseilles to Halifax. Much has been written to suggest that he arrived in North America with a false US passport. This is untrue. He traveled on a false Canadian passport.

CHAPTER SIX

1. Author interview with Brik.
2. Ibid.
3. Ibid.
4. Author interview with Brik. This is also supported by declassified top-secret document obtained from the CSIS through Canadian Access to Information and Privacy legislation.
5. It has been reported that Brik destroyed the passport he used when he entered Canada at Halifax and flushed it down the toilet at the Halifax train station. This never happened. Brik was given this same passport again when he returned to Moscow almost four years later.
6. Author interview with Brik.

CHAPTER SEVEN

1. Brik's extensive knowledge of English, which he spoke without any trace of a Russian accent, allowed him to blend into the community without raising suspicion on himself. This ability would stand him in good stead as he traveled throughout the country the following two years.
2. Author interview with Brik.
3. Ibid.
4. Central Station (Montreal), https://en.wikipedia.org/wiki/Central_Station_(Montreal).
5. Author interview with Brik.
6. Ibid.
7. Christopher Andrew and Vasili Mitrokhin, *The Mitrokhin Archive: The KGB in Europe and the West* (New York: Penguin Press, 1999).
8. Author interview with Brik.
9. Ibid.
10. Ibid.

CHAPTER EIGHT

1. Also spelled as Vassili Chitarev. He was identified as being KGB Resident by former KGB Colonel Oleg Gordievskiy, who worked for British Intelligence from 1974 until 1985.

2. "A Station with a Rich History," Toronto.com, https://www1.toronto.ca/wps/portal/contentonly?vgnextoid=2765962c8c3f0410VgnVCM10000071d60f89RCRD.

3. Pseudonym used. See also Christopher Andrew and Vasili Mitrokhin, *The Mitrokhin Archive: The KGB in Europe and the West* (New York: Penguin Press, 1999), 218.

4. Pseudonym used.

5. Author interview with Brik.

6. Ibid.

CHAPTER NINE

1. Author interview with Brik. See also Christopher Andrew and Vasili Mitrokhin, *The Mitrokhin Archive: The KGB in Europe and the West* (New York: Penguin Press, 1999).

2. Ibid.

3. Ibid. See also Andrew and Mitrokhin, *The Mitrokhin Archive: The KGB in Europe and the West*. This is also referenced in John Sawatsky, *For Services Rendered: Leslie James Bennett and the RCMP Security Service* (Toronto: Doubleday Canada Limited, 1982).

4. Declassified top-secret document obtained from the CSIS through Canadian Access to Information and Privacy legislation.

5. Ibid.

6. Author interview with former RCMP Security Service officer who wishes to remain anonymous. See also Sawatsky, *For Services Rendered*.

7. Author interview with former RCMP Security Service officer who wishes to remain anonymous.

CHAPTER TEN

1. Declassified top-secret document obtained from the CSIS through Canadian Access to Information and Privacy legislation.

2. Author interview with Brik.

3. Ibid.

CHAPTER ELEVEN

1. Author interview with former RCMP Security Service officer who wishes to remain anonymous.

2. Author interview with former senior RCMP Security Service officer Mr. Bruce James. Documentation supporting this was received from the RCMP through Access to Information and Privacy legislation.

3. Christopher Andrew and Vasili Mitrokhin, *The Mitrokhin Archive: The KGB in Europe and the West* (New York: Penguin Press, 1999).

CHAPTER TWELVE

1. Declassified top-secret document obtained from the CSIS through Canadian Access to Information and Privacy legislation.
2. John Barron, *KGB: The Secret Work of Soviet Secret Agents* (New York: Readers Digest Press, 1974).
3. Christopher Andrew and Vasili Mitrokhin, *The Mitrokhin Archive: The KGB in Europe and the West* (New York: Penguin Press, 1999).
4. John Sawatsky, *For Services Rendered: Leslie James Bennett and the RCMP Security Service* (Toronto: Doubleday Canada Limited, 1982).

CHAPTER THIRTEEN

1. Declassified top-secret document from Operation FEATHERBED, obtained from the CSIS through Canadian Access to Information and Privacy legislation.
2. Ibid.
3. Christopher Andrew and Vasili Mitrokhin, *The Mitrokhin Archive: The KGB in Europe and the West* (New York: Penguin Press, 1999).
4. Ibid.
5. Author interview with Brik.
6. Author interview with former RCMP Security Service officer who wishes to remain anonymous.
7. Ibid.

CHAPTER FOURTEEN

1. Documentation received from the RCMP through Access to Information and Privacy legislation.
2. Ibid.
3. *Montreal Gazette*, J.R. Lemieux Promoted, August 2, 1956.
4. Supreme Court of Ontario, Court of Appeal, Supplementary Appeal Book: Exhibits in Proceeding in the Provincial Court (Criminal Division). *Her Majesty the Queen vs. James Douglas Finley Morrison: Province of Ontario.* 1984.

CHAPTER FIFTEEN

1. Birth Certificate of James Douglas Finley Morrison obtained from Library and Archives Canada pursuant to an Access to Information and Privacy Act request.
2. Documentation received from the RCMP through Access to Information and Privacy legislation.

3. D. R. Johnson, *On Guard for Thee: The Silver Anniversary of the Security Branch* (Winnipeg: Jostens Canada Limited, 1993).

4. Documentation received from the RCMP through Access to Information and Privacy legislation.

5. Author interview with the late Ryan Vidian-Jones. He was the brother of Gwynneth and brother-in-law to James Douglas Finley Morrison.

6. Ibid.

7. Details obtained from the military file of James Douglas Finley Morrison, which was obtained from Library and Archives Canada through Access to Information and Privacy Act legislation.

8. Author interview with the late Ryan Vidian-Jones.

9. Ibid.

10. Details obtained from the military file of James Douglas Finley Morrison, which was obtained from Library and Archives Canada through Access to Information and Privacy Act legislation.

11. Author interview with the late Ryan Vidian-Jones.

12. Author interview with Sandy McCallum.

13. Ibid.

14. Ibid.

15. Author interview with the late Ryan Vidian-Jones.

16. Documentation received from the RCMP through Access to Information and Privacy legislation.

CHAPTER SIXTEEN

1. Author interview with the late Ryan Vidian-Jones.

2. Out of respect, I have chosen not to provide her name or identify where she resides.

3. Supreme Court of Ontario, Court of Appeal, Supplementary Appeal Book: Exhibits in Proceeding in the Provincial Court (Criminal Division). *Her Majesty the Queen vs. James Douglas Finley Morrison: Province of Ontario.* 1984.

4. Ibid.

CHAPTER SEVENTEEN

1. Author interview with former RCMP Security Service officer who wishes to remain anonymous.

2. Declassified top-secret document obtained from the CSIS through Canadian Access to Information and Privacy legislation.

3. Supreme Court of Ontario, Court of Appeal, Supplementary Appeal Book: Exhibits in Proceeding in the Provincial Court (Criminal Division). *Her Majesty the Queen vs. James Douglas Finley Morrison: Province of Ontario,* 1984.

4. Ibid. This declassified top-secret report, written on April 21, 1971, by (then) Sergeant Jim Warren to Subinspector, the late Archie Barr, has the notation that RCMP Commissioner, William L. Higgitt, saw the report on May 8, 1971. Higgitt was well aware of the case. He had assisted Charles Sweeny in the initial interrogation of Morrison at the Château Laurier in December 1957.

5. Supreme Court of Ontario, Court of Appeal, Supplementary Appeal Book: Exhibits in Proceeding in the Provincial Court (Criminal Division). *Her Majesty the Queen vs. James Douglas Finley Morrison: Province of Ontario*, 1984.

6. The dialogue in this and subsequent chapters between Morrison and Ostrovskiy, with respect to Morrison's act of treachery toward Yevgeni Brik, have been recreated from his statements of confession in December 1957.

CHAPTER EIGHTEEN

1. Declassified documentation received from the RCMP through Access to Information and Privacy legislation.

2. The dialogue in this and subsequent chapters between Morrison and Ostrovskiy, with respect to Morrison's act of treachery toward Yevgeni Brik, have been recreated from his statements of confession in December 1957.

3. Supreme Court of Ontario, Court of Appeal, Supplementary Appeal Book: Exhibits in Proceeding in the Provincial Court (Criminal Division). *Her Majesty the Queen vs. James Douglas Finley Morrison: Province of Ontario*. 1984.

CHAPTER NINETEEN

1. ZIS-110, https://en.wikipedia.org/wiki/ZIS-110.
2. Author interview with Brik.
3. Ibid.
4. Ibid.

CHAPTER TWENTY

1. Documentation received from the RCMP through Access to Information and Privacy legislation. See also: Supreme Court of Ontario, Court of Appeal, Supplementary Appeal Book: Exhibits in Proceeding in the Provincial Court (Criminal Division). *Her Majesty the Queen vs. James Douglas Finley Morrison: Province of Ontario*, 1984.

2. Documentation received from the RCMP through Access to Information and Privacy legislation.

3. Ibid.

4. Supreme Court of Ontario, Court of Appeal, Supplementary Appeal Book: Exhibits in Proceeding in the Provincial Court (Criminal Division). *Her Majesty the Queen vs. James Douglas Finley Morrison: Province of Ontario*, 1984.

CHAPTER TWENTY-ONE

1. Vladimir Kuzichkin, *Inside the KGB: My Life in Soviet Espionage*, translated by Thomas B. Beattie (New York: Pantheon Books, 1990).
2. Author interview with Brik.
3. Ibid.
4. Documentation received from the Canadian Security Intelligence Service (CSIS) through Canadian access to information and Privacy Act legislation.
5. Christopher Andrew and Vasili Mitrokhin, *The Mitrokhin Archive: The KGB in Europe and the West* (New York: Penguin Press, 1999).

CHAPTER TWENTY-TWO

1. Documentation received from the RCMP through Access to Information and Privacy legislation.
2. Hansard, House of Commons Debates, 34th Parliament, 3rd Session 14, March 31, 1993, 17850.
3. Supreme Court of Ontario, Court of Appeal, Supplementary Appeal Book: Exhibits in Proceeding in the Provincial Court (Criminal Division). *Her Majesty the Queen vs. James Douglas Finley Morrison: Province of Ontario*, 1984.
4. Documentation received from the RCMP through Access to Information and Privacy legislation.
5. Supreme Court of Ontario, Court of Appeal, Supplementary Appeal Book: Exhibits in Proceeding in the Provincial Court (Criminal Division). *Her Majesty the Queen vs. James Douglas Finley Morrison: Province of Ontario*, 1984.
6. Ibid.

CHAPTER TWENTY-THREE

1. Christopher Andrew and Vasili Mitrokhin, *The Mitrokhin Archive: The KGB in Europe and the West* (New York: Penguin Press, 1999).
2. Author interview with Brik.
3. Ibid.
4. Brik held no animosity toward his wife with respect to his arrest. He knew she had no choice but to report on his activities to Korznikov. When asked if he forgave his wife, he responded that he was never angry with her.

CHAPTER TWENTY-FOUR

1. Author interview with James Morrison's youngest son. Out of respect to him I have chosen not to identify him or say where he resides in Canada.
2. Ibid.
3. Declassified documentation received from the RCMP through Access to Information and Privacy legislation.
4. Supreme Court of Ontario, Court of Appeal, Supplementary Appeal Book: Exhibits in Proceeding in the Provincial Court (Criminal Division). *Her Majesty the Queen vs. James Douglas Finley Morrison: Province of Ontario*, 1984.
5. Ibid.
6. Declassified top-secret document obtained from the CSIS through Canadian Access to Information and Privacy legislation.

CHAPTER TWENTY-FIVE

1. Author interview with Brik.
2. Supreme Court of Ontario, Court of Appeal, Supplementary Appeal Book: Exhibits in Proceeding in the Provincial Court (Criminal Division). *Her Majesty the Queen vs. James Douglas Finley Morrison: Province of Ontario*, 1984.
3. Christopher Andrew and Vasili Mitrokhin, *The Mitrokhin Archive: The KGB in Europe and the West* (New York: Penguin Press, 1999). See also: Paddy Hayes, *Queen of Spies: Daphne Park Britain's Cold War Spy Master* (New York: Overbrook Duckworth, Peter Mayer Publishers, 2016).
4. Author interview of Brik. Another theory suggested by author Paddy Hayes in his book, *Queen of Spies*, is that the KGB engaged in "operational games" and perhaps used an imposter or a Brik "lookalike." Although this would not be surprising, Brik insisted during our discussions that he flew the warning signal indicating that he was under control.
5. Declassified top-secret document obtained from the CSIS through Canadian Access to Information and Privacy legislation.

CHAPTER TWENTY-SIX

1. Supreme Court of Ontario, Court of Appeal, Supplementary Appeal Book: Exhibits in Proceeding in the Provincial Court (Criminal Division). *Her Majesty the Queen vs. James Douglas Finley Morrison: Province of Ontario*, 1984.
2. Ibid.
3. Ibid.
4. Ibid.
5. Ibid.

CHAPTER TWENTY-SEVEN

1. Author interview with Brik.
2. Ibid.

CHAPTER TWENTY-EIGHT

1. Supreme Court of Ontario, Court of Appeal, Supplementary Appeal Book: Exhibits in Proceeding in the Provincial Court (Criminal Division). *Her Majesty the Queen vs. James Douglas Finley Morrison: Province of Ontario*, 1984.
2. Ibid.
3. Ibid.
4. Declassified documentation received from the Royal Canadian Mounted Police through Access to Information and Privacy legislation.
5. Supreme Court of Ontario, Court of Appeal, Supplementary Appeal Book: Exhibits in Proceeding in the Provincial Court (Criminal Division). *Her Majesty the Queen vs. James Douglas Finley Morrison: Province of Ontario*. 1984.
6. Declassified documentation received from the RCMP through Access to Information and Privacy legislation.
7. Ibid.
8. Ibid.

CHAPTER TWENTY-NINE

1. John Sawatsky, *For Services Rendered: Leslie James Bennett and the RCMP Security Service* (Toronto: Doubleday Canada Limited, 1982).
2. Hansard, House of Commons Debates, 34th Parliament, 3rd Session, 14, March 31, 1993, 17850.
3. Supreme Court of Ontario, Court of Appeal, Supplementary Appeal Book: Exhibits in Proceeding in the Provincial Court (Criminal Division). *Her Majesty the Queen vs. James Douglas Finley Morrison: Province of Ontario*. 1984. A transcript of the *Fifth Estate* program is contained in the documentation that comprises the exhibits in the proceeding against Morrison. His appearance on the *Fifth Estate* and his self-incriminating statements formed the basis of his arrest and charges under the Official Secrets Act.
4. Mike Ward, "Ex-Agent Warns against Charges," *Winnipeg Free Press*, November 13, 1982.
5. Hansard, House of Commons Debates, 32nd Parliament, 1st Session, 18, November 19, 1982, 20826.
6. Ibid.
7. Hansard, House of Commons Debates, 32nd Parliament, 1st Session, 19, January 24, 1983, 22144.

8. Hansard, House of Commons Debates, 32nd Parliament, 1st Session, 20, March 4, 1983, 23449.

9. Supreme Court of Ontario, Court of Appeal, Supplementary Appeal Book: Exhibits in Proceeding in the Provincial Court (Criminal Division). *Her Majesty the Queen vs. James Douglas Finley Morrison: Province of Ontario*, 1984.

10. Ibid.

CHAPTER THIRTY

1. Author interview with John F. Cummings.
2. Author interview with Geoffrey O'Brian.

CHAPTER THIRTY-ONE

1. Author interview with Robbie McLeod.

2. The assistance of Deputy High Commissioner Lavertu and the Canadian ambassador to Sweden went a long way in assuring the success of the exfiltration operation. As they were both fully briefed, they would have been able to intervene on our behalf should any unforeseen problems arise in the United Kingdom and/or Sweden as we transited their respective countries. It was an excellent example of interdepartmental cooperation.

CHAPTER THIRTY-THREE

1. Sandra Grimes and Jeanne Vertefeuille, *Circle of Treason: CIA Account of Traitor Aldrich Aimes and the Men He Betrayed* (Annapolis, MD: Naval Institute Press, 2012).

2. Christopher Andrew and Oleg Gordievsky, *KGB the Inside Story* (London: Hodder and Stoughton, 1990).

3. Author interview with Brik.

4. Ibid.

5. Ibid.

6. Anatoli Sudoplatov, Pavel Sudoplatov, Jerrold Schecter, and Leona P. Schecter, *Special Tasks: The Memoirs of an Unwanted Witness, A Soviet Spy Master* (Toronto: Little, Brown & Company, 1994).

CHAPTER THIRTY-FOUR

1. Author interview with Brik.

2. Anatoli Sudoplatov, Pavel Sudoplatov, and Leona P. Schecter, *Special Tasks: The Memoirs of an Unwanted Witness, A Soviet Spy Master* (Toronto: Little, Brown & Company, 1994).

3. Author interview with Brik.

4. Ibid.
5. Francis Gary Powers with Curt Gentry, *Operation Overflight: A Memoir of the U-2 Incident* (Washington, DC: Potomac Books, 2004).
6. Author interview with Brik.

CHAPTER THIRTY-FIVE

1. Author interview with Robbie McLeod.
2. Ibid.
3. Author interview with Brik.
4. Ibid.
5. Mikhail Volpin, https://en.wikipedia.org/wiki/Mikhail_Volpin. See also: Erdman, Nikolai. https://en.wikipedia.org/wiki/Nikolai_Erdman.
6. Author interview with Brik.

CHAPTER THIRTY-SIX

1. Author interview with Brik.
2. Ibid.

CHAPTER THIRTY-SEVEN

1. Author interview with Brik.
2. Ibid.
3. Francis X. Clines, "Gorbachev, Last Soviet Leader, Resigns; U.S. Recognizes Republics' Independence," *New York Times*, December 26, 1991.
4. Author interview with Brik.

CHAPTER THIRTY-EIGHT

1. Author interview with Brik.
2. Ibid.

EPILOGUE

1. Author interview with the youngest son of James Douglas Finley Morrison. He asked that his name not be given and that no information be provided as to where he resides in Canada. Morrison's oldest son predeceased him on April 22, 1997, due to natural causes.
2. Ibid.

Bibliography

Andrew, Christopher and Oleg Gordievsky. *KGB: The Inside Story*. London: Hodder and Stoughton. 1990.

Andrew, Christopher and Vasili Mitrokhin. *The Mitrokhin Archive: The KGB in Europe and the West*. New York: Penguin Press. 1999.

Barron, John. *KGB: The Secret Work of Soviet Agents*. New York: The Reader's Digest Association, Inc. 1974.

Barron, John. *KGB Today: The Hidden Hand*. New York: The Reader's Digest Association, Inc. 1983.

Berkikow, Louise. *Abel*. New York: Random House. 1970 Reprint. March 1982.

Grimes, Sandra and Jeanne Vertefeuille. *Circle of Treason: CIA Account of Traitor Aldrich Aimes and the Men He Betrayed*. Annapolis, MD: Naval Institute Press. 2012.

Hayes, Paddy. *Queen of Spies: Daphne Park, Britain's Cold War Spy Master*. New York: Overbrook Duckworth, Peter Mayer Publishers, Inc. 2016.

Johnson, D. R., Lt. Colonel. *On Guard for Thee: The Silver Anniversary of the Security Branch*. Winnipeg: Jostens Canada Limited. 1993.

Knight, Amy W. *The KGB: Police and Politics in the Soviet Union*. Winchester, MA: Unwin Hyman, 1988.

Kuzichkin, Vladimir. Translated by Thomas B. Beattie. *Inside the KGB: My Life in Soviet Espionage*. New York: Pantheon Books, 1990. Originally published as *Inside the KGB: Myth and Reality*. London: André Deutsch Ltd. 1990.

Levchenko, Stanislav. *On the Wrong Side: My Life in the KGB*. Washington: Permanon-Brassey's International Defense Publishers, Inc. 1988.

Levchenko, Stanislav and Herbert Romerstein. *The KGB Against the "Main Enemy": How the Soviet Intelligence Service Operates Against the United States*. Lexington, MA: Lexington Books, D. C. Heath and Company. 1989.

Miller, Lawrence. *The Avro Arrow: A Picture History*. Toronto: James Lorimer and Company Ltd., Publishers. 2011.

Peterson, Martha D. *The Widow Spy: My CIA Journey from the Jungles of Laos to Prison in Moscow.* Wilmington, NC: Red Canary Press. 2012.

Powers, Francis Gary with Curt Gentry. *Operation Overflight: A Memoir of the U-2 Incident.* Washington, DC: Potomac Books Inc. 2004.

Sawatsky, John. *For Services Rendered: Leslie James Bennett and the RCMP Security Service.* Toronto: Doubleday Canada, 1982.

Sudoplatov, Anatoli and Pavel Sudoplatov with Jerrold L. and Leona P. Schecter. *Special Tasks: The Memoirs of an Unwanted Witness. A Soviet Spymaster.* New York: Little, Brown & Company. 1994.

Supreme Court of Ontario, Court of Appeal. *Supplementary Appeal Book: Exhibits in Proceeding in the Provincial Court (Criminal Division). Her Majesty the Queen vs. James Douglas Finley Morrison.* Province of Ontario, 1984.

West. Nigel. *The Illegals: The Double Lives of the Cold War's Most Secret Agents.* London: Hodder and Stoughton. 1993.

Whiteside III, John W. *Fool's Mate: A True Story of Espionage at the National Security Agency.* USA: Self-Published. 2013.

A Note about Sources

Operation KEYSTONE is a case that, until 1992, had been resting in the relative quiet of the CSIS and Library and Archives Canada's archives. With only minimal interruption, these historic, top-secret files have been gathering dust since the early 1960s. Yevgeni Vladimirovich Brik returned to Moscow in 1955. The files remained active for a few short years following his departure but gradually were overtaken by other events and other counterintelligence files.

Over the last several years, I have endeavored to identify, locate, and interview those individuals who had direct, firsthand knowledge of Operation KEYSTONE and the people who were directly or indirectly involved with it. Most of those people have been deceased for several years. A number of those that I did interview, some on several occasions, have asked for and have received anonymity. Their reasons for requesting nonattribution are as varied as the individuals themselves. Some are Soviet defectors who have settled in Canada. Others are landed immigrants who do not wish to be identified. Some are family members of those whose names appear in this narrative. And still others, whose positions in national security require that their names not be divulged, have spoken about their historical knowledge of the case or the people in it.

I spent many hours speaking with Yevgeni Vladimirovich Brik, who commonly used the name Eugene. These conversations, years after my retirement, were personal and rewarding. Like so many others within CSIS who developed a professional relationship with him, we lost touch with one another. When I tried to reconnect with him, I learned that he had moved, and later, that he had passed away. Our lengthy conversations formed the basis of some of the narrative in this book.

I also made extensive use of Canadian and US legislation as it relates to Access to Information and Privacy legislation and Freedom of Information Act legislation.

A source of invaluable information was the extensive array of documents, interviews, confessions, photographs, and former classified reports that Crown Counsel introduced as evidence at Morrison's trial, and as such became public documents.

Finally, a comment about existing family members of the late James Morrison: I have had personal meetings, lunches, telephone conversations, and email exchanges with various family and extended family members. Others within the family have chosen not to speak with me or even respond to my attempts to engage them. To those of you whom I have personally met, I am grateful for your time and candor. I also thank those who would only speak with me on the telephone. And I understand and respect those who ignored my telephone calls and email messages all together. It is unfortunate that we didn't connect, as I truly wanted to obtain your unique perspective on this story.

Index

"YB" refers to Yevgeni Vladimirovich
Brik and "JM" to James Douglas
Finley Morrison.
"P" followed by a number indicates
a page in the photospread; for
example, P4 will be located on the
fourth page of photos.

125; contacts with Morrison, 78–79,
82, 91, 108; departure from Canada,
109, 113; meeting with Morrison at
Glenlea Golf Course, 82–84; meeting
with Morrison at Grand Hotel,
76–78, P6; meeting with Morrison at
Orleans Hotel, 99–100, P11; meeting
with Morrison at Royal Ottawa Golf
Club, 79–80; meeting with Morrison
at Somerset Park, 109; meeting with
Morrison in Templeton, 90; post
at embassy in Ottawa, 2, 77; and
RCMP, 74, 81, 83, 120; unknown
end, 188; work with KGB, 77
Ottawa, 56, 63, 76, 124, 131, 137;
Abramov in, 24, 26, 27, 34; Brik in,
39, 159, 163, 169, 185–86; dentist in,
5, 45, 49, 94; Gouzenko's defection
from, 39; Soviet Embassy in, 2, 23,
29, 31, 38, 41, 53, 113–17, 120, 122,
P3, P10
Ottawa International Airport, 150
Ottawa Journal, 58

palace, in The Hague, 69
Panyushkin, Aleksandr Semyonovich
(General), 85, 86–87, 154
Parent, Louis R. (Subinspector), 124–25
Paris, France, 5–7, 21, 149; Morrison
and KGB to meet in, 100, 108, 113,
114
Park, Daphne Margaret Sybil Desirée
(Baroness), 110–11, 126, 151, 188,
P10
paroles, 139, 180
passports: authentic, 19, 24, 55, 158;
diplomatic, 144, 147, 149; false,
1–3, 6–8, 20, 22, 24, 28, 185, 186;
internal, 169, 170
PAUL WILLIAM HAMPEL SVR
Illegals, xvi
Pearson, Lester B. (Prime Minister), 136
Pearson International Airport, 149
Pereslavi, USSR, 170
perestroika, 173, 174

Pete, alias of Morrison, 91, 98
Peterson, J., alias of Nikolai Ostrovskiy,
97
Philby, Kim (SIS officer), 168
Phillips, Michael (Ambassador), 145
photography, 18, 27, 28. *See also
under* Brik, Yevgeni Vladimirovich;
film and coded messages; Germain
School of Photography; portraits by
Soboloff
Pier 21, Halifax, 22
Poland, 19
Politburo, 87
POMOSHCHNIK, 53, 56
Portraits by Soboloff, 1, 2, 102, 172,
P1. *See also under* Bannantyne Ave.
address; Brik, photography studio
cover
Poudrette, Joesph H.T. (Superintendent),
43
Powers, Francis Gary Jr., P13
Powers, Francis Gary Sr., 160, P13
Praemona, Beiramar, 2, 5
Pratt, Frank, 135
Prince Rupert, British Columbia, 78,
131
Provost Corps, No. 1 (RCMP), 65, 67,
68, 69, 72, P5
putsch, 175

Queen Elizabeth Hotel, 93, 94, 103, 110

radio frequencies, 46, 91, 100, 107, 110,
117
RADOV, codename of Hugh George
Hambleton, 55
Ratkai, Stephen Joseph, 132
RCMP (Royal Canadian Mounted
Police), 179, 181; breaches of rules,
124–25; and Brik's triple agency,
41; Headquarters, 40; investigation
of Morrison, 126, 130–31; iterations
of, xv; Mounties, 39, 69, 70, 71, 124;
Musical Ride, 71, 128; and publicity
of Morrison's treachery, 126, 129,

White Rock, British Columbia, 187
Winnipeg, Manitoba: Brik in, 26, 34, 36; Morrison in, 82, 84, 89–91, 97–101, 107–9, 115–16, 126
Winnipeg Free Press, 129, 130, 131
Women's Voluntary Service, 66
Wood, Stuart Taylor (Commissioner), 64, 65
World War I, 32, 132

World War II, 2, 64, 68, 132, P5
writing inks, secret, 115

Yeltsin, Boris, (President), 147, 178
Young Communist League (KOMSOMOL), 11
Yukon Territory, 48

Zaslaosky, Ida, 19

About the Author

Donald G. Mahar served forty-one years in the Royal Canadian Mounted Police (RCMP), Security Service; the Canadian Security Intelligence Service (CSIS); and Communications Security Establishment Canada (CSEC), both in Canada and abroad. His career was primarily spent in counterintelligence against the Soviet KGB/Russian SVR target. He currently serves as national president of the Pillar Society, the retirement/alumni organization for the Canadian Security Intelligence Service and the former RCMP Security Service. He resides in Ottawa, Ontario, with his wife, Carol Anne.